Enjoyable Econometrics

Econometrics can at first appear a highly technical subject, but it can also equip the practitioner with a useful skillset of smart ways to formulate research questions and collect data. *Enjoyable Econometrics* applies econometric methods to a variety of unusual and engaging research questions, often beyond the realm of economics, demonstrating the great potential of using such methods to understand a wide range of phenomena. Unlike the typical textbook approach, *Enjoyable Econometrics* follows in the footsteps of *Freakonomics* by posing interesting questions first, before introducing the methodology to find the answers. Therefore, rather than equation-heavy sections based around complex methodologies, the reader is presented with chapters on "Money" and "Fashion, Art, and Music." Franses writes in a way that will enthuse and motivate the economics student embarking on the essential study of econometrics. Indeed, the book shows that econometric methods can be applied to almost anything.

PHILIP HANS FRANSES is Professor of Applied Econometrics and Professor of Marketing Research at the Erasmus University Rotterdam. He is an elected fellow of the International Institute of Forecasters, the *Journal of Econometrics*, and the Royal Netherlands Academy of Arts and Sciences. He has published several books, including *A Concise Introduction to Econometrics* (Cambridge University Press, 2002), and more than 250 articles in international journals.

Enjoyable Econometrics

PHILIP HANS FRANSES

Erasmus University Rotterdam

CAMBRIDGE
UNIVERSITY PRESS

University Printing House, Cambridge CB2 8BS, United Kingdom

One Liberty Plaza, 20th Floor, New York, NY 10006, USA

477 Williamstown Road, Port Melbourne, VIC 3207, Australia

314-321, 3rd Floor, Plot 3, Splendor Forum, Jasola District Centre, New Delhi - 110025, India

79 Anson Road, #06-04/06, Singapore 079906

Cambridge University Press is part of the University of Cambridge.

It furthers the University's mission by disseminating knowledge in the pursuit of education, learning and research at the highest international levels of excellence.

www.cambridge.org
Information on this title: www.cambridge.org/9781107164611
DOI: 10.1017/9781316691137

© Philip Hans Franses 2018

First published 2018

A catalogue record for this publication is available from the British Library

Library of Congress Cataloging in Publication data
Names: Franses, Philip Hans, 1963– author.
Title: Enjoyable econometrics / Philip Hans Franses.
Description: 1 Edition. | New York : Cambridge University Press, 2018. | Includes bibliographical references and index.
Identifiers: LCCN 2018018449 | ISBN 9781107164611 (hardback)
Subjects: LCSH: Econometrics. | Econometrics – Popular works.
Classification: LCC HB139 .F7224 2018 | DDC 330.01/5195–dc23
LC record available at https://lccn.loc.gov/2018018449

ISBN 978-1-107-16461-1 Hardback
ISBN 978-1-316-61647-5 Paperback

To find your true path, you must be as free as possible to cast adrift.

—Francis Bacon (painter)

Contents

Preface

The Wiki lemma of Econometrics (consulted February 28, 2017) states:

> Econometrics is the application of statistical methods to economic data and is described as the branch of economics that aims to give empirical content to economic relations. More precisely, it is "the quantitative analysis of actual economic phenomena based on the concurrent development of theory and observation, related by appropriate methods of inference."

Anyone who has a look at the content of an introductory textbook of econometrics will surely agree that statistical methods are important for econometrics, because most of these textbooks are full of mathematical notation. So, at first sight, econometrics is considered a highly technical subject that demands substantial skills from its practitioners. At the same time, however, it is not true that econometric methods are designed only for the sake of creating ever more complicated tools. No, the techniques are helpful in many situations: for example, when it comes to forecasting economic variables like gross domestic product (GDP) growth, inflation, and unemployment or when it comes to policy evaluation where the merits of educational programs and tax reform programs can be evaluated.

A closer look at the empirical applications of econometric methods, not only in textbooks but also in scientific articles in international journals, suggests that most applications address issues in macroeconomics and finance. These areas are usually characterized by the availability of an abundance of data, as national statistical institutes and financial institutions collect a wealth of information on an annual to a daily basis.

A first reason for writing this book is to emphasize that econometric methods can also be applied to *all kinds* of settings, where typically the practitioner has to collect his or her own data first. Such collection can be done by carefully combining existing databases, but also by holding surveys or running experiments. A nice by-product of having to collect one's own data is that doing so helps make a proper and educated choice among the wealth of potential methods and techniques to be considered later on. This book therefore contains a range of datasets so that anyone can play around with them, also perhaps to try out alternative methods than those that I chose to use. All data are available via www .enjoyable-econometrics.com.

A second reason for writing this book concerns the very motivation to engage in applying econometric methods. A casual glance at many econometric studies seems to suggest that most practitioners have a solid view on their research questions. Indeed, someone who needs an econometric model to create out-of-sample forecasts usually knows that he or she wants a tool that provides somehow accurate forecasts. And those who evaluate policy programs want to answer the question of whether a program is successful. However, there are many more (and also perhaps slightly unconventional) research questions that also benefit from using econometric methods, and in this book I will address quite a few of those. Indeed, as you may have seen in the table of contents, the chapter titles do not feature econometric concepts, but they do reference a range of research questions.

The two reasons for writing this book come together in the single overall goal: to attract newcomers to the field by showing

that econometrics also involves smart ways of formulating
research questions and smart ways of data collection. So, while
people may shy away from the mainstream applications of
econometrics, it is hoped that this book full of other research
questions and innovative datasets will provide a motivation to
embark on a primer course of econometrics.

HISTORY

It is in this building in Rotterdam, the Netherlands, at the Pieter
de Hooghweg where it all began. The world's first academic program
on econometrics was launched in 1956. Initiated by Jan Tinbergen and
Henri Theil, the Econometric Institute was founded and the first
students embarked on an econometrics bachelor program, which
bore many similarities with the one today. The library looked different in those days, by the way.

Since 1956, the Econometric Institute at the Erasmus University Rotterdam has educated thousands of students, and several of those have pursued academic careers. I am very proud today that I can be a part of this wonderful institute and that I can work with my superbly qualified colleagues and ambitious and very smart students.

THANKS

A first word of thanks is to the editorial team of Cambridge University Press. Phil Good has been very helpful in encouraging and in governing the publication process.

I am also thankful to the students who helped me with the data collection; in particular, I would like to mention Wouter Knecht, Bert de Bruijn, Stephanie Vermeer, Lotje Kruithof, Merel van Diepen, Rogier Potter van Loon, Marjolein van Baardwijk, and Jeanine Kippers.

A special word of thanks goes to Eva Janssens for checking all the computations and her help with the website and to Christiaan Heij for his keen eye on the equations.

Since 2006, I have served as Dean of the Erasmus School of Economics, a school with more than 6,000 bachelors and masters students in economics and econometrics. Usually, when someone becomes a dean, his or her research output will vaporize quickly, as the administrative duties require much time. I was lucky though, in the past years, to have a wonderful team to help me lead the school, which made it possible for me to have some spare moments to work on this book. I therefore conclude these words of thanks by expressing my enormous gratitude to Harry Commandeur, Saskia Krijger, Margaretha Buurman, Nine van Gent-van der Feltz, Bert de Groot, Ben Schotpoort, Reino de Boer, Ivo Arnold, Casper de Vries, Shirley May, Ylaise Herwig-Djojokarso, Ellen Baaij-van der Hoven, Ronald de Groot, Charles Hermans, and of course Tineke Kurtz-Wierenga, who has been my wonderful personal assistant for many years. Without all of you, this book could never have been completed.

1 Introduction

Pleasure in the job puts perfection in the work.

—Aristotle

AT A GLANCE

This book deals with applications of econometric methods and techniques to a variety of questions, often and on purpose outside the realm of economics. Usually, econometric methods are considered for questions in macroeconomics, labor economics, or finance, among others. However, admittedly, when you are a novice to the field, the examples and illustrations in econometric textbooks may not be that entertaining, and hence the very fact that illustrations are chosen as such may reduce your wish to master the methods yourselves. Well, in plain English, several examples in textbooks do not look very challenging.

At the same time, econometric textbooks also seem to have some knowledge content that is difficult to grasp for a novice. These books usually introduce a method and then they apply it, always with great success, to a case at hand. Now, how did the authors know in advance which method would work best for a certain question? And, even more so, is it not the case that, *first*, there is a question and *then* there is a method that could come in handy? And could it be that someone first has tried a variety of methods and that then after some time it is found that one method is more useful than another?

That brings me to the main idea of this book, and that is that questions come first and econometric methods come next. As a consequence and as you will see, the chapters in this book therefore have a format opposite to the one that is commonly used. The main text of each chapter discusses empirical questions, and each appendix collects the relevant methods and techniques for these questions. The questions collected in the chapters all have a topic in common. Chapters therefore have titles like "Money" and "Fashion, Art, and Music" instead of what you can commonly find like "Generalized Least Squares" and "Autocorrelation." Of course, this book will not claim to be a general introduction to econometric methods and techniques. The main claim is that this book hopes to arouse enthusiasm for the application of those methods and techniques and in fact to illuminate a little bit how econometric science proceeds. New methods have always been designed and developed just because someone believed that a question or a type of data required a new method. Textbooks usually turn it around, and there may be good reasons for that. But, in this very introductory book, the ordering is first the question and then the method.

MORE DETAIL

This first chapter provides the motivation and a brief outline. Econometric methods and techniques can often be applied in practice, but they usually come in third place. First, there is a question. Then there need to be data to be analyzed. Textbooks usually present an overwhelming array of methods and techniques but rarely address how to collect relevant data, let alone that the books provide creative inspiration for the formulation of questions. This book seeks to provide some such inspiration by examining a range of questions, many of which one perhaps would not have thought about in the first place, and then to illustrate how relevant data can be acquired such that basic econometric methods and techniques can be applied. It is not difficult to make econometric methods more difficult. It is more difficult to try to make matters easier.

Motivation

The title of this book may sound like an oxymoron. Wiktionary (consulted March 11, 2016) gives for "enjoyable":

Enjoyable (comparative more enjoyable, superlative most enjoyable)

1. Pleasant, capable of giving pleasure.
   That was an enjoyable day; I had a lot of fun.

At the same time, the Wikipedia lemma of "Econometrics" (also consulted March 11, 2016) reads as

> Econometrics is the application of mathematics, statistical methods, and computer science, to economic data and is described as the branch of economics that aims to give empirical content to economic relations. More precisely, it is "the quantitative analysis of actual economic phenomena based on the concurrent development of theory and observation, related by appropriate methods of inference."

Well, I know that this summary describes matters well, but I can readily appreciate that it does not arouse much warmth and enthusiasm. For many students, academics, and practitioners, it therefore may seem that the two words in the book title are disconnected. The "econo" part of the second word seems OK, but the "metrics" part makes the combined term somewhat daunting. One could wonder whether "economics," which to many people already seems like an applied mathematics discipline, can be made even more quantitative by adding even more metrics.

One cause for the seeming disconnection may be a cursory look into an introductory textbook on econometrics, where one may bump into "text" like the following:

The final expression for b is

$$b = \frac{\sum_{i=1}^{n}(x_i - \overline{x})(y_i - \overline{y})}{\sum_{i=1}^{n}(x_i - \overline{x})^2}$$

With $a = \overline{y} - b\overline{x}$, you can now compute the residuals

$$e_i = y_i - a - bx_i$$

with their variance

$$s^2 = \frac{1}{n-2} \sum_{i=1}^{n} e_i^2$$

and

$$E(s^2) = \sigma^2.$$

Now, what could this possibly mean? And, notably, this kind of text usually comes in one of the first chapters, while then there still are hundreds of pages to come in a textbook. So, why do we need all this?

Another possible cause for the felt disconnection can be that most textbooks on econometrics typically focus on economic relations in the macroeconomic world or in finance. So, the focus often is on gross domestic product, unemployment, and inflation or on the New York Stock Exchange and the Nikkei index. In the present book, where the intention is to give meaning to the title, this second potential cause for believing enjoyable econometrics is an oxymoron is addressed in a particular way. As you may have seen in the table of contents, some of the questions that I will address are not the very standard ones.

Clearly, anyone who has a glance at the content of an introductory textbook of econometrics will surely agree that mathematics is important for econometrics because most of these textbooks are full of mathematical notation. In fact, also in the forthcoming Chapter 2, some of such notation will be used too, although the intention is to keep it to a minimum. So, at first sight, econometrics is considered a highly technical subject, which demands substantial skills from those who practice it in real-life situations. At the same time, it is *not* true that econometric methods are only designed for the sake of creating ever more complicated tools. No, in many situations the techniques are really very helpful, for example, when it comes to forecasting economic variables like, indeed, gross domestic product (GDP) growth, inflation, and unemployment or when it comes to evaluate, for example, the merits of educational programs or tax reform programs.

Yet a closer look at the empirical applications of econometric methods, not only in textbooks but also in scientific articles in international academic journals, also reveals that many applications apparently address issues in macroeconomics and finance, with some exceptions concerning labor economics or microeconomics. These areas are usually characterized by the abundant availability of data, as national statistical institutes and financial institutions collect a wealth of information on a daily to an annual basis.

This suggested abundance of accessible data is not common in all economic areas, and in many cases students and practitioners have to collect their own data. And then rarely it is told in the textbooks how one should collect such data. How do you start? Which data are the proper ones? How many do you need?

Now, here is the key idea. The collection of data is preceded by a question. Students may believe that the model comes first because textbooks seem to only discuss the ins and outs of models, but in the real world it does not work that way. In fact, in the real world it starts with a question. It is important that people learn to formulate such a question. Textbooks usually assume that there was a question from the onset and then start with methods to find some apparently relevant estimates. Examples of questions for macroeconomics and finance could be "Is turmoil on American stock markets contagious for European stock markets?" or "Do lower inflation levels spur economic growth?," but seldom are they formulated in this way.

When a question is well articulated, the next step is to collect the relevant data, and then only at the end does an econometric method or model come into play. Sometimes these data are available in a clean and nice format (again in macro and finance), or they are available in a messy and noisy format (discourses on social media, the mentioning of the word "recession" in Google Trends), but quite often they are not available at all. Or worse, there are data collected but for another purpose or inappropriately, and then the subsequent analysis could be impossible or difficult.

A typical response of students is that everything seems to work well in those nice and shiny textbooks, but, and I quote one of my own undergraduate students, when "I analyze my data, nothing seems to work." Another response is that the nice and simple regression model (more on that in Chapter 2) never adequately fits the data; there always seems to be a problem with the data. So, here is the challenge!

Combining technical mathematics with data that do not work well and perhaps also questions that are less interesting to the novice can make people to feel that econometrics can hardly be enjoyable.

This book intends to change this perspective by doing a couple of things. First, Chapter 2 outlines the two main tools of econometrics, that is, correlation and the regression model. We do need these two tools, as almost everything proceeds from there. With various illustrations, I will show that basic tools can already be quite handy for interesting research questions, even such a basic tool as an average value of various numbers. One such question is at what age creative individuals make their best work. It seems that, on average, novelists, composers, and painters make their best work around the age of 40, but that is not so interesting, in particular because various artists have already died by that age – think of Jimi Hendrix and Amy Winehouse. So, perhaps a more interesting figure is not the absolute age but the relative age, that is, at which fraction of their lives did these creative individuals make their best work? There is a surprising outcome to this question, and join me later on to have a look in Chapter 2 at what it is. An illustration of correlation in that chapter concerns the link between fouls and yellow cards in football. When all fouls would be punished with a yellow card, then this correlation would be equal to 1, right? Well, is that the case? We will see. A third illustration in Chapter 2 concerns the regression model and seeks to answer the question of whether men and women could possibly run the marathon in less than two hours, sometime or ever in the future. We will see that this might happen for men, but it most likely will take a while, and we will have to wait for a few more Olympics or championships.

Chapter 2 concludes with a lucid discussion of what else is in econometric textbooks by mainly using very simple notation. Correlation and regression will always be useful, but the form of the tools will change depending on the question and on the properties of the data. In all further chapters, I will put some of those adapted versions in the appendix so that you can get an impression of how that works. If you decide to skip each appendix, it is perfectly fine, as the main text can be read without the appendix. On the other hand, the appendices do give you an indication how questions and data help to shape econometric models and methods. The level of mathematics is always at a high school level, as it basically involves the operators "adding up," "subtracting," "multiplying," "dividing," and "raising to the power."

The key message of this book is, with emphasis, that it all starts with asking a question. Thus, this book will be full of questions. As is evident from the just-mentioned Chapter 2 questions, the questions will not be the mainstream questions that one typically encounters in econometric articles and books. Deliberately, questions will be considered that sometimes may seem awkward, and it is hoped that this partly may help to introduce the joy into applying econometric methods. Indeed, who does not want to know if hemlines have any predictive value for the economic cycle? Well, Chapter 6 will show that they do not, by the way, but it is good to know anyway. This book also highlights the subsequent collection of relevant data. It is important for anyone applying econometric methods to make, so to speak, dirty hands. This means, for example, to collect data and then to find out that there are all kinds of issues with the data (typos and missing data). To have personal practical experience is very relevant because it helps to learn how and when basic tools need further refinement.

When you look at textbooks, it seems that the ordering is "method," "data," and "illustration." That is, here we have a model, and let us illustrate it on the following data. This sequence obviously suggests that the model or method comes first. Of course, in reality, the ordering is "question," "data," "model," and "answer to the question," and this is what I follow here too.

A potential consequence of the first ordering of "method, data, and illustration" is that students and practitioners may believe that more complicated methods also require more sophisticated questions. If the econometric method is highbrow, so should be the question, right? Well, I can tell you that this is not necessarily the case. In fact, usually when models get more complicated, it is because the data have certain features. For example, sales data typically obey an S-shaped pattern; that is, first the innovators take a try with the new product, then an early majority, which makes the sales levels take off, and way at the end there is a group of laggards who adopt the product when it has almost disappeared from the stores. Such an S-shaped pattern does suggest an upward trend in the data, and a trend that does not move on forever and eventually dies out. We will see that econometric models exist that allow for this feature and that these models are a little more involved than the simple regression model. So, features of the data can suggest new models and methods.

CHAPTERS 3 TO 8

The six chapters after Chapter 2 all address topical questions, all arranged in chapters with a specific theme. Chapter 3 deals with money, quite literally in fact. In early 2002, something happened in Germany that triggered some of my questions in this chapter. What happened was the exchange of a banknote of 300 euros for payment at a gas station, where the customer received 250 euros in notes of 100 and 50 in return. The euro had just been introduced, and people apparently needed time to adjust to the new notes, and certainly that one of 300 euros. Well, as you might have guessed, there is no such thing as a 300-euro banknote! This smart but illegal construction, however, triggered me. Why do we have 10, 20, and 50 on our banknotes and not 30 or 40? And how do we make payments anyway? What is it that we do when we want to make a cash payment and look into our wallets to make a choice among the available notes and coins?

In Chapter 3, we will also ask ourselves whether we suffer from money illusion, that is, does it matter if we have banknotes of 10 or of 10,000, for example? Next we move to the issue of how we pay with cash. I will show that, even before data are collected, it helps to think deeply about the choice process when you look into your wallet and make a decision. You may of course always choose the largest banknote, if it is available, but after some transactions, you will always end up with a wallet containing smaller notes and coins. And what do you do when some notes are missing? That is, what happens if only notes of, say, 10 and 50 are available and no notes of 20? And, rounding, does that matter? Anyway, Chapter 3 has lots of very practical questions.

In a sense, Chapter 4 continues with money, but now about money in the future, possibly with interest. In our daily lives, we have to make decisions about current situations, like the choice among coins in our current wallet, but in many other cases, we have to make decisions that have consequences that persist for a long time in the future. For example, we can choose to pay the full amount for a new television set now, but we may also decide to postpone our payments by resorting to a scheme of monthly payments during the next few years. Therefore, we pay 480 USD now for a television set, or we pay 25 USD per month for the next two years. Both options have their benefits, but beware that the second option can mean that you still have to pay for the old television when you may have already purchased a new model. This example by the way does involve interest rate payments. Usually, when payments are postponed, the one who receives the money in the future wants to have some interest on his or her money. Now, a notoriously difficult exercise concerns computations with interest rates. This is because you need quite some numerical skills to solve interest rate equations. Such skills are usually summarized under the header of financial literacy and numeracy, which gives the title of Chapter 4. With some simple ways of data collection and with the use of two new econometric models beyond those of Chapter 2, I will show how questions on numeracy can be answered simply. Data collection is key here, and the examples give you some idea how this works in practice. The two new econometric tools are multiple regression and the logit model, both of which are highlighted, as promised, in the appendix.

We stay close to money in the next chapter, as Chapter 5 deals with banknotes and postage stamps, where now the focus is on their potential use as collectibles. At times, people wonder what are the best ways to invest money and to have some returns at a later stage, perhaps to be used as savings for a rainy day. In economics, it is usually assumed that people invest in companies buy holding stocks or countries by having bonds, but people can also invest in art or in rare collector's items. Stocks and bonds have various specific features, and one of them is that their prices may suddenly go up, in a race to the top, and after that show a price nadir of substantial size. These patterns are usually called bubbles, and the most famous ones are the Tulip Bubble in seventeenth-century Netherlands and the South Sea Bubble in early eighteenth-century England. In Chapter 5, it is asked whether postage stamp prices also face bubbles and what might cause these bubbles. It turns out that scarcer stamps keep on having their high investment value, whether there are bubbles or not. Now, how can we estimate which stamps are more rare than others are? And how does this work for banknotes? Some banknotes were issued only for a short while, and perhaps these are scarce? As there may be a link between inflation rates and the values on banknotes, would there be any relation between these, that is, does inflation make the number of zeroes to go up, or is it the other way around? Chapter 5 introduces, yes again in the appendix, a multi-equation version of the simple regression model. This model is called a vector autoregression, and it is very often used in practice because it is simple to apply. This model can also prevent finding spurious relations across two or more variables. The appendix to Chapter 5 shows how that works.

Chapter 6 addresses a range of quite different questions. The first question deals with a well-known urban legend. It is said – or, better, it is believed – that the current state of the economy is visible from the length of a woman's dress. When the economy is doing well, skirts get shorter (where somehow people have the roaring twenties and the hippy sixties in mind), and when the economy is going down, dress lengths increase. This phenomenon is called the hemline index, and it regularly gets attention in popular media and also in professional media. Well, one day I decided (together with a student) to collect the data and to put the urban legend to an econometric test.

In Chapter 6, we also return to the peak years of creative artists. There the focus is on whether people who peak later also get older. That would make sense from an experience point of view, but is there also some evidence for that?

Going back to the sixties and seventies of the twentieth century brings up an interesting question about music. Being over 50, I notice myself sometimes saying to students that "many things were better in the past," and then I usually refer to music. I mention Pink Floyd, Queen, the Rolling Stones (never was very fond of the Beatles, by the way), Led Zeppelin, and the like, and then they usually gaze at me with this misty look like "What is he talking about?" Well, for a long time, these rock bands dominated the charts, and to many these days, these bands are still the main favorites. In the Netherlands, there is, each year, a chart called the Top2000, and it features the 2000 most favorite songs, as indicated by and voted for by the Dutch public. Often this list is called a list for old men (where, for students, old means over 40), as for many years now, those bands mentioned have topped the lists. So, the question is, is older music better indeed? Looking at many years of data in the Top2000 lists should somehow provide an answer. In part, the analysis relies on an alternative econometric model, which is a model that allows for S-shaped patterns, a model that is introduced in the appendix.

In Chapter 7, the move is toward the academic process itself. Scientists are expected to publish their work in academic journals, usually in the format of a paper. Papers can range from 5 to 40 printed pages in those academic journals, and there is a ranking of the quality of these journals. A publication in a top journal can advance one's career, and such publications usually mark the start of a successful career. Now, getting one's work published is one thing, but to have colleagues and the media pay attention to your work is quite another thing. Among other numbers, one number that I will present in this chapter is the fraction of my own articles that effectively were ignored completely. I will not give away the fraction yet, but if I would have known it in advance, I could have saved more than 1500 pages of typing. Anyway, sometimes articles do receive attention, and it would be interesting to know which features these successful articles have. So, one question to be addressed is which types of econometrics-based articles get the most attention? Is it new data? Is it a new econometric method, or is it the research question itself? And does it help to be more productive, as an academic? Does the writing of more articles lead to more attention for those articles? And, as one part of the publication process involves judgment and suggestions by reviewers, do the implemented modifications based on their suggestions lead to more citations? In the technical appendix, I will present another model for S-shaped data.

To end this book, there will be chapter on trends and hypes. In economics, when we think of trends, we consider trends in economic prosperity, in populations, in prices, and in, for example, production. Often, the trends go up, and the question typically is whether these trends will go up forever and whether events can change recent trends and make the trend wander away in another direction. In the appendix to Chapter 8, I will address a few simple econometric models for trends, and I will discuss how to choose between these models, if one wishes to do so. Much academic research in econometrics in the past few decades has addressed this seemingly simple issue because it was found to not be simple. In the appendix, I will direct some attention to the underlying reason why this is the case. And, because common trends are such an important and Nobel Prize–worthy topic, the appendix contains a concise discussion on those.

Otherwise, Chapter 8 will try to answer various other questions about trends. Trends in the climate, for example, are a hotly disputed topic. But is local or global warming equally distributed throughout the year, or could it be that only winters are getting warmer? Anecdotal evidence and personal memories about summers in the Netherlands do not suggest that summers are getting warmer.

Another trend can be found in prescribing medication, in particular for attention deficit hyperactivity disorder symptoms. Recent years have seen a tremendous growth in the use of methylphenidate and atomoxetine, in particular in young children. Are these trends going to persist?

The prices and salaries of top football players are on the rise too. In 2016, Paul Pogba came to Manchester United for 105 million euros, and one may wonder: Where will this end?

Finally, sometimes a trend turns out to be hype. By the late 1990s, there was much buzz about a phenomenon called "The New Economy." One feature of this was the declared and foreseen end of unemployment. Well, with a recent worldwide crisis just recently experienced and the rise of unemployment fresh in our memory, one may wonder: Was it hype? Moreover, if it was, when will we stop talking and writing about it?

TO CONCLUDE

One motivation for writing this book is to emphasize that econometric models and methods can also be applied to more unconventional settings, which are typically settings where the practitioner has to collect his or her own data first. Such collection can be done by carefully combining existing databases but also by holding surveys or running experiments. A nice by-product of having to collect one's own data is that this helps to make a proper and educated choice among the wealth of potential methods and techniques to be considered.

Another motivation for writing this book concerns the recommendation to engage in applying econometric methods. A casual glance at many econometric studies seems to suggest that most practitioners have a solid view of their research questions. Indeed, someone who needs an econometric model to create out-of-sample forecasts usually knows that he or she wants a tool that somehow provides accurate forecasts. And those who evaluate policy programs want to answer the question of whether the program was successful. However, there are many more perhaps slightly unconventional research questions that also benefit from using econometric methods, and in this book I will address quite a few of those.

These two reasons for writing this book come together in the single overall goal, and that is to attract newcomers by showing that econometrics also can involve smart ways of formulating research questions and smart ways of data collection. So, while some may shy away from the mainstream applications of econometrics, it is hoped that this book, full of alternative research questions and innovative datasets, will provide a motivation to embark on a primer course of econometrics. Digging into technicalities will then prevail, so, first for now, let us have some fun!

2 Correlation and Regression

"Begin at the beginning," the King said, gravely, "and go on till you come to the end; then stop."

—*Alice in Wonderland*

AT A GLANCE

This chapter starts with the introduction of two basic econometric methods and techniques. Most other methods and techniques build on these two. The first is called correlation, and it deals with the coherence or relation between two variables. Wikipedia's definition of a variable is

> Variable (mathematics), a symbol that represents a quantity in a mathematical expression, as used in many sciences[1]

and this is what it is. In economics, such a quantity can be income, interest rate, exports, imports, and gross domestic product (GDP), but also a stock price, sales levels, annual turnover, almost anything. Outside economics, one can think of temperature, rainfall, and time to run the marathon, also almost anything. A variable typically has variation: that is, stock prices have different values during a trading day, rainfall can be much or a little, and yearly exports can go up or down. When two variables have variation, one may want to measure to what extent this variation overlaps. Do two stock prices go up and down in approximately similar swings, or is an increase in GDP associated with lower unemployment, and vice versa? A correlation measures to what extent two variables have their variation in common.

The second basic concept is the regression model. This builds on the notion of correlation with now the explicit purpose to use any common variance to predict the outcome of one variable using the other. So, if GDP increases by 1%, can we predict a reduction of unemployment of 0.5%? Or, if prices are reduced, can we foresee by how much sales will go up? Or, when the wind comes from the south-west, might that mean more rainfall?

In this chapter, I will illustrate these two concepts with three detailed examples. The first concerns data on Dutch soccer teams, and the question is whether there are any relevant correlations between fouls and yellow cards or between goal attempts and points in the ranking. The regression model will be illustrated using data on the record times for marathons, and the question is if we will see marathon times below two hours in the near future.

Another illustration of the regression model deals with the salaries of chief executive officers (CEOs) of 100 Netherlands-based companies and their ranking. We will see that there is a remarkable relation between these two, a relation that is often called the law of Zipf.[2]

DATA AND PROPERTIES

In brief, econometric methods seek to make sense out of economic data, but in principle, these methods are useful to make sense out of any type of data on variables. A basic premise of this sense making while using econometric techniques is that you need a benchmark. Years ago, my oldest son, who then was five years old, asked me: "Daddy, is four a lot?" Even by then, I could already teach him some key ideas of statistics, which are, first, you need to know what the unit of measurement is. Second, you need to have some kind of benchmark. So in reply I asked him whether he meant four children in a family or perhaps four Nissan GTRs in front of our house. In the Netherlands, families with four children have become rare over the past decades; two children seems to be the most common situation. At the same time, there are not many Nissan GTRs in the Netherlands in the first place, and being the owner of four of those supercars seems to be quite unlikely, certainly for a professor at a university. So, what we basically need is (1) a benchmark value and (2) some kind of a range of values around that benchmark that would be associated with reasonably commonly observed numbers. If you have that, then you can tell whether the number four is a lot or not.

The first mentioned benchmark and very commonly used value is usually the average, whereas the second benchmark deals with variation or the range.

Average

Consider the availability of N observations on a variable Z, where Z can refer to the number of children in a family or ownership of a Nissan GTR by each of those N households. Denote the observations as $z_1, z_2, \ldots, z_N$. For example, there could be 10 households and suppose that these families have 1, 3, 2, 3, 1, 2, 2, 4, 2, and 1 children. So, the range is from 1 to 4, where 4 occurs only once, whereas 1 occurs three times. The average of these 10 observations is

$$\frac{1 + 3 + 2 + 3 + 1 + 2 + 2 + 4 + 2 + 1}{10} = \frac{21}{10} = 2.1.$$

Hence, the average number of children in these families is 2.1. Note that thus the average number of children does not have to be equal to one of the observations, as indeed having 2.1 children is not possible, and thus the average can be a fractional number. The median, which is another kind of benchmark that looks a bit like the average, is obtained by ordering the 10 observations, like 1, 1, 1, 2, 2, 2, 2, 3, 3, 4, and looking for the middle number, which here is 2, as it is the average of the fifth and sixth number. If there would have been 11 families in our sample, then the middle number would have been the sixth number. A third benchmark could be the mode, which is the number that most often occurs. Here, we have four observations with value 2, so that is the mode. I will come back to the median and mode later on, but now I will first address the average.

When there are N observations on Z, denoted as $z_1, z_2, \ldots, z_N$, then the average of the 10 observations is given by

$$\bar{z} = \frac{z_1 + z_2 + z_3 + z_4 + z_5 + z_6 + z_7 + z_8 + z_9 + z_{10}}{10} = \frac{1}{10}\sum_{i=1}^{10} z_i,$$

where Σ, the Greek letter for capital S, means summation, here a summation from the first number to the tenth number.

In general, we have

$$\bar{z} = \frac{1}{N}\sum_{i=1}^{N} z_i.$$

The average of a sample of observations can be informative in itself. In an article in the British newspaper *The Guardian*,[3] the author addressed the issue of whether there would be an ideal age for authors and novelists to write a masterpiece. The article collects data on 65 authors who appear on bestseller lists, and a reproduction of these data is provided in the table in the Appendix to this chapter. As of April 2016, 34 authors have died.

Figure 2.1 concerns the basic statistics[4] of the age at which these 65 authors produced their key work. The average (mean) age turns out to be 40.9 years, whereas the median age is 41.0, which is very close. The range of the 65 age observations goes from 26 to 65. Clearly, the histogram in Figure 2.1 suggests that the mode of these age observations is within the range of 40 to 42.5 years, visible from the obvious spike in the histogram.

Now, that all seems well, but the second column of the table in the Appendix shows that at least one author (Charlotte Brontë) died before the age of 41, so perhaps a more interesting average to compute could be the relative age at which an author composed the best work. This relative age is defined as

$$\text{Relative age} = \frac{\text{Age at peak work}}{\text{Age at death}}.$$

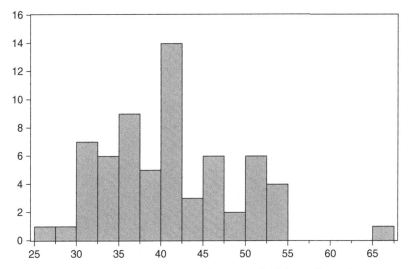

FIGURE 2.1 Basic statistics on the age at which bestseller authors composed their best work.

Figure 2.2 provides some basic statistics of this variable, which is now provided for only 34 of the 65 authors.

The average relative age appears to be 0.633, whereas the median is 0.573. Apparently, about 0.6 into an author's life, the best work is created, and this may be viewed as the age of peak creativity.[5]

The average can be used as a benchmark as it is informative about what someone can expect. Going back to the number of children in families, if one were going to observe a new family, one could perhaps beforehand expect that the most likely number of children for that family is equal to two. At the same time, one is likely too, but four is perhaps less likely. And, using the data for the novelists, one could use these results to guesstimate an average age for other creative individuals, which could be about 40 as well. So, an average of observations in one sample can provide a prediction for a property of a new sample. Such a prediction based on the average is usually called the expected value.

One may now wonder whether a sample of ten families is large enough to have confidence in the prediction of two children per family. This doubt certainly holds for the Nissan GTRs. There are

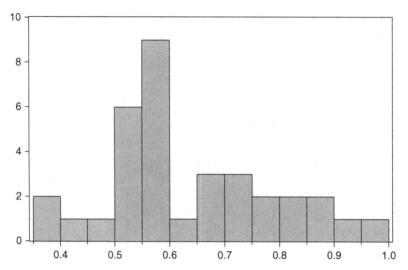

FIGURE 2.2 Basic statistics on the relative age at which bestseller authors composed their best work.

6.5 million households in the Netherlands and there are perhaps 100 of those supercars around; one may need on average to interview or observe 65,000 households to be lucky enough to find 1 such a car. Of course, one may reduce the number of households by looking at income levels (indeed, Nissan GTRs are quite expensive), but then still a fair amount of observations would be needed. Indeed, the average ownership of this car would perhaps be $\frac{1}{40,000}$.

Getting back to my son's question, observing four supercars in one family is very rare, and then the answer to the question "Is four a lot?" would be a "yes," while the answer to this question would be somewhere in between "yes" and "somewhat" in the case of the number of children.

Variance

One way to make the answers a bit more informative is to rely on the second benchmark, which concerns the range of values. For the sample with the number of children, we saw that the range is from 1 to 4. If we had collected not 10 observations but 10,000, then it may have occurred that there would be families with 6 or 7 children. The frequency would be small, but still, they could have been observed. For the Nissan GTRs, one could perhaps collect data on all Dutch households, but then still the range would be from 0 to 1. That is, it is quite unlikely that someone owns two of those supercars.

The range is one way to measure the spread of the observations, but it is a little inconvenient, as it does not benchmark the range relative to the mean. So, one would want to have a measure of the spread of the observations around that expected value, and this measure exists and is called the variance. When there are N observations on Z, denoted as $z_1, z_2, \ldots, z_N$, and the average is given by $\bar{z}$ as before, the variance is defined as

$$s_z^2 = Variance(Z) = \frac{1}{N}\sum_{i=1}^{N}(z_i - \bar{z})^2.$$

For the 10 families and their children, this would be

$$\frac{(1-2.1)^2 + (3-2.1)^2 + (2-2.1)^2 + \cdots + (2-2.1)^2 + (1-2.1)^2}{10}$$
$$= 0.890.$$

Note that this variance is always positive due to the fact that it amounts to a summation of squares. The square root of the variance of the variable Z, s_z, is called the standard deviation. For the 10 families, this would be $0.890^{\frac{1}{2}} = 0.943$.

Empirical Distribution

To be able to informatively answer the question "Is four a lot?" we need an average, we need a standard deviation, and we also need some kind of impression of the shape of the histogram of the data, or something like an empirical distribution. If we were to have histograms like in Figure 2.3, then the average (here around 25 apparently) would not be very informative. Clearly, Figure 2.3 depicts something like two very different samples of households.

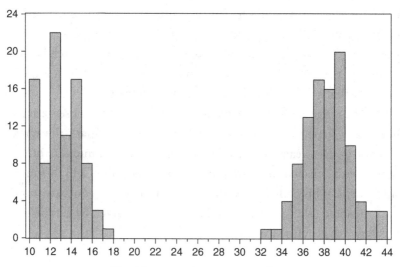

FIGURE 2.3 Two histograms in one, apparently.

And you may not want to have a distribution like the one in Figure 2.4, where there is a clear asymmetry with a hint of large-valued observations toward the right.

Preferably, one wants to have a histogram like the one in Figure 2.5, which seems symmetric around the mean and where the mean and the median are about equal.

The average age that the 34 best-selling authors died is 66.2, and the median age is 65. The maximum age is 94, which is 29 years away from the median, and the minimum age is 38, which is 27 years away from the median. Given the nature of this variable, one could also perhaps not expect anything other than a symmetric distribution. The standard deviation for these 34 observations in 15.0.

THEORETICAL DISTRIBUTION

To learn about the properties of the data, one needs to match an empirical distribution with a theoretical one. Figure 2.6 presents one such theoretical distribution, which is the Gaussian distribution, sometimes also called the normal distribution. The normal distribution has

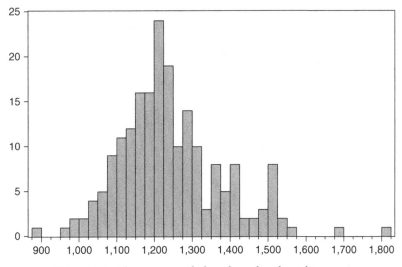

FIGURE 2.4 A histogram with data skewed to the right.

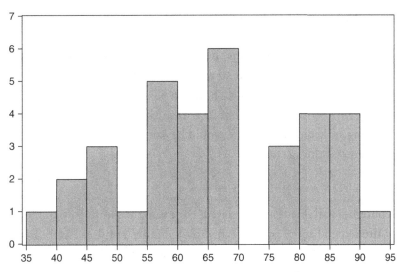

FIGURE 2.5 Age at which bestseller authors have died.

the property that how many observations you may expect within certain intervals around the mean can be easily estimated.

The intervals are defined by the standard deviation, and this is very convenient. One can say that you may expect 95% of all the

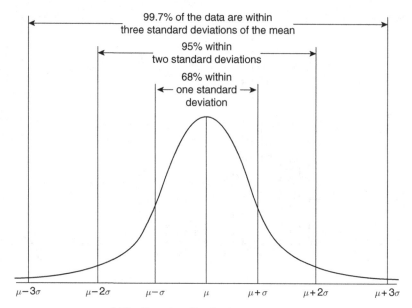

FIGURE 2.6 The Gaussian distribution.

observations to lie in between the mean minus two standard deviations and the mean plus two standard deviations. For the novelists,
95% of the data would then be in between 65 − 2 times 15 = 30 and 65 +
2 times 15 = 95. Here all data fall within this area. In other words,
observing someone dying at 27 would be exceptional,[6] as is someone
who achieves the age of 99.

PROPERTIES ACROSS VARIABLES

(Economic) variables can be related. For example, families with more
children spend more on groceries than smaller families. And larger
families do not fit into a Nissan GTR; one usually sees such families in
bigger cars like a Chrysler Voyager. Note that people who spend a lot
on groceries do not necessarily have many children. And a large family
may have two cars, one for family outings and one for the parents to
drive around without their children.

   Sometimes it is evident that when one variable obtains larger-
valued observations, another shall too. Think of tall people who typically

also have big feet. Or, think otherwise, if a grocery store lowers its prices for detergent, then sales may go up due to these lower prices. In that sense, there is some kind of causality, that is, because prices go down, sales goes up. It can also be that such causality is not obvious or is even absent. National economies may show similar growth patterns, but it might be unclear which of the countries makes it possible for others to grow. Think of China: Is China's economic growth in part due to increased exports to the United States because the US economy is doing well and it can afford them, or is the US economy doing well because it can import cheaper products from China and therefore China can grow? Disentangling what comes first and what comes next can thus be difficult.

Covariance

A useful measure to describe co-movement or common properties is the sample covariance. Suppose you have N observations on a variable X, denoted as $x_1, x_2, \ldots, x_N$, with an average given by

$$\overline{x} = \frac{1}{N} \sum_{i=1}^{N} x_i$$

and another set of N observations on a variable Y, denoted as $y_1, y_2, \ldots, y_N$, with an average given by

$$\overline{y} = \frac{1}{N} \sum_{i=1}^{N} y_i;$$

then the sample covariance between X and Y is defined by

$$s_{xy} = \frac{1}{N} \sum_{i=1}^{N} (x_i - \overline{x})(y_i - \overline{y}).$$

So, suppose we would have observed for the 10 families not only their number of children, namely, 1, 3, 2, 3, 1, 2, 2, 4, 2, and 1 (call these now X), but also their grocery expenditures (Y) for this month, say, 500, 1,000, 800, 900, 400, 700, 700, 1,100, 600, and 300 USD. The average of Y is 700. The sample covariance can now be computed as

$$s_{xy} = \frac{(1-2.1)(500-700)+(3-2.1)(1,000-700)+\cdots+(1-2.1)(300-700)}{10}$$
$$= 220.$$

This sample covariance is positive, and hence this means that apparently larger-sized families are associated with higher grocery spending.

Correlation

A drawback of the covariance is that it is not scale-free. If the measurements on grocery spending would have been recorded not in USD but in 1,000 USD, meaning that the observations would have been 0.5, 1.0, 0.8, and so on, then s_{xy} would have become 0.22.

A scale-free measure of the strength of a relationship between two variables X and Y is the correlation. The correlation between these variables is defined by

$$r_{xy} = \frac{\frac{1}{N}\sum_{i=1}^{N}(x_i - \bar{x})(y_i - \bar{y})}{\sqrt{\frac{1}{N}\sum_{i=1}^{N}(x_i - \bar{x})^2 \cdot \frac{1}{N}\sum_{i=1}^{N}(y_i - \bar{y})^2}} = \frac{s_{xy}}{\sqrt{s_x^2 s_y^2}} = \frac{s_{xy}}{s_x s_y},$$

which in words means that the sample covariance is scaled by the two standard deviations of X and Y. For the families and their spending, we have

$$r_{xy} = \frac{220}{\sqrt{0.89^*60,000}} = 0.952.$$

The upper bound of a correlation is 1, and the lower bound is –1, so 0.952 is close to 1. This confirms the notion that larger-sized families are associated with higher grocery spending.

ARE FOULS CORRELATED WITH YELLOW CARDS IN FOOTBALL?

Of course, these numbers on families are all made up and serve just for illustration, but to see how dependencies across variables can occur in real settings, consider the data in Appendix on 18 Netherlands-based

Table 2.1 *Statistics on club characteristics.*

Variable	Mean	Median	Minimum	Maximum
Players	22.2	22.5	17	28
Points	24.7	23.5	15	37
Attempts	232	225	167	301
Corners	94	95	68	126
Fouls	241	239	158	314
Yellow	33.9	35	19	43
Red	2.28	2	0	6
Offside	37.6	27	20	59

football clubs, all playing in the Dutch premier league, after 17 matches in the 2013–14 season.

Table 2.1 reports various statistics on the performance of these teams halfway through the 2013–14 season. Although during a match each team consists of 11 players, the coach can rely on various substitutes, and the range of players used in the first part of the season is between 17 and 28. The average amount of points at that time in the season per club was 24.7, where the leading club attained 37 points. A team obtained 3 points when it won, 1 point when it drew, and 0 points when it lost. During the matches, also recorded was how often clubs make an attempt to score a goal. The median number of attempts was 225. Furthermore, also measured were the total number of corners; the number of fouls, where some led to yellow or red cards; and finally the number of times a player was offside.

Table 2.2 gives the correlations between the various variables, where of course the "self-correlation" is equal to 1. A correlation that likely amounts to a causal relationship (abstaining from the unfortunate own goals) concerns the attempts and the points. Indeed, without an attempt, one cannot score, and without scoring, the number of points will be low. A draw of a match yields just 1 point. And indeed, the correlation between the attempts and the points is 0.814. So, here you might safely conclude that goals occur because players make an

Table 2.2 *Correlations across variables with club characteristics* (N = 18).

Variable	Players	Points	Attempts	Corners	Fouls	Yellow	Red	Offside
Players	1							
Points	0.121	1						
Attempts	0.079	0.814	1					
Corners	0.241	0.691	0.713	1				
Fouls	-0.061	-0.347	-0.280	-0.055	1			
Yellow	-0.196	-0.513	-0.291	-0.307	0.644	1		
Red	-0.131	-0.347	-0.507	-0.424	0.231	0.350	1	
Offside	0.218	-0.379	-0.413	-0.220	0.219	0.324	0.396	1

attempt to score. If you do not try, you most likely will not score a goal.

For other correlations in Table 2.2, the story is perhaps less clear. The correlation between points and yellow cards is –0.513, which is large and negative. In words, this says that more winning games are associated with less misbehavior. This could sound reasonable, as in if you apparently do not need to make fouls, your team is apparently superior. On the other hand, a foul that leads to a red card can also prevent goals.[7]

SIMPLE LINEAR REGRESSION

The relationship between two variables can be represented by a covariance and a correlation, which then suggests that there may be a relationship that differs from 0. However, if one has the impression that values of one variable come prior to values of another variable, one may want to do a little more than just get an estimate of a correlation. In fact, one may want to use values of one variable to predict values of the other variable. Look at the scatter plot of points versus attempts in Figure 2.7. Clearly, more attempts are associated with more points, which seems reasonable. Now, for the next season with new teams and new players, one may perhaps predict how many points a team will achieve when it has 250 attempts. One may also want to predict what happens when the number of attempts is, say, 350. A useful tool for this purpose is called simple regression.

Simple regression is the starting point for many econometric methods and techniques. The method of simple regression does not require advanced technical tools. Still, the ideas of simple regression are fundamental. Consider again the attempts and points in Figure 2.7. One would expect that more attempts lead to more points. An econometrician tries to quantify the magnitude of changes in points due to changes in attempts. When we go back to the scatter diagram in Figure 2.7, we see that a straight line can be fitted reasonably well to the points in this diagram; see Figure 2.8. The actual points are the dots, and the predicted points are on the line. A given number of

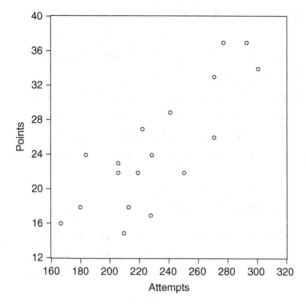

FIGURE 2.7 A scatter plot of points versus attempts.

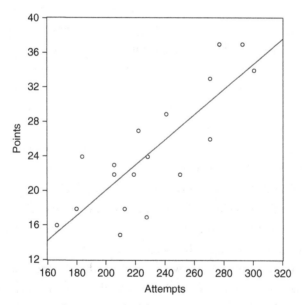

FIGURE 2.8 A scatter plot of points versus attempts with a straight line fitted to them.

attempts is not always associated with the same point level as there are other factors that also cause variation in points. For example, regularly changing the team and adding new players can also influence the number of points. The observed data are reasonably close to the line, but they do not lie exactly on it. This line would be Points = $a + b$ times Attempts or, in short, Points = $a + b$ Attempts.

For a given number of attempts and a given line, the predicted Points are equal to the value of a plus the value of b times Attempts. We denote the difference between actual Points and predicted Points by the residual e. So, we have

Points = $a + b$ Attempts + e.

The coefficient b measures the slope or marginal effect, that is, the change in Points when the number of Attempts changes by one unit. When the slope is nearly equal to zero, this corresponds to observations; for example, in Figure 2.9, where a scatterplot is presented of the

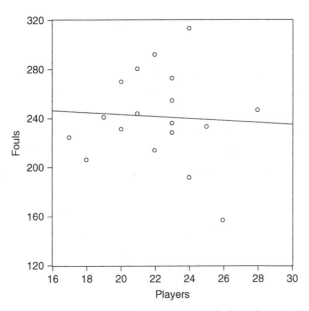

FIGURE 2.9 A scatterplot of players versus fouls with a straight line fitted to them.

number of Players and the number of Fouls. In Table 2.2, we could already see that their correlation is –0.061, which is close to zero (on a scale from –1 to 1).

Going back to the original scatter diagram in Figure 2.7 of Points versus Attempts, the values of the coefficients a and b are of interest to a team manager as they offer the opportunity to predict Points for a given number of Attempts. This helps perhaps to encourage the players to do better, if the number of Points is considered too low. From the scatter plot of Points and Attempts data, you see that different Attempt levels are associated with different Point levels, and this suggests that you can use the number of Attempts to predict Points.

In simple regression, the focus is on two variables of interest that we denote by Y and X, where one variable X is thought to be helpful to predict the other variable Y. This helpful variable X is called the regressor variable or the explanatory factor, and the variable Y that we want to predict is called the dependent variable or the explained variable.

A simple way of modeling the 18 observations on points is written as

Points $\sim N(\mu, \sigma^2)$.

This model means that the observations of points are considered to be independent draws from the same normal (N, Gaussian, see Figure 2.6) distribution with mean μ and variance σ^2. Note that we use the Greek letters μ and σ^2 for parameters that we do not know and that we want to estimate from the observed data. Their data-based equivalents are thus m and s^2. The probability distribution of Points is described by just two parameters, the mean and the variance.

For the normal distribution with mean μ, the best prediction for a new observation on Points is equal to the mean μ. An estimator of the population mean μ is given by the sample mean

$$\bar{y} = \frac{1}{N}\sum_{i=1}^{N} y_i.$$

Obviously, the sample mean is equal to the unconditional prediction of Points, as it does not depend on any other variable. In many cases, however, it helps to use additional information to improve the prediction. In our example, Attempts may help to predict Points because fewer Attempts will most likely lead to fewer Points.

When $y_i \sim N(\mu, \sigma^2)$, the expected value (with notation E) of y is equal to μ, and the expected value of the variance of y is equal to σ^2. Or

$$E(y_i) = \mu,$$
$$E(y_i - \mu)^2 = \sigma^2.$$

An estimator of the population mean μ is given by the sample mean and an estimator for σ^2 is the sample variance, so

$$m = \bar{y} = \frac{1}{N}\sum_{i=1}^{N} y_i$$

$$s^2 = \frac{1}{N-1}\sum_{i=1}^{N}(y_i - \bar{y})^2.$$

The idea of using one variable to predict another, instead of just using the sample mean, means that we move from an unconditional mean $E(y_i) = \mu$ to a conditional mean, given a value of x. For example, the conditional mean can be

$$E(y_i) = \alpha + \beta x_i.$$

We thus move from an unconditional prediction to a conditional prediction, that is, we move from

$$y_i \sim N(\mu, \sigma^2) \text{ with } E(y_i) = \mu$$

to

$$y_i \sim N(\alpha + \beta x_i, \sigma^2) \text{ with } E(y_i) = \alpha + \beta x_i.$$

An alternative way of writing the conditional prediction follows from demeaning y by subtracting the linear relation $\alpha + \beta x_i$, such that a normally distributed error term with mean zero emerges, that is,

$$y_i = \alpha + \beta x_i + \varepsilon_i \text{ with } \varepsilon_i \sim N(0, \sigma^2).$$

This rewritten form will become useful when we want to estimate the coefficients α and β from observed data, as will be demonstrated next.

Until now, you acquired insights into two aspects of predicting values of a dependent variable Y based on an explanatory variable X. First, there are coefficients a and b that can be useful in practice for actual data, and there are parameters α and β that only exist for hypothetical data. We will now see how to obtain values for a and b from a given set of observations. We will use observed data on X and Y to find optimal values of the coefficients a and b. The line $y = a + bx$ is called the regression line. We have N pairs of observations on (x_i, y_i), and we want to find the line that gives the best fit to these points.

The idea is that we want to explain the variation in the outcomes of the variable y by the variation in the explanatory variable x. When we use the linear function $a + bx$ to predict y, we get residual e. We want to choose the fitted line such that these residuals are small. Minimizing the residuals seems a sensible strategy to find the best possible values for a and b, and a useful objective function is the sum of squared residuals, that is,

$$S(a,b) = \sum_{i=1}^{N} e_i^2 = \sum_{i=1}^{N}(y_i - a - bx_i)^2.$$

This way of finding values for a and b is called the method of least squares, abbreviated as LS. Minimizing $S(a, b)$ to a and b gives[8]

$$b = \frac{\sum_{i=1}^{N}(x_i - \overline{x})(y_i - \overline{y})}{\sum_{i=1}^{N}(x_i - \overline{x})^2} = \frac{s_{xy}}{s_x^2}$$

$$a = \overline{y} - b\overline{x}.$$

The first expression shows that b is equal to the sample covariance of Y and X divided by the sample variance of X. Clearly, there is a link between the expression for b and the expression of the correlation we saw earlier!

When we fit a straight line to a scatter of data, we want to know how well this line fits the data. One measure for this is called the R^2 (pronounced as "R squared"). The line emerges from explaining the variation in the outcomes of the variable Y by means of the variation in the explanatory variable X. The R^2 is defined as 1 minus the fraction of the variation in Y that is not explained by the regression model, that is,

$$R^2 = 1 - \frac{\sum_{i=1}^{N} e_i^2}{\sum_{i=1}^{N} (y_i - \overline{y})^2}.$$

When the R^2 is 0, there is no fit at all, and when the R^2 is 1, the fit is perfect. Finally, the variance of e_i is estimated as

$$s^2 = \frac{1}{N-2} \sum_{i=1}^{N} e_i^2.$$

Let us see how this all works out for the data on the Dutch soccer teams. The average of Points is 24.67, and the average of Attempts is 231.6. The variance of Attempts, s_x^2, is 1,428, and the covariance between Attempts and Points, s_{xy}, is 208.6. Taking these numbers to the equations for a and b, we get $a = -9.15$ and $b = 0.146$. The $\sum_{i=1}^{N} e_i^2$ is 279.7, and hence s is equal to 4.18. Finally, s_y^2 is equal to 46, and this makes the R^2 equal to $1 - \frac{279.7}{18*46} = 0.662$.

With these numbers, we can now also make a prediction, given a certain value for X. That is, we can find for x_0 a prediction for y_0, written as $\hat{y}_0$, like

$$\hat{y}_0 = a + bx_0.$$

As we are uncertain about this prediction, we can also report the prediction interval for y_0, which is

$$(\hat{y}_0 - ks, \hat{y}_0 + ks).$$

So, if the number of Attempts is 400, the prediction for the number of Points would be $-9.15 + 0.146*400 = 49.25$. When we set $k = 2$, the associated prediction interval is $(49.25 - 2*4.18, 49.25 + 2*4.18) = $

(40.89, 57.61). As the number of Points is an integer, this prediction interval would then be (40, 58). The number $k = 2$ is obtained from the Gaussian distribution in Figure 2.6, and hence one can say that with 95% confidence the predicted number of Points, given 400 Attempts, is between 41 and 58.

IS β PERHAPS EQUAL TO 0?

The key idea behind the simple regression model is that we assume that in reality the Y and X are connected via

$$y_i = \alpha + \beta_{xi} + \varepsilon_i \text{ with } \varepsilon_i \sim N(0, \sigma^2)$$

and that we have fitted a line

$$y_i = a + bx_i + e_i.$$

Under a range of assumptions,[9] it is possible to derive the following results. First, it can be shown that b is an unbiased estimator of β, that is,

$$E(b) = \beta.$$

This is a great result, as it means that the value of b obtained via the least squares method is informative for the unknown but assumed link between Y and X, that is, β.

But there is more. When it comes to making predictions, it is actually relevant to know if β is perhaps equal to 0. Or, even though b will always give a number, can we say that it is close enough to 0 to call it 0? Look again at Figure 2.9, where we try to connect Players with Fouls. Even though the line seems to slope a little downward, can we perhaps say that the true but unobserved relation would relate to a line that eventually is perfectly horizontal?

To be able to say something on the closeness of β to zero while actually only having a value for b, we need a confidence interval around β. If that confidence interval would include 0, we can then say that β is not significantly different from 0. With some extra derivations, it is possible to show that when the number of observations N is sufficiently large,

$$\frac{b - \beta}{s_b} \sim N(0, 1),$$

where $N(0,1)$ is the standard normal distribution and where

$$s_b = \sqrt{\frac{s^2}{\sum_{i=1}^{N}(x_i - \overline{x})^2}} = \sqrt{\frac{1}{N}}\sqrt{\frac{s^2}{s_x^2}}.$$

This last expression suggests that the larger N is, the more reliable is our estimate b.

Finally, given the $N(0,1)$ distribution, an approximate 95% confidence interval of $\frac{b-\beta}{s_b}$ is $(-2, 2)$, and hence we have in case of the true $\beta = 0$ that

$$b - 2s_b, \, b + 2s_b$$

includes 0.

For the Points–Attempts relationship, we have that s_x^2 is 1,428 and that s^2 is $(4.18)^2 = 17.5$, such that s_b is 0.026. Together with $b = 0.146$, we thus have a 95% confidence interval of $(0.146 - 2^*0.026, 0.146 + 2^*0.026) = (0.094, 0.198)$, which indeed does not include 0. So, we now say that this b is significantly different from 0.

CAN MEN AND WOMEN RUN MARATHONS WITHIN TWO HOURS?

Let us turn to a more extensive example for the simple regression model. The Appendix to this chapter gives the data on men's marathon record times. The first recorded record dates back to April 10, 1896, and is 2 hours, 58 minutes, and 50 seconds, which is close to 3 hours. The last record (available at the time of writing) can be attributed to Kenyan Dennis Kimetto and is 2 hours, 2 minutes, and 57 seconds, which is close to 2 hours.

So, in more than a century, the record time has decreased by almost an hour; see a graphical impression in Figure 2.10. For women,

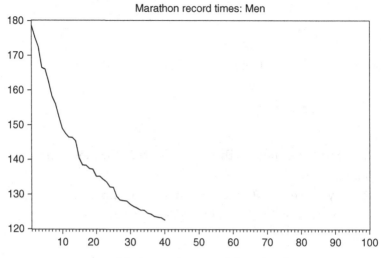

FIGURE 2.10 Men's marathon record times in minutes.

see Figure 2.1, progress is even larger, where the difference between the first record time (October 3, 1926, at 3 hours, 40 minutes, and 22 seconds) and the current record (April 13, 2003, by Paula Radcliffe at 2 hours, 15 minutes, and 25 seconds) is much more than an hour.

The question one now may ask is whether men or women could run a marathon in less than 2 hours in the near future.

Let us see what a regression model can tell us. As the data do not seem to obey a straight line, one may choose to transform the data using the natural logarithmic transformation. Next, a scatter of the current versus the previous records shows a nice straight line, as in Figure 2.12 for men (the scatter for women is very similar).

When we use the least squares methods from earlier, relying on the software package EViews (but any other package would come up with the same results), the model with its estimated coefficients looks like

log(Record men) = 0.263 + 0.945 log(Record men, last time).

Figure 2.13 displays the fit and the errors, and it is clear that the fit is excellent. In fact, the R^2 is 0.995.

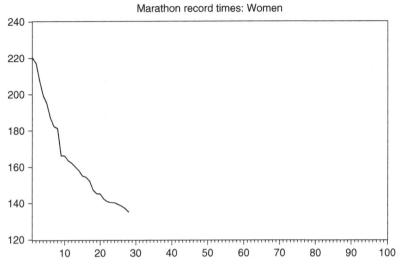

FIGURE 2.11 Women's marathon record times in minutes.

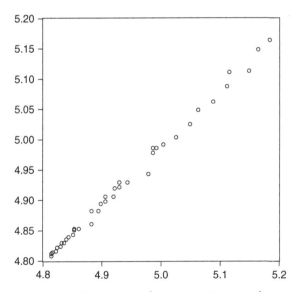

FIGURE 2.12 Current record versus previous record.

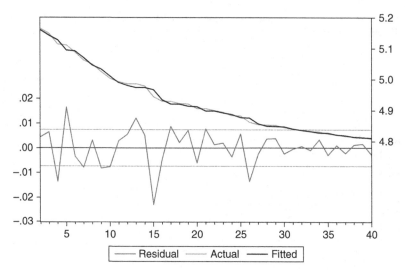

FIGURE 2.13 Actual data, the fitted data from the regression model, and the errors for male record times.

When we run similar computations for the data on the women's records, we get

log(record women) = 0.318 + 0.934 log(record women, last time)

with an R^2 of 0.987.

Given the high-quality fit, it is now quite tempting to see if we can predict records in the future or can see if the record times can ever come below 2 hours. The models for the records in more formal notation are given by

$$y_i = \alpha + \beta y_{i-1} + \varepsilon_i.$$

Such a model is called a first-order autoregression, as the values of Y depend on their own past, just one record ago. Such a model is very useful for forecasting into the future, as you can plug in the current Y on the right-hand side to predict the next value of Y. More formally, one can compute the one-step-ahead forecast made at time N as

$$\hat{y}_{N+1|N} = \alpha + \beta y_N.$$

A two-step-ahead forecast is then given by another plug-in and becomes

$$\hat{y}_{N+2|N} = \alpha + \beta\hat{y}_{N+1|N} = \alpha + \alpha\beta + \beta^2 y_N.$$

When this goes on for K steps, one obtains

$$\hat{y}_{N+K|N} = \alpha(1 + \beta + \cdots + \beta^{K-1}) + \beta^K y_N.$$

And when K goes to infinity, then β^K goes to 0 when $|\beta| < 1$, as we have here, and then we end up with a forecast for the infinite horizon of

$$\hat{y}_{N+\infty|N} = \alpha(1 + \beta + \cdots + \beta^\infty) = \frac{\alpha}{1 - \beta}.$$

With the numbers as noted and transforming the logs back to levels, we obtain a long-run forecast for men of 1.57:32 and for women of 2.03:88. This suggests that the men's records will fall below 2 hours sometime in the future. Figure 2.14 suggests that this record will be

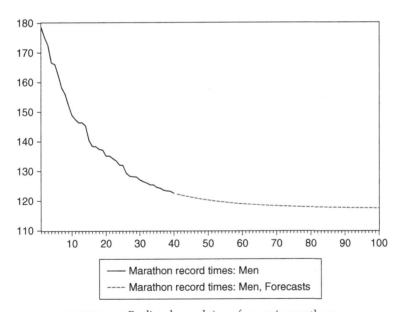

FIGURE 2.14 Predicted record times for men's marathons.

obtained around record 52. For the data on 40 records, where thus 39 records are broken, I can compute that the average time between the records is $(2014 - 1986)/39 \approx 3.0$ years. So, 12 times 3.0 years from 2014 would amount to about the year 2048.

DO RANKED SALARIES SHOW A SPECIFIC PATTERN?

A second illustration of the simple regression model involving two variables Y and X is given by the following data.[10] The histogram in Figure 2.15 presents the annual salaries (in euros for 2015) of the top 100 highest-paid chief executive officers (CEOs) in the Netherlands.

The histogram in Figure 2.15 clearly shows a distribution that is very skewed to the right. The mean is about twice a large as the median, and the standard deviation is about three times as large as the median. So, apparently, a few of these CEOs earn a fortune while many others have much lower salaries (still a lot by the way, as the minimum is 399,000 euros). The highest salary is indeed more than 15 million euros!

The distribution of these salaries has quite a peculiar shape, but when the data are put in a scatter plot against their rank (in the ranking

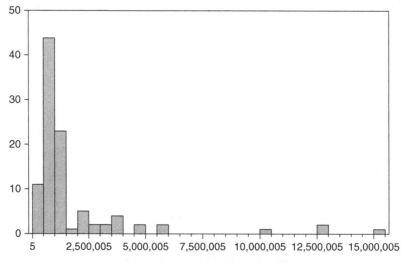

FIGURE 2.15 Salaries (in euros) of the 100 highest-paid CEOs in the Netherlands.

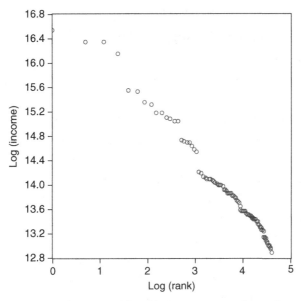

FIGURE 2.16 A scatter plot of log income versus log rank.

1 to 100) after the natural logarithmic transformation,[11] something special appears; see Figure 2.16.

The 100 points all lie around a straight line. Note that the top-left observation has log (rank = 1) = 0, and hence concerns the number 1 salary. Fitting the regression line using the least squares method as before, we get

$$\log (\text{Income}) = 17.096 - 0.872 \log (\text{Rank})$$

with an R^2 equal to 0.983. This strong link between the rank and the variable is associated with what is called Zipf's law; according to Wikipedia, "Zipf's law states that given some corpus of natural language utterances, the frequency of any word is inversely proportional to its rank in the frequency table. Thus the most frequent word will occur approximately twice as often as the second most frequent word, three times as often as the third most frequent word, etc.: the rank-frequency distribution is an inverse relation." Clearly, this law of Zipf also holds for incomes of CEOs. We will see more of this law later in the book.

In the present book, as promised, I will put all further technical aspects in the appendices to the forthcoming chapters. Usually, these aspects concern variations or extensions of the regression model that are then relevant for the questions and data in each of these chapters. Examples of what you can expect are the regression model with not just one variable on the right-hand side but two or more and the regression model, which is associated with S-shaped data. I will also present a multi-equation first-order autoregression where y depends on its own past $Y(-1)$ but also on the past of X, that is, $X(-1)$, while at the same time X also depends on $Y(-1)$ and $X(-1)$.

Econometric textbooks usually have the format that they first introduce the regression models and then continue with a range of extensions of that model. Many textbooks also address the cases where the important assumptions underlying the simple regression model are violated.

Now, to give an impression of those violations, consider again the regression model in its simplest format, that is,

$$y_i = \alpha + \beta x_i + \varepsilon_i$$

with $\varepsilon_i \sim N(0, \sigma^2)$.

Suppose that it is not

$$y_i = \alpha + \beta x_i + \varepsilon_i$$

that one should look at but

$$y_i = \alpha + \beta x_i + \gamma z_i + \varepsilon_i,$$

which means that one has ignored z_i. So, this is an example of a violation of an assumption, which here is that the model involves only a single explanatory factor, while in reality there are two such factors. Alternatively, what happens if it is not

$$\varepsilon_i \sim N(0, \sigma^2)$$

but

$$\varepsilon_i \sim N(\rho \varepsilon_{i-1}, \sigma^2),$$

which means that the errors show first-order autocorrelation? Or what happens to the estimator b for β if it is not

$$\varepsilon_i \sim N(0, \sigma^2)$$

but

$$\varepsilon_i \sim N(0, \sigma_i^2),$$

which says that the variance of the errors is not the same for all errors?

A nasty one is the case when it is unclear whether it is

$$y_i = \alpha + \beta x_i + \varepsilon_i$$

or

$$x_i = \alpha + \beta y_i + \varepsilon_i.$$

And how should one handle

$$y_i = \alpha + \beta x_i^7 + \varepsilon_i,$$

which is a nonlinear regression model?

The list of deviating features is endless. You can also think of the case where Y is either 0 or 1 or where Y is A, B, C, or D or where Y counts like 3, 1, and 0 for the points in football matches.

Anyway, many econometric textbooks deal with a variety of these cases. In some chapters, I will deal with a few of them (always in the appendix!) when they are necessary to answer a question. As indeed, it is question, data, and model, in that order.

APPENDIX: DATA

Fata on authors in *The Guardian*, retrieved from www.theguardian .com/books/2015/jan/13/is-there-an-ideal-age-to-write-a-master piece-infographic.

Author	Key work	Died at
Jack Kerouac	26	47
Douglas Adams	28	49
F. Scott Fitzgerald	30	54
Stella Gibbons	31	87
Charles Dickens	32	58
Charlotte Brontë	32	38
Daphne du Maurier	32	81
Nicholas Sparks	32	
Stephen King	32	
JK Rowling	33	
Stephenie Meyer	33	
Haruki Murakami	34	
Martina Cole	34	
Meg Cabot	34	
Robert Louis Stevenson	34	44
LM Montgomery	35	67
Salman Rushdie	35	
Thomas Hardy	35	87
John Steinbeck	36	66
Terry Pratchett	36	
John Grisham	36	
Louisa May Alcott	37	55
Patrick Suskind	37	
Wilkie Collins	37	65
Raymond E Feist	38	
Aldous Huxley	39	69
Helen Fielding	39	
Jane Austen	39	41
Joseph Heller	39	76

(*cont.*)

Author	Key work	Died at
Dan Brown	40	
Jeffrey Archer	40	
Mervyn Peake	40	57
Colleen McCollough	41	
Gabriel Garcia Marquez	41	87
James Joyce	41	58
John Fowles	41	79
Ken Follett	41	
Louis de Bernieres	41	
Sebastian Faulks	41	
Leo Tolstoy	42	82
Nora Roberts	42	
Paulo Coelho	42	
Danielle Steel	42	
Evelyn Waugh	43	62
George Orwell	43	46
William Golding	44	81
Alexandre Dumas	45	68
Jean M. Auel	45	
Frank Herbert	46	65
Fyodor Dostoyevsky	46	59
JRR Tolkien	46	81
James Patterson	47	
John Irving	48	
Lee Child	48	
Mario Puzo	50	78
Philip Pullman	50	
Anya Seton	51	86
Alexander McCall Smith	52	
Janet Evanovich	52	
Nevil Shute	52	60
CS Lewis	53	64
Richard Adams	53	
Dodie Smith	54	94
George Eliot	54	61
Rosamunde Pilcher	65	

Fata on Dutch Football Teams

Club	Players	Points	Attempts	Corners	Fouls	Yellow	Red	Offside
Ado Den Haag	23	17	228	90	255	43	2	33
Ajax Amsterdam	26	37	277	107	158	19	1	28
AZ Alkmaar	19	24	229	99	241	25	2	39
Cambuur	21	16	167	94	281	33	2	44
Feyenoord	23	33	271	102	229	28	3	38
Go Ahead Eagles	18	23	206	77	207	30	1	20
FC Groningen	20	27	222	89	270	40	5	42
Heerenveen	22	29	241	112	293	39	3	43
Heracles Almelo	24	22	251	99	314	42	0	31
NAC Breda	20	22	206	78	232	37	1	44
NEC Nijmegen	25	15	210	68	234	36	2	59
PEC Zwolle	24	22	219	95	192	29	1	30
PSV Eindhoven	23	26	271	115	237	30	2	33
Roda JC	17	18	213	75	225	43	6	46
FC Twente	22	34	301	126	214	36	0	36
Utrecht	28	24	184	95	247	34	4	57
Vitesse Arnhem	21	37	293	99	244	30	0	24
RKC Waalwijk	23	18	180	72	273	37	6	30

40 World Marathon Records, Men

Date	Athlete	Time	
April 10, 1896	Spiridon Louis	2:58.50	
July 24, 1908	John Hayes	2:55.18,4	
January 1, 1909	Robert Fowler	2:52.45,4	
February 12, 1909	James Clark	2:46.52,6	
May 8, 1909	Albert Raines	2:46.04,6	
May 26, 1909	Frederick Barrett	2:42.31	
May 12, 1913	Harry Green	2:38.16,2	
May 31, 1913	Alexis Ahlgren	2:36.06,6	
August 20, 1920	Hannes Kolehmainen	2:32.35,8	
October 13, 1925	Albert Michelsen	2:29.01,8	
March 31, 1935	Fusashige Suzuki	2:27.49	
April 3, 1935	Yasou Ikenaka	2:26.44	
November 3, 1935	Sohn Kee-chung	2:26.42	
April 19, 1947	Suh Yun-bok	2:25.39	
June 14, 1952	Jim Peters	2:20.42,2	
July 13, 1953	Jim Peters	2:18.40,2	
October 4, 1953	Jim Peters	2:18.34,8	
July 26, 1954	Jim Peters	2:17.39,4	
August 24, 1958	Sergej Popov	2:15.17	
September 10, 1960	Abebe Bikila	2:15.16,2	
February 17, 1963	Toru Terasawa	2:15.15,8	
June 15, 1963	Leonard Edelen	2:14.28	
June 13, 1964	Basil Heatley	2:13.55,2	
October 21, 1964	Abebe Bikila	2:12.11,2	
June 12, 1965	Mono Shigematsu	2:12.00	
December 3, 1967	Derek Clayton	2:09.37	
May 30, 1969	Derek Clayton	2:08.34	
December 6, 1981	Robert de Castella	2:08.18	
October 21, 1984	Steve Jones	2:08.05	
April 20, 1985	Carlos Lopes	2:07.12	(Rotterdam)
April 17, 1988	Belayneh Densamo	2:06.50	(Rotterdam)
September 20, 1998	Ronaldo da Costa	2:06.05	
October 24, 1999	Khalid Khannouchi	2:05.42	
April 14, 2002	Khalid Khannouchi	2:05.38	

(cont.)

Date	Athlete	Time
September 28, 2003	Paul Tergat	2:04.55
September 30, 2007	Haile Gebrselassie	2:04.26
September 28, 2008	Haile Gebrselassie	2:03.59
September 25, 2011	Patrick Makau Musyoki	2:03.38
September 29, 2013	Wilson Kipsang	2:03.23
September 28, 2014	Dennis Kimetto	2:02.57

28 World Marathon Records, Women

Date	Athlete	Time	
October 3, 1926	Violet Piercy	3:40.22	
December 13, 1963	Merry Lepper	3:37.04	
May 23, 1964	Dale Greig	3:27.45	
July 21, 1964	Mildred Sampson	3:19.33	
May 6, 1967	Maureen Wilton	3:15.22	
September 16, 1967	Anni Pede-Erdkamp	3:07.26	
February 28, 1970	Caroline Walker	3:02.53	
May 9, 1971	Beth Bonner	3:01.42	
August 31, 1971	Adrienne Beames	2:46.30	
October 27, 1974	Chantal Langlace	2:46.24	
December 1, 1974	Jacqueline Hansen	2:43.55	
April 1, 1975	Liane Winter	2:42.24	
May 3, 1975	Christa Vahlensieck	2:40.16	
October 12, 1975	Jacqueline Hansen	2:38.19	
May 1, 1977	Chantal Laglace	2:35.16	
September 10, 1977	Christa Vahlensieck	2:34.48	
October 22, 1978	Grete Waitz	2:32.30	
October 21, 1979	Grete Waitz	2:27.33	
October 26, 1980	Grete Waitz	2:25.42	
April 17, 1983	Grete Waitz	2:25.29	
April 18, 1983	Joan Benoit	2:22.43	
April 21, 1985	Ingrid Kristiansen	2:21.06	
April 19, 1998	Tegla Loroupe	2:20.47	(Rotterdam)

(cont.)

Date	Athlete	Time
September 26, 1999	Tegla Loroupe	2:20.43
September 30, 2001	Naoko Takahashi	2:19.46
October 7, 2001	Catherine Ndereba	2:18.47
October 13, 2002	Paula Radcliffe	2:17.18
April 13, 2003	Paula Radcliffe	2:15.25

REFERENCES AND FURTHER READING

Here is a list of textbooks on econometrics. The best textbook I can recommend (nudge, nudge, say no more) is

Christiaan Heij, Paul de Boer, Philip Hans Franses, Teun Kloek, and Herman K. van Dijk (2004), *Econometric Methods with Applications in Business and Economics*, Oxford: Oxford University Press.

But, of course, I am biased here.

Useful textbooks that can be studied without knowledge of matrix algebra (tools that make notation easier) are

Damodar N. Gujarati (2003), *Basic Econometrics*, Boston, MA: McGraw-Hill.

R. Carter Hill, William E. Griffiths, and George G. Judge (2001), *Undergraduate Econometrics*, New York, NY: Wiley.

Peter Kennedy (1998), *A Guide to Econometrics*, Oxford: Blackwell.

George S. Maddala (2001), *Introduction to Econometrics*, London: Prentice Hall.

Robert Pindyck and Daniel L. Rubinfield (1998), *Econometric Models and Economic Forecasts*, Boston, MA: McGraw-Hill.

James H. Stock and Mark W. Watson (2015), *Introduction to Econometrics*, Harlow: Pearson Education.

Jeffrey M. Wooldridge (2000), *Introductory Econometrics*, Australia: Thomson Learning.

And textbooks that use matrix algebra and are of a bit higher level are

Gregory G. Chow (1983), *Econometrics*, Auckland: McGraw-Hill.

William H. Greene (2000), *Econometric Analysis*, New York, NY: Prentice Hall.

Marno Verbeek (2012), *A Guide to Modern Econometrics, Fourth Edition*, Chichester: Wiley.

3   Money

Phoney as a Three Dollar Bill!!!

—Hy Gardner's "Broadway Newsreel" column in the Brooklyn (NY)
Daily Eagle on March 19, 1937

AT A GLANCE

This chapter is about money, real money. Quite literally, in fact, it
is about the coins and notes that we have in our hands when we
pay for something. Of course, many payments these days are done
with credit and debit cards, but still, a substantial fraction of
payments worldwide involves a transaction with cash. Typically,
these transactions involve reasonably small amounts, like amounts
below 100 EUR or 100 USD. The largest euro banknote is EUR 500,
and it is this note that will no longer be produced by the European
Central Bank as it is typically used in very large but illegal
transactions.[1]

Interestingly enough, there has never been much interest in
what it is that people do when they actually pay with cash, although
there are some exceptions.[2] This could be a lack of interest in the topic
itself, but it could also be that data collection is not straightforward.
In fact, if you want to study what people do when they pay with cash,
then you should also observe the contents of their wallets. Moreover,
you can imagine that the question "Can I see the content of your
wallet?" does not always lead to an enthusiastic "Yes, of course!"
Unless, as will become clear later in this chapter, you either make
students ask this question with the additional text that it is required
for a school project or collect such data when the data are visible to
anyone, like during a game of Monopoly, for example.

One focus point in this chapter is the collection of data and how this collection influences the subsequent application of econometric methods. Often we believe that people collect data for us, and we just analyze them, but it may sometimes be much better to collect the data ourselves. Indeed, in 1998 the Dutch Central Bank (DNB) commissioned a large-scale data collection of cash transactions, where it collected information on no fewer than 38,330 cash payments.[3] A careful selection of retail outlets across the country and also across a range of categories, like supermarkets, specialized food stores, and so on, should allow for a systematic analysis of payment behavior. What was recorded was the amount that needed to be paid, the number of notes and coins that people gave to a cashier, and the number of notes and coins that they received in return. In the Netherlands in those days, one could pay with the Dutch guilder (NLG), which had 12 denominations: 1,000, 250, 100, 50, 25, and 10 for notes and 5, 2.5, 1, 0.25, 0.10, and 0.05 for coins. Even though the sample size was very large, certainly for those days, there was one little problem with these data collected by DNB. Due to "privacy reasons," the data collectors did not observe nor ask what the wallet contents were in these 38,330 situations. Therefore, in the end, there were many data available, but the subsequent analysis was seriously hampered by an omitted variable, the wallet content. This wallet content is of course very relevant because when we observe which notes and coins are used by an individual, we should also know between which notes and coins he or she could choose. To understand how people pay with cash, we therefore should be able to observe the full choice process.

In the previous chapter, we discussed the mean, variance, correlation, and simple regression model, and these are all methods, which are useful once one has the data. Now it is time to address the importance of data collection itself. Sometimes data collection is helped by an event that makes the world change in some dimension. Think of the introduction of the euro (EUR) on January 1, 2002. That introduction is interesting for various reasons, one of them being that the denominational range changed, that is, the EUR has 15 denominations: 500, 200,

100, 50, 20, 10, and 5 as banknotes and 2, 1, 0.50, 0.20, 0.10, 0.05, 0.02, and 0.01 as coins. Therefore, for the Netherlands, the number of denominations increased from 12 to 15. The conversion rate of EUR to NLG was 2.20371, that is, one euro was 2.20371 guilder. Not only the number of denominations changed; the value of the denominations did as well. The denominations 250, 25, 2.5, and 0.25 did not return with the euro.[4]

A second key message from this chapter is that an event can allow you to collect data before and after that event to see if things have changed. Hence, you may think twice before you start to collect data. It too often happens that one first collects data and then thinks about how to analyze them. Here we will see that the other way around can be more useful and may save time. Indeed, we will see that there is no need at all to collect 38,330 observations to learn about individual payment behavior. However, before one can do that, like before, we need a benchmark. Therefore, similar to answering the "Is four a lot?" question, we need to wonder beforehand what it is we are actually observing. We will see that a key concept relevant for cash payments is the efficiency of a payment. Remember a time when you stood in line to check out behind someone who emptied a wallet with an overwhelming amount of coins to pay a small amount. Well, that transaction with a large amount of coins was *not* an efficient transaction. Therefore, before we can collect relevant data, we need to think about what it is that we want to observe.

Before we get to the wallets, let us first have a look at the face value of banknotes. We tend to believe that big numbers also imply something big. Think of the question "Is 4,000 a lot?," which sounds quite different from "Is four a lot?" With money we have the same phenomenon, that is, higher-valued denominations seem to have a larger value (in the sense that you may feel you can buy more with them) than lower-valued denominations. Mid-2016, the exchange rate between the euro and the Indonesian rupiah was about 15,000. Therefore, when you go to Jakarta, you need many bills with high numbers on them. One effect of these additional zeroes is that we are

FIGURE 3.1 A banknote of 100,000,000,000,000,000,000 Hungarian Pengö.

tempted to spend less. Each time you see something like a bag or a souvenir and it costs 300,000 rupiah, you feel that the gift is very expensive. This phenomenon is called *money illusion*. In times of hyperinflation, these additional zeroes would suggest that the money is useless. Look at the Hungarian banknote of 10^{20} Pengö in Figure 3.1, which was issued July 11, 1946, and withdrawn July 31, 1946.

So, apparently, it matters what is on a banknote. Let us start with that.

DO WE SUFFER FROM MONEY ILLUSION?

By the time the euro was introduced on January 1, 2002, many people were curious about this new currency. Others were worried. The worry was that prices would go up because people would start to spend the euro as if it were a Dutch guilder. Indeed, in those days it did happen that restaurant meal prices changed from 20 NLG to 15 EUR, which basically implies a serious price increase. The link between prices and what is on the banknotes could exist, and people had horror stories of Germany in the 1920s in mind, where inflation approached 1,600% (see Figure 3.2).

Now, it could well be that the introduction of a new currency like the euro would trigger inflation, but whether this was true for the

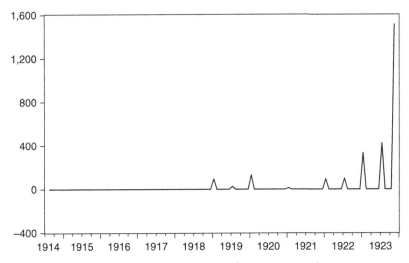

FIGURE 3.2 Inflation (month to month, in percentages) in Germany from January 1914 to December 1923.

Netherlands was doubtful. Figure 3.3 shows the monthly inflation rate (the current month versus the same month in the previous year), and intriguingly, it seems that inflation started to increase about a year before the introduction of the euro. And, what is more, inflation seemed to fall right after the introduction of the euro.

So, prices were high indeed, as an inflation rate of 4 or 5 is quite high, at least for the Netherlands, and it is far from hyperinflation figures like in Figure 3.2. Hence, it seems that perhaps other reasons also would make people to feel that prices were on the rise. It could be that the Dutch public suffered from money illusion.

There are various ways to design measures of money illusion, and here let us have a look at a very simple way, which makes use of a little deceit.[5] It is not the intention to advocate data collection methods based on deceit, but here it was only a little, and it did work out quite well.

Thirty-six individuals (within the realm of family, friends, and sports teammates; with a range of different ages; and gender equally balanced) were contacted,[6] and they were presented the question in Survey 1. The data were collected in the summer of 2004.

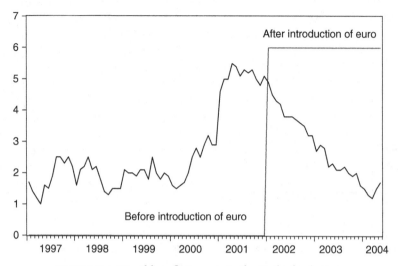

FIGURE 3.3 Monthly inflation rate in the Netherlands, January 1997 to May 2004.

Survey 1: Assume that you will go to a holiday park the upcoming weekend, where the rent of a two-person lodge will be 769 NLG for the entire weekend and where the prices go down for more individuals, that is, a four-person lodge is 893 NLG in total and a six-person lodge is only 1,025 NLG. The park offers various facilities to make your stay more pleasant, and the question that we have is what would you be willing to pay for these facilities?

Facility		Willingness to pay (in NLG)	
Beauty day (one full day)	NLG	. . . ..	per person
Bowling alley (one hour)	NLG	. . . ..	per alley
Tennis court (one hour)	NLG	. . . ..	per court
Bicycle (two days)	NLG	. . . ..	per bicycle

Two weeks later, the very same 36 individuals were contacted again with the message that unfortunately we had made a mistake. Even though it was already halfway through 2004, the researchers erroneously put NLG amounts in the survey, and they should of course be EUR. So, whether the 36 individuals would be so kind to answer the four questions in the survey again? Survey 2 (same people): Assume that you will go to a holiday park the upcoming weekend, where the rent of a two-person lodge will be 349 EUR for the entire weekend and where the prices go down for more individuals, that is, a four-person lodge is 405 EUR in total and a six-person lodge is only 465 EUR. The park offers various facilities to make your stay more pleasant, and the question that we have is what would you be willing to pay for these facilities?

Facility	Willingness to pay (in EUR)		
Beauty day (one full day)	EUR	. . . ..	per person
Bowling alley (one hour)	EUR	. . . ..	per alley
Tennis court (one hour)	EUR	. . . ..	per court
Bicycle (two days)	EUR	. . . ..	per bicycle

Our 36 individuals were actually kind enough to complete the questionnaire again. The data are listed in the Appendix to this chapter.

The results are quite interesting when comparing the two surveys, as we can see from Table 3.1. In all four cases, the individuals were clearly willing to pay more in euros than in guilders. The last two columns show that one would be willing to pay about 5.5 euros more for the beauty day, about 3 euros more for a bowling alley, about 2.5 euros more for a tennis court, and again about 2.5 euros more for a bicycle. Note that these were the very same 36 individuals and that the time between the two surveys was just two weeks.

Table 3.1 *Average willingness to pay for additional facilities.*

	NLG	EUR	NLG as EUR
Beauty day (one full day)	64.75	35.94	29.38
Bowling alley (one hour)	17.90	11.06	8.124
Tennis court (one hour)	15.92	9.79	7.22
Bicycle (two days)	25.29	14.25	11.48

Table 3.2 *Differences of willingness to pay in terms of EUR and NLG as EUR (in boldface are the 5% significant test values).*

	EUR minus NLG as EUR			Percentage
	Average	SD	t test[8]	
Beauty day (one full day)	6.562	11.45	**3.439**	+38.19%
Bowling alley (one hour)	2.932	6.513	**2.701**	+60.59%
Tennis court (one hour)	2.569	3.555	**4.336**	+52.57%
Bicycle (two days)	2.773	6.245	**2.664**	+39.63%

Zooming in on the specifics of the differences, as in Table 3.2, we can see that the differences in Table 3.1 are statistically significant, which is because the t test values in the penultimate column exceed 2. And what is more, people are willing to pay 40% to 60% more for the same facility when they are forced to think in terms of euros.[7]

This example shows that with not that much effort one can collect informative data, which then can be analyzed using a rather simple statistical method. Indeed, the econometric method here only involves the computation of an average. One could of course say, should one not collect many more data than just 36? Well, more data would of course always be more informative, but given the expression in the appendix on the t test, we see that the first term is $\sqrt{N}$. Hence, one may expect that when N increases, the associated t test values only will become larger, at least when the additional individuals answer in the same way as our 36 do. So, it seems that this size of a sample is already quite informative. One could also ask, does the collection of data among family and friends not bias the outcomes? Well, why should that be? What is the chance that only family members and friends would suffer from money illusion and others perhaps not? Is there a reason to believe that these 36 individuals would behave very differently from others? Of course, 36 is not representative for the public in the Netherlands, along various dimensions, but why would it not be representative for the dimension "money illusion"?

Now that we have seen that money illusion can matter, it becomes interesting to see how people would pay with cash in the real world.

HOW DO WE PAY WITH CASH?

A very interesting quote appeared on NOS Teletext Page 192, May 31, 2002 (a Netherlands-based television channel), and it reads as follows:

> Some people still have to get used to the Euro. A gas station cashier in Erbach, Germany, turned out not to be completely familiar with the new denominations. A client paid with a note of 300 Euro, and the cashier happily returned him the amount of 250 Euros.

At first sight, not much seems to be strange about this message, but apparently it is, as otherwise it would not have been posted on Teletext. The key issue of this message is of course the number 300. Even though it does not sound strange, well, there actually is no 300 EUR banknote! So, this banknote was obviously fake. See Figure 3.4 for an example. A closer look at the note shows that it must be fake, but then still, 300 would not be such a strange denomination. One may wonder why the forger did not fake a 500 EUR note or 1,000 EUR, for that matter, as that would have delivered much more in return, but that is another issue. So, plausible denominations may feel like valid currency.

This brings me to the question how people pay with coins and banknotes and what cashiers do. One may also wonder what happens if certain banknotes are not available. Or what happens if certain coins, like those of the 1 and 2 EUR cents, are not introduced or removed from day-to-day transactions?[9] Indeed, for the Netherlands from September 1, 2004 onward, all transaction amounts were rounded to 5 cents, making the 1- and 2-cent coins legal tender but less useful.

To learn more about how we pay with cash, we need a benchmark, just like in the case of the question "Is four a lot?"

FIGURE 3.4 A fake banknote of 300 EUR.

Here the benchmark is not an average or a variance or a theoretical distribution; here the benchmark is called "efficiency." Before we can potentially understand what it is that people do when they pay with cash, and for that purpose look into their wallet to make a choice among the available amounts of notes and coins, we need to assume that individuals have the intention to make an efficient payment. So, we have to reduce the potential variation in the data somewhat. Obviously, an inefficient payment is something like having to pay an amount of 5 euros and then give three bills of 5 euros to a cashier, who will return two of those bills to you. This transaction then involves four unnecessary actions, that is, your superfluous two bills and the return of each of these. A very useful algorithm to retrieve efficient payment schemes was developed by J.S. (Mars) Cramer.[10] For infinite-sized wallet contents, Cramer's method[11] works as follows.

Denote with P the payment amount and with $n(P)$ the amount of tokens (notes and or coins) to be used for cash payment. The denomination range is given by the set $\{1, 2, \ldots, D\}$, and an element of this set is denoted by d. Denote with $n(P,d)$ the number of tokens of denomination d, so

$$n(P) = \sum_{d=1}^{D} n(P,d)$$

Finally, denote with $v(d)$ the value of denomination d.

The objective is now to minimize $n(P)$ by choosing the "right" notes and coins out of the set $\{1,2,\ldots,D\}$. More formally, one should solve

$$\text{minimize } n^*(P) = \sum_{d=1}^{D} |n(P,d)|$$

$$\text{subject to } \sum_{d=1}^{D} n(P,d)v(d) = P.$$

Note that we have to use the absolute value of $n(P,d)$ to allow for the possibility that notes and coins are returned as change.

Cramer's algorithm to obtain all efficient payment schemes proceeds as follows. We take a range of payment amounts that are of potential interest, say, 0.01 EUR (which is 1 eurocent) until, say, 100 EUR with intervals of 0.01 EUR. The goal of the algorithm is to find for each of these amounts the efficient combinations of notes and coins.

Step 1: The algorithm starts by taking all amounts that can be paid with only one note or one coin. For the euro, the amounts 0.01, 0.02, 0.10, 0.20, 0.50, 1, 2, 5, 10, 20, 50, and 100 are now covered.

Step 2: All amounts that can be paid with two tokens, either two given by the individual as payment or one returned by the retailer as change, are next to be computed. For example, 15 EUR can be paid with 10 and 5 euro notes or with a 20 euro note with a 5 euro note as change. If we now observe an amount that was already covered with only one token in the previous step, we do not add this pair of two tokens to the list as those tokens are obviously not efficient for this amount.

Step 3: To the pairs that were found efficient in the previous two steps, we add each token once, with both positive and negative signs, the latter indicating change. For example, to a 10 and 5 euro note we add a 0.20 coin, covering the amounts 15.20 and 14.80 (where in the last case the 0.20 is given as change). For a given pair in Step 2, this gives 2*d* extra combinations with an additional token each. Adding a token with a positive sign to a combination, which has this same token with a negative sign, would yield a combination with fewer tokens and is therefore ignored. Note also that there is the restriction that the highest-valued token always has a positive sign. With these combinations we cover all resulting amounts, provided they were not already covered by efficient payments with lesser tokens.

Step 4: Repeat Step 3 by increasing each time the number of tokens until all amounts between 0.01 EUR and 100 EUR are covered.

This algorithm results in efficient combinations (note that there can be more than one!) for each possible amount in the specified range of 0.01 EUR to 100 EUR. Table 3.3 gives some statistics about these efficient payment schemes.

The original Crame's algorithm assumes that an individual has available all possible notes and coins. This is not realistic, and hence we better modify the algorithm, which is now based on

$$\text{minimize } n^*(P) = \sum_{d=1}^{D} |n(P,d)|$$

$$\text{subject to } \sum_{d=1}^{D} n(P,d)v(d) = P$$

$$n(P,d) \leq w(d) \text{ for all } d$$

Table 3.3 *Statistics on all payment schemes for amounts between 0.01 EUR and 100 EUR.*

Efficient payment schemes	All euro denominations
Number	36,591
Average number of tokens exchanged	5.83
Median	6
Minimum	1
Maximum	8

where we use $w(d)$ to denote the amount of available notes and coins of denomination d.

If a wallet allows for paying according to an efficient scheme, we take this efficient scheme. Otherwise, we need to find the restricted efficient scheme, that is, the combination of notes and coins that minimizes the numbers of tokens used given the wallet contents. The modified algorithm then is as follows.

Step 1: The algorithm starts by computing all amounts that can be covered by a single token. Only if the wallet contains the relevant tokens is the combination stored.

Step 2: All amounts that can be paid with two tokens, either given by the individual or partly returned by the cashier as change, are computed. Again, only if the wallet content allows it is the combination stored.

Step 3: To the pairs that were found as efficient in the previous step, we add each token once, with both positive and negative signs (indicating change). With these combinations, we fill the list with the resulting amounts, provided they are not already covered by lesser tokens and provided the combination fits in the wallet.

Step 4: We repeat Step 3 for increasing numbers of tokens until the amount P is covered. Note that it is not sufficient to only store the combination that pays the given amount P exactly. We need to store each combination that fits in the individual's wallet, as we use these as the starting point for the schemes in the next step.

As an example, suppose a wallet contains three notes of 5 euros and an individual has to pay 15 euros. The efficient combinations 10 and 5, and 20 and –5 are not available, but the combination 5, 5, and 5 is efficient *given* this wallet content. Now, all this may seem irrelevant, but really, it matters!

An Econometric Model for Payments

In the previous chapter, we learned that in reality Y and X are connected via

$$y_i = \alpha + \beta x_i + \varepsilon_i \text{ with } \varepsilon_i \sim N\left(0, \sigma^2\right)$$

and that for actual data we could fit

$$y_i = a + b x_i + e_i$$

and assign a meaning to the numbers a and b, which would help us to say something about α and β. Over here, trying to make sense out of data on actual transactions, we have to do something similar, that is, we have to think about a model for actual data that could reflect (an unobserved) reality.

Now that we know whether a wallet of an individual contains notes and coins that allow for an efficient payment, the next step is to think about a theoretical version of the payment process so that we later on can arrive at a model that can be considered for actual data. That is, what could it be that people do when they open up their wallet? We could assume a sequential process,[12] where larger-valued denominations are considered prior to lower-valued ones. It assumes that an individual first checks if the payment amount requires one or more of the highest-valued notes or coins available in the wallet and then he or she proceeds to adjacent lower-valued notes and coins. A second feature is that it contains a sequence of regression models, each time for the number of notes or coins that are used.[13] A third feature is that it includes the amount of the payment left that needs to be paid.

To illustrate this third feature, assume that the amount to be paid is 15 euros and that the wallet contains one note of 20, one of 10, and one of 5. If the individual pays with a note of 20, the amount left to pay with notes of 10 or 5 is zero. If the individual chooses not to pay with a note of 20, the amount left to pay is 15 euros, which is paid with a note of 10 and a note of 5. Thus, we can compute, for each note and coin in the payment process, what amount still has to be paid after a choice concerning this note or coin has been made. We expect that the larger the amount left relative to a specific note or coin, the higher the probability that the individual will select it.

If cash payment behavior of individuals reveals no preference for any denomination, then the probability of choosing a denomination for payment would be equal for all denominations in similar payment situations and defined by wallet content and amounts to be paid. Therefore, the question of whether individuals are indifferent toward denominations can be answered statistically by testing if the parameter values (intercepts and coefficients on the amount left to pay) are equal across denominations.

Basically, the model is in the spirit of a simple regression model, and it reads as

Number of notes or coins used of denomination $d = \alpha_d + \beta_d$ times (Amount left to be paid, given that denominations $d+1$ have been used)

The test on the null hypothesis

$$\beta_1 = \beta_2 = \cdots = \beta_D$$

is an extension of the t test in the Appendix. Rejection of the null hypothesis suggests that the parameters significantly differ across denominations. In that case, some denominations are more or less preferred than others, and the denominational structure of the currency can be regarded as suboptimal. Indeed, one would want to have a denominational range such that all notes and coins are equally often used when they are necessary. If not, one can perhaps remove a denomination from the range.

So, we now have a method that can be used to analyze data, which, by the way, still need to be collected.

IS THE EURO DENOMINATIONAL RANGE OPTIMAL?

The final issue before we can reliably answer the question on optimality is of course how many observations we need to collect to have somewhat reliable inference. It is important to decide on this upfront, as we have to collect data on wallets and hence have to ask individuals to open up their wallets and tell us what is in them. That is quite a time-consuming activity, and it is also unlikely that we will be able to collect the more than 30,000 (admittedly incomplete) observations that DNB collected. The theoretical econometric model for payments with cash can now be used to create artificial data, given certain choices for the parameters α_d and β_d. The artificial data are then the input for an empirical econometric model. The parameters in the latter model are estimated, and the crucial test on the equality of these parameters is performed. When the empirical distribution of the test values comes close to the normal distribution, given a certain number of artificial observations, one can conclude that that number of observations might give reliable estimates in practice. Here it turns out that about 250 observations would be enough to have reliable estimates.

An application to data for the Netherlands guilder[14] showed that the guilder denominational range was suboptimal. That is, individuals tended to have a higher preference for using the NLG 100 note and a smaller preference for using the NLG 50 note.[15]

An application to 272 observed transactions with wallet content with the euro, carried out in October 2002, resulted in the conclusion that the euro denominational range effectively *is* optimal.[16] The differences across the guilder and the euro could be due to the fact that the guilder had denominations of 250, 25, and 0.25 whereas the euro has 200, 20, and 0.20. In sum, in terms of ease of use of the notes and coins, a transition from NLG to EUR was beneficial to the Dutch public.

HOW DO WE PAY WITH EURO NOTES WHEN SOME NOTES ARE MISSING?

Now that we have a theoretical model and a model that we can use to analyze actual transaction data, we can also ask other questions concerning how we pay with money. One relevant question is what we would do if certain notes or coins were missing. It is now good to bear in mind that asking someone to open up a wallet is quite an issue, but to ask a bank or ATM to stop issuing certain denominations is virtually impossible! Perhaps playing a game can alleviate this issue. We will see.

First, let us think about this issue from a theoretical perspective.[17] January 1, 2002, marked the launch of the euro in 12 European countries, and since then a few more countries have introduced the euro and still more countries will do so in the future. The euro banknotes are 500, 200, 100, 50, 20, 10, and 5. The euro coins consist of denominations 2, 1, 0.50, 0.20, 0.10, 0.05, 0.02, and 0.01. Ever since the euro's inception, countries have questioned the relevance of having 1- and 2-euro cent coins. Indeed, rounding at 5 euro cents has been common in Finland for a long while and also became common in the Netherlands in the past few years.

The question thus is whether all euro denominations are necessary for efficient payments. In other words, can we do without some denominations without loss of efficiency? For that purpose, we can again rely on Cramer's theoretical concept of efficient payments and compare the outcomes of the relevant algorithm to compute the number of efficient payment schemes. Like before, the theoretical model of individual payment behavior is based on the "principle of least effort." If individuals would behave according to this principle, each amount would be paid such that the number of notes and coins exchanged is minimized. Such payment schemes are then called efficient payments.

Each payment amount has one or more efficient payment schemes. An illustration is the amount of 11.30 EUR that can be efficiently paid using three different schemes, that is, (1) 10 + 1 + 0.20 + 0.10, (2) 10 + 1 + 0.50 and 0.20 returned, and (3) 10 + 2 and 0.50 + 0.20 returned.

In practice, it is unlikely that all actual payments are efficient because individuals might not behave according to the principle of least effort, nor will they all have the necessary denominations in their wallet. However, the Cramer model does provide a simple way to illustrate basic differences between denominational ranges because it can be applied to any denominational range.

In comparing the efficient payment schemes of two denominational ranges (with or without certain notes or coins), one can distinguish between two aspects of efficiency. First, the smaller the number of tokens that is exchanged on average, the more efficient is the range. Second, the more efficient payment schemes that exist for an amount, the more opportunities for individuals to make an efficient payment. Otherwise stated, the higher the probability that an efficient payment is made, the more efficient is the range. If we look at all efficient payment schemes and at the number of tokens used in each payment, we combine the two aspects of efficiency. That is, the more efficient payment schemes with a small amount of tokens, the higher the efficiency of the range.

Leaving Out a Single Note

It is generally accepted that a banknote range should not contain too many different denominations. This might cause confusion and perhaps inefficient payment behavior. If empirical analysis would show this is indeed the case for euro cash payments, it might be worthwhile to investigate the possibility of withdrawing a banknote denomination from circulation. Next, in cases of emergency it might be necessary to temporarily put one banknote denomination out of use (for example, due to a counterfeiting attack, strikes, or delivery failure). With the concept of efficient payments, one can understand the theoretical effects of removing one denomination from the current euro banknote range.

The starting point for the calculations is the complete euro banknote range complemented by a 1-euro coin. The resulting (virtual) range consists of the following denominations: 500, 200, 100, 50, 20, 10, 5, and 1 euro. Our focus is on banknote denominations, and by limiting the range to the smallest denomination of 1 euro, I reduce computational efforts. Cramer's algorithm again gives efficient payment schemes for all amounts between 1 and 1,000 euros for six different denominational ranges. The first is our basic range, which includes all denominations listed previously. Later on, we subsequently remove 200, 100, 50, 20, and 10 euros from the denominational range. Therefore, these five ranges have one denomination less than the basic range.

Table 3.4 shows some characteristics of the resulting efficient payment schemes for each of the denominational ranges. The first row of the table shows that the number of efficient payment schemes decreases rapidly if a single banknote denomination is removed from the range. For example, in the full range, amounts can be paid efficiently with up to a maximum of 18 different payment schemes, while this maximum decreases to 10 or less if a single denomination is left out of the range. This means that individuals have fewer opportunities to make an efficient payment. As can be expected (see the last row of Table 3.4), the average number of tokens exchanged, in an arbitrary amount that is paid efficiently, increases when the denominational range becomes smaller. This effect is largest when the 200- or 20-euro note is removed from the range, with an average of 4.8 tokens required to pay an amount efficiently, in contrast to the 4.5 tokens with the full range available.

If we consider the tokens exchanged per payment scheme, in which both aspects of efficiency are combined, we find the differences to be small. In all cases, the maximum number of tokens used in a payment scheme is 8. The average number of tokens exchanged in a payment scheme even decreases if the 100- or 10-euro note is removed from the full range. This is explained by the fact that the reduction in efficient payment schemes, when the 100- or 10-euro note is removed from the range, mainly concerns those efficient payment schemes that involve many tokens (7 or 8).

In sum, this theoretical analysis shows that the removal of one banknote denomination does have a negative effect on the payment system, but the effect is not as dramatic as one might expect. If we compare across the different denominational ranges, we can conclude that the withdrawal of the 100 EUR or 10 EUR banknotes has the smallest negative effects. It will reduce the number of efficient payment schemes by 25% and the average number of tokens exchanged per amount by only 2% to 2.5%. The 50 EUR banknote, on the other hand, seems to be more important. Removing this banknote from the denominational range will increase the average number of tokens exchanged by 7%.

Table 3.4 *Statistics on efficient payment schemes for all ranges (amounts are between 1 and 1,000 euros with multiples of 1 euros)*

	All denominations	Leaving out a single note				
		200	100	50	20	10
Efficient payment schemes						
Number	2,553	1,766	1,873	2,034	1,862	1,964
Maximum	18	6	9	8	8	10
Tokens used						
for each payment scheme						
Average	5.18	5.26	5.10	5.34	5.27	5.12
Median	5	5	5	5	5	5
Minimum	1	1	1	1	1	1
Maximum	8	8	8	8	8	8
Tokens used for each amount						
Average	4.52	4.83	4.62	4.84	4.82	4.65

How Does This Work in Practice?

To make an ATM stop giving certain notes is too much of a hassle and most likely undoable. So, to collect data on payments and transactions where we could safely remove one of the denominations, we decided to play games of Monopoly (the European version). Knowing that about 250 observations would provide reliable inference, we estimated that, each time, we need to play the game twice with three or four players for a period of about two hours.[18]

The person who played as the banker kept records of all transactions. In my office at the Erasmus School of Economics, we had various people play games with all denominations, that is, with 500, 200, 100, 50, 20, 10, 5, and 1 EUR notes, and we had five additional games where each time we removed one of the notes. The 500 EUR note, the 5 EUR note, and the 1 EUR coin turn out to be mandatory for their use in all relevant transactions, that is, there is no choice but to use them. We thus had these five games played without the 200 EUR note, without the 100 EUR note, without the 50 EUR note, without the 20 EUR note, and finally without the 10 EUR note. Hence, in total we had 12 games played, six times two.

The individuals who participated in the games ranged in age from 18 to 56, and there were equal numbers of men and women. The players had different educational backgrounds, as they consisted of undergraduate students, academic colleagues, and administrative assistants, all associated with the Erasmus School of Economics. In total, there were 51 participants. None of them were informed that they were participating in an experiment. We informed them that the data were being collected to understand strategic behavior in games.

The European edition of the Monopoly game uses EUR notes of 500, 100, 50, 20, 10, and 5 and a coin of 1. As the actual denominational range of the euro also contains a 200 EUR note, we had to make a new note. It turned out that none of the participants had played the game ever before, so none of them were aware that our 200 EUR note

FIGURE 3.5 A newly created Monopoly note of 200 euros.

was not original to the game. We had the note made specifically for this purpose, and it is depicted in Figure 3.5. In reality the size of this note is the same as the size of all other toy notes, and hence it is obvious that it is not a genuine note; it is also only printed on one side. In order to make sure that we would never run out of notes of any value, we had additional copies made of the available notes. Hence, in all situations, the bank (within the game) would have no shortage.

There were two more modifications to the game as it is outlined in the booklet of the European edition of Monopoly. Sometimes people play with an additional fund where fines can be deposited. This possibility was excluded. Also, we issued wallets to all players, and they were told not to inform the other players what was in their wallets. This prevented them from helping match payment amounts. Naturally, all players started with the same amount in their wallets. Furthermore, the possibility of changing notes with the bank was excluded.

In the end, we collected between 210 and 280 observations across the six cases of interest. The data cover the wallet contents prior to each transaction, the payment at the transaction occasion, and the money received in return. The return cash was used to keep track of the wallet contents.

When we use the same model as before, that is, the model that allows for a sequential decision process, we obtain the following results. If all notes are available, the participants of the game use the 50 EUR note more often than expected, in particular to pay higher amounts. So, apparently, the setting of the Monopoly experiment induces preferences that do not exist in real-life payment situations. Further, when we remove the 100 EUR or 10 EUR note, this has a positive influence on payment behavior, and this is in accordance with the theoretical results in Table 3.4. A third conclusion from the experiments is that the 200 EUR and 20 EUR notes are the most crucial notes, and these cannot be left out as payment behavior does not improve in these cases.

WHAT HAPPENS IF WE ROUND ALL PAYMENTS TO 0.05 EUR?

Now that we are talking anyway about deleting notes or coins from the denominational range, we could just as well look at the situation that has already occurred in some countries, that is, what happens if 0.01 EUR and 0.02 EUR coins are not needed anymore to make payments.[19] In Finland and in the Netherlands, all amounts to be paid in cash are rounded to the nearest multiple of EUR 0.05. Although the coins 0.01 EUR and 0.02 EUR remain legal tender, their need is reduced due to rounding. Applying Cramer's algorithm to all amounts between 0.01 EUR and 100 EUR, where the amounts are multiples of 0.01 EUR in one case and multiples of 0.05 EUR in another, thus starting with the amount 0.05 EUR, can tell us more about the effects on payment efficiency.

The results shown in Table 3.5 are quite striking. The average number of tokens exchanged per payment scheme decreases from 5.83 to 4.93. Also, the maximum number of required tokens decreases from 8 to 7. This exercise implies that payments apparently can be done more efficiently without the 0.01 and 0.02 coins.

Table 3.5 *Statistics on all payment schemes for amounts between 0.01 EUR and 100 EUR.*

Efficient payment schemes	All euro denominations	Without 1 and 2 cents
Number	36,591	5,957
Average number of tokens exchanged	5.83	4.93
Median	6	5
Minimum	1	1
Maximum	8	7

To examine how these theoretical insights in Table 3.5 carry on through actual wallets of individuals, we collected data on wallet contents before and after September 2004, when retail stores and the like could round all amounts to 0.05 EUR in the Netherlands. Before we describe the data in more detail, we summarize a few assumptions that we need in order to be able to perform such an analysis.

The main assumption is again that an individual always intends to make an efficient payment, that is, he or she aims at exchanging the smallest possible amount of coins and notes when making a payment. Next, we assume that individuals intend to make efficient payments on average, and hence that their wallets contain coins that allow them to do so, again on average. How would such wallets look? Again, we can rely on the algorithm of Cramer, and we can see for all efficient payment schemes (where we limit from earlier the amounts to 100 EUR) how many coins are required on average. The results are displayed in the left-hand column of Table 3.6. These numbers indicate that in order to make any efficient payment, on average one needs 2 EUR coins most and 1 and 0.10 EUR coins the least.

Table 3.6 suggests an easy-to-implement method for practical data collection. Indeed, we only need to collect wallet contents and

Table 3.6 *Theoretical fraction and observed fractions of coins in an average wallet.*

Coin	Theory	Cross section Before	After	After
		I	II	III
2	0.152	0.083	0.122	0.110
1	0.091	0.096	0.108	0.102
0.5	0.116	0.104	0.119	0.117
0.2	0.146	0.135	0.144	0.147
0.1	0.091	0.127	0.169	0.149
0.05	0.116	0.162	0.151	0.183
0.02	0.156	0.143	0.100	0.099
0.01	0.122	0.150	0.089	0.092

compare these contents with theoretical fractions. In the spring of 2004, I became aware that the DNB was investigating the possibility of rounding to 0.05 EUR. Therefore, I decided to collect wallet contents of a large number of individuals. With the help of a few students, we collected data at the Erasmus University Rotterdam, at a soccer club, and in a waiting room of a physiotherapist. In the period February to June 2004, we collected 240 observations this way. The next cross section was collected in October 2004 and comprises 211 observations. Finally, in January 2005, we collected yet another sample of 273 observations. We label the three samples as I (before rounding) and II and III (both after rounding). The main question we had for all times that we collected the data was "Can I see your wallet content?" Interestingly, we did not encounter any problems whatsoever getting an answer to this question.

Some basic statistics on samples I, II, and III are given in the other columns of Table 3.6. The average wallet contents in these three samples were 13.5, 11.6, and 9.9 coins, respectively. What we see from Table 3.6 is that the number of 1- and 2-cent coins is decreasing rapidly, thereby supporting the theoretical conjectures that the fractions of 5 cents and 10 cents are rapidly going up. Otherwise, differences seem to be small.

TO CONCLUDE

This chapter has presented a few examples of relevant and detailed questions that could be addressed using simple tools and in one case with an extended version of the regression model and that the way the data are collected matters much. It is not claimed that this was all done in the best possible way and also not that the econometric model chosen is the best possible model. However, the claim is that if one wants to answer a question, it helps to think first about a potential theoretical model that could be used to generate hypothetical data that look like the data at hand. This model can then also be instrumental to examine how many actual observations one may need to draw reliable inference. After that, one may decide to collect the data. This is particularly relevant in cases like the ones in this chapter, where the question "Can I see your wallet content?" may create some resistance. So, we see that question, model, and data can interact. At the same time, we learned that an econometric model is not always known in advance, and some thinking about how the data could look in theory helps.

You now have seen a few examples of how research using econometric methods and techniques may proceed. At the same time, you saw that seemingly simple questions about how we deal with money do require specific data to be collected and, then, as always, an econometric method to analyze the data.

ID	Beauty day NLG	Beauty day EUR	Bowling alley NLG	Bowling alley EUR	Tennis court NLG	Tennis court EUR	Bicycle NLG	Bicycle EUR
1	150	60	35	25	15	7.5	50	15
2	100	50	20	5	20	10	25	20
3	100	50	15	10	25	20	20	10
4	40	20	20	7	25	8	7.5	5
5	150	50	35	17.5	35	17.5	15	7
6	0	0	30	15	30	20	15	10
7	25	25	15	7.5	15	10	20	15
8	70	30	30	15	25	15	20	15
9	75	50	40	7	20	10	40	20
10	65	40	15	7	15	7.5	30	20
11	50	40	15	12	10	15	20	25
12	75	30	30	10	10	2.5	30	10
13	30	15	2	5	10	7.5	30	15
14	40	25	10	13	10	10	25	10
15	30	17.5	30	10	15	5	50	15
16	135	75	18	10	6	10	16	7
17	80	22.5	20	10	20	12.5	20	12.5
18	15	30	7.5	12	7.5	12	20	15
19	100	50	17.5	17.5	12.5	10	7	8

(cont.)

ID	Beauty day		Bowling alley		Tennis court		Bicycle	
	NLG	EUR	NLG	EUR	NLG	EUR	NLG	EUR
20	75	50	30	17	18	15	0	0
21	125	80	0	0	0	0	25	10
22	0	0	10	7.5	10	0	30	12
23	35	17	20	10	20	10	15	7
24	30	15	15	7	15	7	15	7
25	150	65	0	0	0	0	50	20
26	0	0	35	24	50	25	10	10
27	25	20	7.5	7	5	5	15	15
28	80	70	15	15	20	15	15	25
29	50	25	2	0	20	8	50	25
30	40	40	20	40	20	15	30	25
31	60	30	10	7.5	10	10	40	12.5
32	100	70	20	15	15	5	40	20
33	50	30	10	10	5	5	30	30
34	75	22	10	8	9	7	40	15
35	60	45	10	7.5	10	7.5	25	20
36	46	35	25	7	20	8	20	5

t tests on Mean and on Two Means

Consider the observations $z_1, z_2, \ldots, z_N$ and the sample average

$$\bar{z} = \frac{1}{N}\sum_{i=1}^{N} z_i.$$

To test for the null hypothesis that the population mean is equal to some value of μ, one can use the t test statistic given by

$$t = \sqrt{N}\,\frac{\bar{z} - \mu}{s_z} \sim t(N-1)$$

where $t\,(N-1)$ is a t-distribution with $N-1$ degrees of freedom. When N gets very large, this distribution comes close to a standard normal distribution, and where s_z is the same standard deviation as in Chapter 2, that is,

$$s_z = \sqrt{\frac{1}{N-1}\sum_{i=1}^{N}(z_i - \bar{z})^2}.$$

When there are two matched samples for the same individuals, with data observations $z_{1,1}, z_{1,2}, \ldots, z_{1,N}$ for the first sample and observations $z_{2,1}, z_{2,2}, \ldots, z_{2,N}$ for the second sample, one can compute

$$\bar{z}_D = \frac{1}{N}\sum_{i=1}^{N}(z_{2,i} - z_{1,i}).$$

To test for the null hypothesis that the population mean is equal to some value of μ_D, one can use the t-test statistic given by

$$t = \sqrt{N}\,\frac{\bar{z}_D - \mu_D}{s_D} \sim N(0,1),$$

where

$$s_D = \sqrt{\frac{1}{N-1}\sum_{i=1}^{N}(z_{2,i} - z_{1,i} - \bar{z}_D)^2}.$$

4 Financial Literacy and Numeracy

Free markets do not just produce what we really want; they also produce what we want according to our monkey-on-the-shoulder tastes.

—*Phishing for Phools: The Economics of Manipulation and Deception*

Me? I'm dishonest, and a dishonest man you can always trust to be dishonest. Honestly. It's the honest ones you want to watch for, because you can never predict when they're going to do something incredibly ... stupid.

—Jack Sparrow, *Pirates of the Caribbean: The Curse of the Black Pearl*

AT A GLANCE

This chapter also deals with money, like the previous one did, but now the focus is no longer what we do with cash money but how we perceive money. Now what do I mean by the perception of money? Such perception involves, for example, our thoughts and understanding when we hear the word "sale" as in price cuts or when we read statements like "buy now, pay later" or when the car salesperson says, "If you buy the car now, we offer you a financial arrangement where you pay just 250 USD per month." Or how about the rental price of a surfboard of 6 euros per hour, 11 euros for half a day, and 19 euros for a full day (24 hours)?[1] If it is your plan to surf, do you intend to do that for 18 hours in a row?

These days, in free markets, people are asked to be self-reliant. Individuals are expected to make sound decisions on all kinds of things, including their personal finances. They are expected to do their grocery shopping and still have money left in the end to pay the rent and other bills. The question is of course whether people actually can do that. Or perhaps some can, but others cannot. At the same time, should we expect that anyone who offers a product is honest about it or at least knows what it is? Toward the end of this chapter, I will present an example of a financial product where the text can easily be misunderstood. And, well, among people who did misunderstand the product (when it was launched for real a few years ago), many ended up in trouble.

This chapter deals with financial literacy, where the definition at Wikipedia (consulted December 2016) is quite a workable one, that is,

> Financial literacy is the ability to understand how money works in the world: how someone manages to earn or make it, how that person manages it, how he/she invests it (turn it into more) and how that person donates it to help others.

One fundamental feature of financial literacy is numeracy, that is, the ability to understand and work with numbers.[2]

For a long time, most economists left behind the old-fashioned notion of *a homo economicus*, which could be defined, again according to Wikipedia (consulted December 2016), by the following:

> In economics, *homo economicus*, or economic man, is the concept in many economic theories portraying humans as consistently rational and narrowly self-interested agents who usually pursue their subjectively-defined ends optimally.

The economics discipline has introduced such concepts as bounded rationality,[3] even irrationality,[4] and all kinds of cognitive biases and heuristics that individuals use (sometimes for good, more often for bad).[5] Arguments have been presented that free markets somehow always also involve people who want to fool you and who are dishonest and make use of your honesty and ignorance.[6] On the positive side, behavioral economists have developed tools and methods to nudge individuals in an appropriate direction.[7]

This chapter will apply some econometric methods and techniques to various sets of data that involve individual decision on financial aspects. I will deal with interest rates and wonder whether people understand how such calculations work. We will see how individuals find it difficult to make proper decisions involving current and future payments. We will see how people can be misled if the amount of information grows, that is, information about products between which they can choose. Think of all the features of a new smartphone or all the features of health insurance. How easy is it to grasp what all these features mean, and how easy is it to compare the attributes against one another? Finally, we will see how the text about a financial product can fool you, or perhaps better, the text that is not revealed can fool you. We will see what that means.

In this chapter, I will introduce two new econometric methods and put these in the appendix to this chapter. The first is the regression model but now for more than one variable on the right-hand side. The second is a regression model where the variable to be explained only takes the values 1 or 0, as in purchase or no purchase. As before, the storyline can be followed without digging into the technical details of the appendix.

Before we start, I present a little question to you. For many years, the Netherlands-based department store chain De Bijenkorf (means "beehive") organized in the fall its so-called "three foolish days." Figure 4.1 shows a line in front of the store right before opening.

The department store chain issues a catalog containing all of its products that are on sale during those three days. For each product, the

FIGURE 4.1 The line for the department store De Bijenkorf at the start of the "three foolish days."

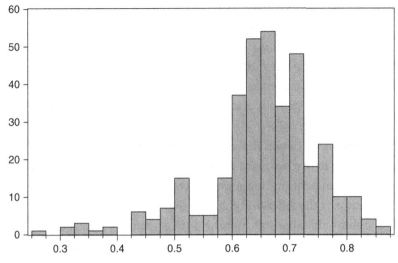

FIGURE 4.2 Price cuts at the "three foolish days."

catalog lists the original price and the price after the price cut. Figure 4.2 presents the histogram of the new price divided by the original price. Now, what is it that you would have expected in terms of price cuts, and what is that you learn from this histogram? We will get back to this question at the end of the chapter.

CAN PEOPLE DEAL WITH INTEREST RATES?

The first question that I address in this chapter is a very basic one. It is also a relevant one, as many people use credit cards or debit cards that require them to pay interest when the available sum is not sufficient for purchases. They then borrow from the credit card company. Also, when people buy a car, they are sometimes offered a financial arrangement in which they do not have to pay the full amount immediately but can spread their payments over an often quite lengthy period, perhaps in monthly terms. Quotes like "buy now and pay later" are quite common in various areas. People also need to deal with interest rates when they buy a house and take a mortgage. And, on the positive side, if people put money in a savings account, they may receive interest. But of course, usually, the interest on debts is higher than the interest on credits, as this is in part how banks make money.

As interest is such an important factor in our day-to-day lives, it is interesting to see to what extent people can handle computations with interest rates; as we shall see, they cannot at all.[8] At least, the second-year students of Methods and Techniques of the Erasmus School of Economics cannot.

How do we obtain this outcome? First, let us see what exactly the question is that we want to answer, which should illustrate if an individual can perform computations with interest rates.[9] One example question is the following: Suppose that you have a loan amount of 10,000 euros, that there is a monthly interest rate of 0.6%, and that the payback sum per month is 250 euros. Now, how many months do you think it will take for you pay back the loan in full? We then present the following answer categories: (a) less than 40 months, (b) 40–45 months, (c) 46–50 months, (d) 51–55 months, (e) 56–60 months, (f) 61–65 months, and (g) more than 65 months. We provide seven possible answer categories and do not ask for the exact answer, as nobody can provide that. The correct answer for this example, by the way, is 46 months, so answer category (c) is correct.

Now, how do we compute this correct answer? For that purpose, we use the following mathematical expressions. For a loan size of Y euros and given a monthly interest rate of x% and a monthly payment of M euros, it goes like this. In Month 1, the debt has become $(1+x)Y$. When M is paid, the amount left at the beginning of Month 2 is $(1+x)Y - M$. With interest, this amount becomes $(1+x)[(1+x)Y - M]$ during Month 2, and if again M is paid at the end of that second month, the amount left at the start of Month 3 is $(1+x)[(1+x)Y - M] - M$. This goes on and on, and generally at the beginning of Month K the amount that is left is

$$(1 + x)^K Y - \sum_{i=0}^{K-1}(1 + x)^i M.$$

Here you see the difficulty of the computations involved. These computations involve adding, subtracting, raising to the power, multiplying, and summing, all in one single expression! Indeed, students should figure out the value of K where the final amount is equal to 0. One person's brain is quite unlikely to be able to solve this, but let us see if the wisdom of the crowd helps, and that the average answer is almost correct.

A survey was begun in 2010 at the start of the course on Methods and Techniques for second-year bachelor students at the Erasmus School of Economics, which is sometime in March. These students all should have about the same general computational skills. They all passed their first bachelor year, which contains courses in mathematics. Many students have experience with borrowing money to pay for tuition, accommodation, and general expenses. Most students additionally borrow money to afford car-driving lessons or to have smartphones and various other electronic gadgets. In sum, one may see these students as regular consumers who also make decisions concerning interest rates.

We did ask the students not to use a machine calculator. The entire questionnaire took less than 15 minutes to fill in, and after that, there were 433 mostly complete questionnaires. We repeated the preceding question six times, where the amount Y was either 10,000 or 20,000 euros, the interest rate was either 0.6% per month or 0.8% per month, and the monthly payment M was either 200 or 250 euros. Prior testing of the survey revealed that these numbers match with numbers that these consumers (in this age category) can encounter in real life. In the end, thus there are seven questions, which we call Q1 to Q7.

Before I turn to some first results, it is again important to have some kind of benchmark. That is, we need to know what their general numeracy skills are because otherwise we cannot see whether the question on interest rates is difficult in itself or whether students' failure is due to a general lack of numeracy. Indeed, if the sample contains many people who lack numerical skills in the first place, it is unclear whether not being able to deal with interest rates is caused by a general lack of numerical skills. Therefore, we also asked four general questions of the students to see how they would fare on general numeracy.

Question 1 was "One chair costs 75 euros. When you buy four chairs, you get a 5% overall discount. How much do you need to pay when you buy eight chairs?"

    Less than 600 euros

    600 euros

    More than 600 euros

    I do not know

where "Less than 600 euros" is the correct answer.

Question 2 was "You buy five chairs for 100 euros each. Again, you receive a 5% discount. However, you have to pay 19% tax on the total amount. Approximately how much do you need to pay?"

    425 euros

    595 euros

    565 euros

    I do not know

The correct answer category here is the third. Five chairs for 100 euros is 500, and the 5% discount is 25 euros, so you pay 475. The 19% tax on the total amount means 1.19 times 475, which is 565.25 euros.

Question 3 was, "In the supermarket there is a promotion for detergent. The promotion is that you can acquire a second package for half the price. How much do you need to pay if you buy four packages and one package costs 5 euros?"

    7.50 euros

    12.50 euros

    15 euros

    20 euros

    I do not know

The correct answer is 5 + 2.5 + 5 + 2.5 euros, so the correct category is the third.

Finally, Question 4 is "The weather forecast says that the average temperature for the next three days is 30 degrees Celsius. Tomorrow and the day after, the temperature is predicted to be 28 and 29 degrees, respectively. What will be the forecast for the third day?"

30 degrees

31 degrees

32 degrees

33 degrees

34 degrees

I do not know

The correct answer is 33 degrees, as 28 + 29 + 33 divided by 3 is 30. Each question involves only two or three types of computations (and not five, as is the case for the interest rates!).

Among the 433 students who we interviewed, the fractions of correct answers were 0.942, 0.737, 0.907, and 0.812 for Questions 1 to 4, respectively. There were 258 students with all answers right. We will later on see if these 258 perhaps give different (read better) answers than the other students.

In Table 4.1, I present for all students the frequencies of correct answers to the interest rate questions Q1 to Q7. Also, I present the fraction where the indicated number of months was too low and where the indicated number of months was too high. Note that the correct answer among the answer categories (a) to (g) also varied across those categories so that students could not believe that, for example, the middle category was always the right answer, as it was not.

Table 4.1 *Frequency of answers to questions Q1 to Q7.*

Question	Sample size	Too low	Correct	Too high
Q1	432	0.382	0.256	0.362
Q2	431	0.244	0.197	0.559
Q3	429	0.548	0.148	0.268
Q4	428	0.484	0.178	0.339
Q5	428	0.266	0.231	0.509
Q6	429	0.795	0.205	0.000
Q7	428	0.381	0.154	0.465
Average		0.443	0.201	0.357

Table 4.2 *Frequency of answers to questions Q1 to Q7, computed for those respondents who gave the correct answers to all four general numeracy questions.*

Question	Too low	Correct	Too high
Q1	0.338	0.274	0.338
Q2	0.212	0.177	0.612
Q3	0.510	0.189	0.305
Q4	0.432	0.193	0.375
Q5	0.247	0.243	0.510
Q6	0.768	0.232	0.000
Q7	0.367	0.174	0.459
Mean	0.411	0.212	0.378

Table 4.1 tells a very clear story. On average, the fraction of correct answers is about 0.2. Now this is quite interesting, as when one simply would have guessed an answer at random, out of 7 answer categories, the hit rate would have been equal to $\frac{1}{7} = 0.14$. Hence, the answers of these students is quite close to a random guess.

Now, Table 4.1 contains the answers by all students (except in case of some missing answers), but let us have a look at the answers for only those 258 students who had all the general numeracy questions right. Their fractions of correct answers are presented in Table 4.2.

The intriguing result in this table is that the mean fraction with correct answers is about the same as before, that is, it is again about 0.2. Hence, whether students have strong computing skills does not seem to matter much when it comes to computations with interest rates.

A second conclusion that can be drawn from the two tables is that the fraction of "too low" answers exceeds that of "too high." In words, more people believe that it takes fewer months (than the correct number of months) to get rid of a debt than that it takes more time. People (or here: students) thus seem to be optimistic in their calculations and slightly underestimate the time it takes to pay off debts. This is important as such optimism may imply that people start too early with new loans, as they believe the running debts will be cleared sooner than they really are. Later on we will see how those overlapping debts also can occur when one "buys now and pays later."

IF BORROWING MONEY COSTS MONEY, LET US TELL HOW MUCH!

Consumers in industrialized countries often have credit debts. There is a large literature on the potential sources of those debts.[10] One potential source of overindebtedness could be that consumers face difficulties performing the actual calculations when they decide to purchase on credit. Indeed, we already saw that consumers will find it hard to compute the exact final amount when they have to pay off a loan of 10,000 euros with a 0.6% interest rate per month over 72 months. We also saw that subjects were found to believe that debts are paid off earlier than they really are. To warn consumers of consequences of borrowing money and against too high a debt, in the Netherlands a campaign was initiated to increase awareness. The tag line in this Dutch situation is "Borrowing money costs money." Despite its apparent success in creating such awareness, one may wonder whether such a campaign could have been made even more effective if the moneylender would be forced to precisely say exactly how large these borrowing costs really are. Exact information about the total amount paid instead of information in monthly terms (and often in small print) should make people more aware of the total costs of the loan. Hence, one would then read, for example, that a television set costs 338 euros, but if a consumer decides to borrow the money and pay back in monthly terms, the total costs would increase to 384 euros. That seems fair to consumers.

Let us see[11] if this conjecture stands a simple empirical test. In 2010, we ran two rounds of experiments; in the first, consumers faced payment options that also involved buying on credit, and the second round concerned only true monetary amounts.

The research design is based on the familiar and rather basic version of what is called a conjoint experiment. We ask individuals to choose between two hypothetical choice options. Each choice option involves values for attributes including the method of payment. We have two runs of our experiments. First, we issue the questionnaire in which the payment options involve cash payments as well as payments in monthly terms (with interest). We do not create additional difficulties by forcing people to calculate percentages, so we simply let people evaluate, say, a cash price of 338 euros against 59 monthly payments of 8 euros (which is 472 euros). In the second set of the experiments, we simply translate the first-round credit payments into the actual monetary value; that is, following the same example, it then becomes 338 euros versus 472 euros.

The text for the survey reads as:

> We kindly ask you to cooperate with the following survey. This survey is about making choices in the purchasing process of a durable good, like television sets, audio equipment, and other household appliances. In each question, you can choose between two different products. The features of each product differ from each other, like brand of the product, screen size, or price. For each question, we ask you to draw a circle around the product you prefer.
>
> Many thanks for your kind help.

Suppose you (the survey taker) want to buy an LCD TV, and on the Internet, you see various offers. Each question displays two products between which you can choose. For each choice set, we ask you to draw a circle around the product that you prefer.

Choice set 1		
Brand	Samsung	LG
Screen size	94	81
Hertz	50	50
Payment	338 euros cash	59 monthly payments of 8 euros

Choice set 2		
Brand	Samsung	Samsung
Screen size	94	81
Hertz	50	60
Payment	338 euros cash	24 monthly payments of 16 euros

Choice set 3		
Brand	LG	Samsung
Screen size	81	94
Hertz	60	50
Payment	24 monthly payments of 16 euros	59 monthly payments of 8 euros

Choice set 4		
Brand	LG	Samsung
Screen size	81	94
Hertz	60	50
Payment	439 euros cash	73 monthly payments of 9 euros

Choice set 5		
Brand	LG	Samsung
Screen size	81	94

(*cont.*)

Choice set 5		
Hertz	50	50
Payment	439 euros cash	24 monthly payments of 8 euros

Choice set 6		
Brand	LG	LG
Screen size	94	81
Hertz	50	60
Payment	24 monthly payments of 21 euros	73 monthly payments of 9 euros

On November 25, 2010, we circulated the questionnaire that is similar to the preceding one, except that the order of choice sets was changed and the prices were all in euros, as follows.

Choice set 1		
Brand	LG	Samsung
Screen size	81	94
Hertz	50	60
Payment	439 euros cash	657 euros cash

Choice set 2		
Brand	Samsung	LG
Screen size	94	81
Hertz	50	50
Payment	338 euros cash	472 euros cash

Choice set 3		
Brand	LG	Samsung
Screen size	81	94
Hertz	50	50
Payment	439 euros cash	504 euros cash

(*cont.*)

Choice set 4		
Brand	Samsung	Samsung
Screen size	94	81
Hertz	50	60
Payment	338 euros cash	384 euros cash

Choice set 5		
Brand	LG	LG
Screen size	94	81
Hertz	50	60
Payment	504 euros cash	657 euros cash

Choice set 6		
Brand	LG	Samsung
Screen size	94	81
Hertz	60	50
Payment	384 euros cash	472 euros cash

We spent time to make sure that the hypothetical products looked realistic. This also involved the payment amounts. Indeed, large screen sizes and more hertz should also come with higher prices. So, whereas brand, screen size, and hertz only have two levels per attribute, the payment seems to have many more. A closer look reveals that for the prices there are effectively three levels: the first is cash, the second is 24 months with some amount per month, and the third is the maximum number of months with a somewhat smaller amount per month. We tested the survey on a few sample individuals (always wise to do!), and we consulted Internet retail stores selling those televisions (in those days) to confirm that these hypothetical products actually made sense.[12]

On the first day of data collection – November 8, 2010 – we surveyed 375 students, which thus resulted in 4,500 (375 times 12) answers of which 2,250 are 1 for "preferred" and 0 for "not preferred." On the second day – November 25, 2010 – we surveyed

285 different students, which yielded 1,710 values of 1 and 1,710 observations with a 0. The students were following different bachelor courses, so there was no overlap between the individuals in the two samples.

The data are analyzed by a new type of regression model, which is called the binary (logit) regression, with the dependent variable y_i taking values of 1 or 0, where here 1 means preferred product and 0 the not-preferred product. In the appendix, I present some of the key features of this particular model. Before I do that, I present in the appendix first the case where the regression model contains more than one explanatory variable, as here we have four such variables.

As the payments can take three levels, each time I consider two logit models, each with a pair of potential levels of payment. What would we expect a priori from the experiments? First, we could see that cash payments would be preferred over credit payments. So, we would expect that consumers would prefer to pay 338 euros over payments in 24 months (which is 384 euros). Second, we would expect that when the actual monetary amounts are given (in the second round of experiments), the differences in preferences would become even larger. We have two settings; one concerns the prices 338, 384, and 472, and the other the prices 439, 504, and 657. Clearly, the differences between the first two are much smaller than between the first and the last, so we would expect that most prominent differences in preferences would appear for the cash price versus payments during the maximum amount of months.

The estimation results for the two logit models for LCD television sets appear in Table 4.3. Students appear to favor LG because the parameters are positive (although not always significant), screen size 94 (all parameters positive and significant), and hertz 50, as their associated parameters usually take a positive and significant value. Payment in 24 months is less preferred over cash, and payments in the maximum amount of months are even less preferred, which can be seen from a comparison of the absolute values of the parameter estimates (–0.641 versus –3.706 in the first survey).

Table 4.3 *Estimation results for LCD television sets (all data 4,500 and 3,420 analyzed).*

Variable	Estimate (standard error)	Estimate (standard error)
	Survey of November 8, 2010	Survey of November 25, 2010
Intercept	−1.733 (0.111)	−1.331 (0.109)
LG (not Samsung)	0.994 (0.132)	0.648 (0.124)
Screen 94 (not 81)	0.661 (0.145)	0.749 (0.132)
Hertz 50 (not 60)	2.453 (0.105)	1.563 (0.098)
24 months (not cash)	−0.641 (0.095)	−0.299 (0.089)
Intercept	0.788 (0.159)	1.321 (0.174)
LG (not Samsung)	0.163 (0.152)	0.224 (0.168)
Screen 94 (not 81)	1.223 (0.164)	1.934 (0.178)
Hertz 50 (not 60)	1.069 (0.109)	0.589 (0.129)
Maximum months (not cash)	−3.706 (0.121)	−4.211 (0.135)

When we compare the results for November 8 versus November 25 of 2010, we see differences across the parameters, but as these estimates are correlated, we resort to an alternative method to highlight the differences across the results for the November 8 and 25 surveys. Table 4.4 gives the estimated probabilities from the logit model for the cases where the LCD television sets are of the type "LG, screen size 94 and hertz 50" across the three levels of prices. The probability of purchasing this product using cash money is 0.915, while it is reduced to 0.850 when one can pay using a 24-month period. This is not a very large difference – only 0.065 – and also for the November 25 survey, where the respective probabilities are 0.836 and 0.791, the difference 0.045 is not large.

However, matters change dramatically for the comparison of cash payments with payments during the maximum amount of months. The purchase probability now is reduced from 0.949 to 0.313 (which is a 0.636 reduction) when only monthly terms are

Table 4.4 *Estimated probability of purchase for LCD television sets (all data 4,500 and 3,420 analyzed).*

	Survey of November 8, 2010	Survey of November 25, 2010 (with actual monetary value)
Type LG, screen size 94, hertz 50		
Cash	0.915	0.836
Or 24-month payments	0.850	0.791
Cash	0.949	0.947
Or maximum months payments	0.313	0.211

used, and it is reduced from 0.947 to 0.211 (which is a 0.736 reduction) when actual monetary values are mentioned. Comparing 0.313 to 0.211 entails about a 30% reduction of probability of purchase.

So far, we relied on a model where individuals were analyzed jointly. When we estimate the parameters of the same models for males and females separately, we do not find any noteworthy differences for the numbers in the current Table 4.3. The same holds when we consider the models for younger and older students and for different income levels. Hence, at least for these samples, we find that demographics do not matter much for purchase preferences related to payment methods.

To see if the results in Table 4.3 are reasonably robust, we had a second product evaluated, parallel to the television sets, and this concerned couches. Couches could be beige or gray, have seat size 45 or 46, and have normal or special comfort, and, again, at three levels of payment (methods). The key results appear in Table 4.5. Again, we see not very large differences between cash and 24 months (from 0.761 to 0.685 in the first experiment and from 0.741 to 0.726 in the second). But, like in Table 4.4, the differences in preferences become salient

Table 4.5 *Estimated probability of purchase for couches (all data 4,500 and 3,420 analyzed).*

	Survey of November 8, 2010	Survey of November 25, 2010 (with actual monetary value)
Type Color gray, seat size 46, normal comfort		
Cash	0.761	0.741
Or 24-month payments	0.685	0.726
Cash	0.873	0.882
Or maximum month payments	0.271	0.146

when we evaluate cash payments against the maximum amount of months. There the reduction in preferences is from 0.271 to 0.146, which is about 50%.

We conjectured that actually mentioning the price that one has to pay would make consumers less prone to opt for credit payments, where I should say that we abstained from high levels of inflation. More precisely, when one would have consumers evaluate a cash price of 338 euros versus 472 euros, we would expect less preference for the 472 euros product then when one would have consumers evaluate 338 euros against 59 months with only 8 euros per month. Our experiments show that this indeed happens. In fact, the reduction in the preference ranges somewhere around 30% to 50%.

These results seem to beg for a rather straightforward recommendation, which involves the idea that the tag line "Borrowing money costs money" needs additional text. An example might be "When you purchase this television set, it costs you 338 euros if you pay with cash, and it eventually costs you 472 euros when you pay 8 euros per month in 59 monthly terms." Hence, it would be recommendable that product offerings consist of not only the amount in cash but also the total amount paid when you pay in monthly terms.

So, we have seen that depending on the way numbers and prices are presented or framed, people are tempted to make different decisions.

CAN WE FOOL PEOPLE A LITTLE BIT?

Apparently, framing prices and numbers matters in the way we make financial decisions. The illustration in the introduction on the three foolish days suggested that the words "sales," "price cut," and "discount" make people line up. To see how this works, we set up a range of experiments back in 2009,[13] and they look rather similar to those on the LCD televisions. Now the products concern smartphones, and forgive me the choice for the levels of the attributes, but those were the parameters of smartphones in those days.

Consider the following three choice sets, where each set involves two hypothetical smartphones and we asked various individuals to make a choice between the two. To make matters close to reality, we considered for each smartphone six attributes, where each of the attributes has various levels. For example, the price of an SMS message has only two levels, that is, 17 and 23 cents, while the extras have three levels, that is, games; games and Internet; and games, Internet, and a camera. Our focus however is on the price. Have a look at the price levels in the following three choice sets.

Choice set 1	A	B
Price	170 euros	100 euros
Network	KPN or Vodafone	Other
Price per minute	35 eurocents	30 eurocents
Price of SMS	23 eurocents	17 eurocents
Design	Trendy	Trendy
Extras	Games	Games and Internet

(cont.)

Choice set 2	A	B
Price	135 euros	125 euros with 20% discount
Network	Other	KPN or Vodafone
Price per minute	35 eurocents	30 eurocents
Price of SMS	17 eurocents	23 eurocents
Design	Basic	Basic
Extras	Games and Internet	Games, Internet, camera

Choice set 3	A	B
Price	189 euros with 10% discount	135
Network	Other	Other
Price per minute	25 eurocents	30 eurocents
Price of SMS	17 eurocents	23 eurocents
Design	Trendy	Basic
Extras	Games, Internet, camera	Games, Internet, camera

It seems that the price attribute has a lot more levels than three, right? There are 170 euros, 100 euros, 135 euros, 125 euros with 20% discount, and 189 euros with 10% discount, so that looks like five levels. Are there indeed five levels? Have a look again! Now you see it! Of course, 125 euros with 20% discount is equal to 100 euros, while 189 euros with 10% discount is almost equal to 170 euros. So, there are in fact just three levels of the price attribute.

An analysis of the responses of individuals to our questions to indicate their preferences for either option A or B in each of the choice sets revealed that individuals did not see that there were just three price levels but rather believed there were five such levels. Additionally, it was found that there is a preference for products with a price cut mentioned.

So, when you frame a product such that people feel that they are somehow rewarded, in this case by a discount, then you can arouse interest for your product. This effect is of course known to the millions of street vendors all over the world who make you feel happy when you have negotiated the price down to a fraction of the original price. Indeed, it may well be that the original and first quoted price never existed at all. Would that perhaps also be the case for the prices at the three foolish days?

CAN WE FOOL PEOPLE A LOT?

By the late 1990s, stock markets boomed all over the world. It was the time of the Internet bubble, which, like other bubbles all too often, was visible only afterward, and it was the time that lots of money were floating around. Companies that never made any profits or had any annual reports made an entry on the stock market, and individual consumers were looking for possibilities to profit from all these glorious developments. It was the time of the so-called "New Economy." This concept promised days and times without inflation, without unemployment, and a fully Internet-based economy where trade was free and anyone could participate. Wikipedia defines that period as follows:

> The new economy is the result of the transition from
> a manufacturing-based economy to a service-based economy. This
> particular use of the term was popular during the dot-com bubble of
> the late 1990s. The high growth, low inflation and high
> employment of this period led to overly optimistic predictions and
> many flawed business plans.

I will come back to this wonderful idea in Chapter 8.

It was also in those days that new financial products were developed, some of which fooled people, and in 2012 we showed[14] that one such product could still be sold, even though the concept received bad press.

What we did is the following. We copied and pasted a prospectus of a financial product that was much in demand by the late 1990s and translated the numbers to the situation in 2012. Stock markets were no longer going up 18% to 20% on average, but instead 2% to 4%, and a few other numbers were changed. In all other aspects, the product was the same, although we came up with a new name; this time the product was called the Profit Multiplier. Now, who would not want to have a product like that?

The story stripped off all kinds of distracting details is the following. A company called Profit Bank (as we called it) offers a new product. You borrow from it a sum per month, it will invest the money in the stock market, and you choose whether you want to have this product for some years. More precisely, you can borrow 500 or 250 euros per month for a period of five or two years. Next, we present, as in those Internet-bubble days, a fictitious numerical example, which goes like this for a 250 euro-per-month deposit.

Average stock returns	Result after five years	Minus net investment
–2%	NA	NA
0%	NA	NA
2%	NA	NA
4%	13,541 EUR	4,728
6%	21,139 EUR	12,326 EUR
8%	29,333 EUR	20,520 EUR
10%	38,156 EUR	29,343 EUR
15%	63,209 EUR	54,396 EUR

Well, that seems like a very interesting result after these five years, does it not? This is also after all kinds of tax refunds, and you know, it is only with just 250 euros per month. Now, wait, what does the "NA" mean? Does that mean "zero" or what? Well, it turns out that NA means a negative number, which in other words means that you owe Profit Bank some money instead of receiving it. So, you did not only borrow money, you now need to pay additionally.

In the 1990s, stock markets went up, but very soon after 2000, they went down rapidly. Many individuals saw their investment disappear, and not only that, they had to pay extra to a company like Profit Bank.

In our experiments, we showed individuals various prospectuses with a range of hypothetical fictitious numerical examples. In one we revealed what was under the NA. Look here:

Average stock returns	Result after five years	Minus net investment
–2%	–6,005 EUR	–14,818 EUR
0%	0 EUR	–8,813 EUR
2%	6,505 EUR	–2,308 EUR
4%	13,541 EUR	4,728 EUR
6%	21,139 EUR	12,326 EUR
8%	29,333 EUR	20,520 EUR
10%	38,156 EUR	29,343 EUR
15%	63,209 EUR	54,396 EUR

So when the stock market returns are 0, you would lose 8,813 euros.

Now, you would think that revealing the monetary losses (instead of NA) would make people not buy this product. However, when we presented the choice sets to various individuals, we obtained the regression-based estimation results in Table 4.6.

The striking outcome in Table 4.6 is that people seem to prefer NA instead of losses, so they seem to prefer not to know than to see that the investment will disappear and even turn into a debt. Even though this matches with well-known findings in behavioral economics,[15] it might come as a surprise. Perhaps

Table 4.6 *Factors that make people prefer a financial product.*

Variable	Parameter	Standard error
Intercept	2.238	0.167
Expected return (1 is 8%, 0 is 5%)	–0.021	0.152
Not mentioning losses (1 is NA, 0 is amount)	0.536	0.151
Monthly deposit (1 is 500 euros, 0 is 250 euros)	–0.378	0.151
Period (1 is 5 years, 0 is 2 years)	0.351	0.151

recently developed tools in nudging can be helpful here because one may want to add an extra column to the figures in the table, which tells us, based on historical evidence, how likely it is that stock markets go up or go down with certain percentage rates. Indeed, stock markets going up 15% over a period of five years is exceptionally rare, while 0% or 2% for such a period is observed much more often.

EPILOGUE

This chapter dealt with issues concerning the way that people can be fooled when it comes to financial transactions. Of course, I highlighted only very few examples; there must be many more. And, also, the way the data were collected was very rudimentary, and much improvement can be obtained when systematic, longitudinal data are collected for panels of individuals over time. Also, the econometric methods were very simple, and there one can also recommend improvements, perhaps allowing for better designed samples and data collection methods.

However, what remains is the impression that simple data collection can already be quite informative, and that rather basic econometric methods sometimes already suffice.

And, indeed, sometimes only a simple histogram of the data can already be quite suggestive. Look again at Figure 4.2 with the price cuts for 359 products during those three foolish days. Now what kind of histogram would you most likely have expected for regular price discounts? Would you not have expected a histogram with spikes at, say, 0.5, 0.6, and 0.8, implying discounts of 50%, 40%, or 20%? In contrast, the data in Figure 4.2 seem to be all over the place, suggesting that the discounts are just random numbers. It could however also be that there were not any discounts in the first place. That is, there is an advertised discounted price, and there is just a random number reflecting the "original price." This practice would adhere to the overall theme of the three shopping days. Were these days not called the "three foolish days"?

APPENDIX: ECONOMETRIC METHODS

MULTIPLE REGRESSION

In Chapter 2, we dealt with the simple regression model, where a single dependent variable Y_i is explained by a single independent variable X_i. The assumption in this simple regression model is that the true link between these two variables is given by

$$y_i = \alpha + \beta x_i + \varepsilon_i$$

with

$$\varepsilon_i \sim N(0, \sigma^2).$$

In practice, the parameters α, β, and σ^2 are of course unknown. These parameters can be estimated using the least squares routine when it is assumed that the sample equivalent of the simple regression model is

$$y_i = a + bx_i + e_i.$$

The multiple regression model extends the simple regression model by assuming that there is more than a single explanatory variable and in fact that there are k such variables. For actual data, this so-called multiple regression model then reads as

$$y_i = a + b_1x_{1,i} + b_2x_{2,i} + b_3x_{3,i} + \cdots + b_kx_{k,i} + e_i.$$

With similar assumptions as for the simple regression model,[16] least squares estimates for the parameters can be obtained. And then, similar to the simple regression model, we have

$$\frac{b_j - \beta_j}{s_j} \sim N(0, 1)$$

with s_j is the standard error of b_j, $j = 1, 2, \cdots, k$. The t test each time concerns a single explanatory variable. It is also possible to test the joint relevance of more than a single variable. For example, one may want to compare

$$y_i = \alpha + \beta_1x_{1,i} + \beta_2x_{2,i} + \beta_3x_{3,i} + \beta_4x_{4,i} + \varepsilon_i$$

against

$$y_i = \alpha + \beta_1x_{1,i} + \beta_2x_{2,i} + \varepsilon_i$$

where in the latter model the third and fourth variables are not included. One can also test the relevance of the entire model by testing the four-variable model against

$$y_i = \alpha + \varepsilon_i.$$

When the residual sum of squares of the larger model (F for full) is written as

$$\sum_{i=1}^{N} e_{F,i}^2$$

and the residual sum of squares of the smaller model that has g less variables is written as

$$\sum_{i=1}^{N} e_{R,i}^2$$

where the R is for restricted, then the F test for the null hypothesis that both models are equally accurate is

$$F = \frac{N-k-1}{g} \frac{\sum_{i=1}^{N} e_{R,i}^2 - \sum_{i=1}^{N} e_{F,i}^2}{\sum_{i=1}^{N} e_{F,i}^2} \sim F(g, N-k-1)$$

where $F(g, N-k-1)$ is an F distribution with g and $N-k-1$ degrees of freedom.

INTERPRETATION OF THE MULTIPLE REGRESSION MODEL

There are two interesting additional issues with the multiple regression model, and these issues concern the interpretation of the parameters. Take, for example,

$$y_i = \alpha + \beta_1 x_{1,i} + \beta_2 x_{2,i} + \varepsilon_i.$$

Then the elasticity of y_i with respect to $x_{1,i}$ is the percentage change in y_i due to a percentage change in $x_{1,i}$, and it reads as

$$\frac{\partial y_i}{\partial x_{1,i}} \frac{x_{1,i}}{y_i} = \beta_1 \frac{x_{1,i}}{y_i}$$

where ∂ means partial derivative. Note that this elasticity depends on the value of both $x_{1,i}$ and y_i. This implies that this measure of elasticity is dependent on the scale of the variables, that is, the way they are measured. If one would want to have a scale-free measure of the elasticity, then one better transform the data using the natural logarithmic transformation and subsequently consider the regression model

$$\log y_i = \alpha + \beta_1 \log x_{1,i} + \beta_2 \log x_{2,i} + \varepsilon_i.$$

In that case, the elasticity is

$$\frac{\partial y_i}{\partial x_{1,i}} \frac{x_{1,i}}{y_i} = \beta_1 \frac{y_i}{x_{1,i}} \frac{x_{1,i}}{y_i} = \beta_1.$$

So, now the estimated parameter b_1 can be straightforwardly be interpreted as a scale-free elasticity.

When there are more variables in a regression model, and also when these variables have different scales or measurement units, it may not be easy to interpret the coefficients. It may then help to create hypothetical combinations of values of explanatory variables and to arrange the predicted values of the dependent variable. Take for example the case where the first explanatory variable is a continuous variable, say, x_i; the second variable is a dummy variable that can take the value 1 or 0, denoted as z_i; and there is a third variable w_i that is associated with three categories A, B, and C. Two dummy variables must then summarize this third variable (three minus one) 1/0 dummy variables as follows: $w_{1,i} = 1$ if w_i is associated with category A and $w_{1,i} = 0$ if not A and a similar variable $w_{2,i} = 1$ if w_i is associated with category B and $w_{2,i} = 0$ if not B. Naturally, if both variables take a value 0, then category C is at stake.

Suppose that the regression model with these variables looks like

$$\log y_i = \alpha + \beta_1 \log x_i + \beta_2 z_i + \beta_3 w_{1,i} + \beta_4 w_{2,i} + \varepsilon_i.$$

With the estimated parameters and after transforming back by taking exponents of both sides, assuming the predicted value of ε_i to equal 0, one gets

$$\hat{y}_i = \exp\left(a + \frac{1}{2}s^2\right)x_i^{b_1}\exp(b_2 z_i)\exp(b_3 w_{1,i})\exp(b_4 w_{2,i}),$$

where the added term $\frac{1}{2}s^2$ follows from the expected value of y_i when it obeys a log-normal distribution.[17] As three of the variables are 1/0 dummy variables, it is easy to see how they contribute to the forecast of y_i, that is, when for example $z_i = 1$, the contribution is $\exp(b_2)$, and when $z_i = 0$, the contribution is $\exp(0) = 1$. For the continuous variable x_i, this is not straightforward, as there is no benchmark value, like the 0 for the dummy variables. Denote $x_{i,B}$ as a benchmark value; then it is convenient to write the prediction of y_i as

$$\hat{y}_i = \exp\left(a + \frac{1}{2}s^2\right)x_{i,B}^{b_1}\left(\frac{x_i}{x_{i,B}}\right)^{b_1}\exp(b_2 z_i)\exp(b_3 w_{1,i})\exp(b_4 w_{2,i}).$$

Now, let us have a look at a numerical example. Suppose we ask various students how much they spend per week when they are on vacation. Further, suppose the answer to the question about their age is either 18, 19, 20, 21, or 22, where $z_i = 1$ when the respondent is a male student, where $w_{1,i} = 1$ when the student traveled to a country in Europe outside the Netherlands, and where $w_{2,i} = 1$ when the student traveled to any country in the world outside Europe. Clearly, the benchmark category here is the Netherlands. Now, suppose further that the parameter estimates obtained using the least squares method are $a = 6$, $\frac{1}{2}s^2 = 1$, $b_1 = 0.05$, $b_2 = 0.02$, $b_3 = 0.03$, and $b_4 = 0.05$, where the benchmark age value is set at $x_{i,B} = 18$. With these numeric values, one can compute that the basic spending amount is

$$\exp\left(a + \frac{1}{2}s^2\right)x_{i,B}^{b_1} = 1268.$$

The multipliers $\left(\frac{x_i}{x_{i,B}}\right)^{b_1}$ are 1.003, 1.005, 1.008, and 1.100 if a student is 19, 20, 21, or 22, respectively; the multiplier $\exp(b_2 z_i)$ is 1.020 if it is a male student; and the multipliers for destination are 1.030 for Europe and 1.051 for the rest of the world. Now one can simply compute the prediction that a male student of 22 who traveled to, say, Thailand spent 1,268 times 1.100 times 1.020 times 1.051, or 1,495 euros per week.

BINARY LOGIT REGRESSION

Suppose that the variable that you want to explain only takes the value 1 or 0. That is, for example, $y_i = 1$ if someone prefers option A and $y_i = 0$ if option B is preferred.[18] And suppose one adopts the regression model

$$y_i = \alpha + \beta x_i + \varepsilon_i$$

with

$$\varepsilon_i \sim N(0, \sigma^2).$$

Clearly, this model does not map a continuous variable x_i on a dependent variable that can only take the values 0 and 1. Hence, a standard regression model does not seem to be appropriate for such data. This is visualized in Figure 4A.1, which shows an estimated regression line to a scanner with binary data for y_i.

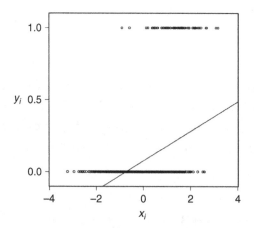

FIGURE 4A.I A least squares regression line to a scatter of points where the dependent variable can be only 1 or 0.

A solution now is to assume another distribution for y_i. The regression model assumes that y_i is distributed as conditionally normal, that is,

$$y_i \sim N(\alpha + \beta x_i, \sigma^2)$$

but for data that take only two values, it seems more appropriate to think of a conditional Bernoulli distribution (B). This works as follows. If

$$y_i \sim B(\pi)$$

with $0 \le \pi \le 1$, there is only a single parameter that characterizes the distribution and that is the probability π, that is

$$\pi = \text{Prob } (y_i = 1)$$

and

$$\text{Prob } (y_i = 0) = 1 - \pi.$$

The probability function of y_i is then

$$f(y_i) = \pi^{y_i} (1 - \pi)^{1-y_i}.$$

It is unlikely that π is known beforehand and that it is constant across individuals. Therefore, we can make π dependent of an explanatory variable x_i like

$$y_i \sim B \left(F \left(\alpha + \beta x_i\right)\right)$$

where the function F somehow maps $\alpha + \beta x_i$ onto the interval $[0, 1]$. An example of a density function is in Figure 2.6. An obvious choice for F is a cumulative density function of a continuous distribution because this always gives a value between 0 and 1.

We now focus on the probability that $y_i = 1$ given the outcome of $\alpha + \beta x_i$, that is,

$$\text{Prob } (y_i = 1) = F \left(\alpha + \beta x_i\right)$$

and

$$\text{Prob } (y_i = 0) = 1 - F \left(\alpha + \beta x_i\right).$$

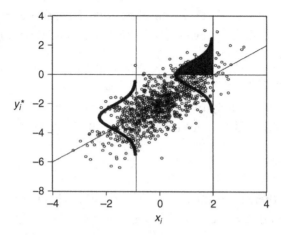

FIGURE 4A.2 The black shaded area above the $y_i^* = 0$ line is the probability that an individual with $x_i = 2$ chooses option 1.[19]

Another way to look at this setting is to assume that there is something like a continuous latent (unobserved) variable y_i^* that then measures the difference in preferences (utility difference if you like) between the two choice options. Assume that we model y_i^* by

$$y_i^* = \alpha + \beta x_i + \varepsilon_i.$$

This latent continuous variable now gets mapped to y_i by the rule

$$y_i = 1 \text{ if } y_i^* > 0 \text{ and } y_i = 0 \text{ if } y_i^* \leq 0$$

and
$$Prob(y_i = 1) = Prob(y_i^* > 0)$$

Figure 4A.2 illustrates this alternative view.

By the way, why do we take the threshold equal to 0? Suppose that the threshold equals δ. The same decision rule can now be obtained if we replace α by $\alpha - \delta$. In econometrics this situation is called a case where α and δ are not jointly identified and therefore one sets δ equal to 0.

Consider again the regression model for the latent variable, that is,

$$y_i^* = \alpha + \beta x_i + \varepsilon_i$$

and assume that ε_i has a symmetric distribution, like in Figure 2.6. The probability that $y_i = 1$ is

$$\text{Prob}(y_i = 1|x_i) = \text{Prob}(y_i^* > 0|x_i)$$
$$= \text{Prob}(\alpha + \beta x_i + \varepsilon_i > 0|x_i) = \text{Prob}(\varepsilon_i \leq \alpha + \beta x_i|x_i).$$

The last term on the right-hand side refers to a cumulative distribution function F of ε_i, that is,

$$\text{Prob}\,(y_i = 1|x_i) = F\,(\alpha + \beta x_i).$$

There are many choices for F, but in practice, one usually considers the normal or the logistic distribution. The logistic function has a simple expression, that is,

$$F(\alpha + \beta x_i) = \frac{\exp(\alpha + \beta x_i)}{1 + \exp(\alpha + \beta x_i)}.$$

and the model is called a logit model. The model parameters can be estimated using an alternative method to least squares called the method of maximum likelihood. It so turns out that when the number of observations is sufficiently large, then again

$$\frac{b - \beta}{s_b} \sim N(0, 1).$$

where s_b is also obtained using the maximum likelihood method. A multiple regression version of this simple logit model looks like

$$F(\alpha + \beta_1 x_{1,i} + \beta_2 x_{2,i} + \beta_3 x_{3,i} + \cdots + \beta_k x_{k,i})$$
$$= \frac{\exp(\alpha + \beta_1 x_{1,i} + \beta_2 x_{2,i} + \beta_3 x_{3,i} + \cdots + \beta_k x_{k,i})}{1 + \exp(\alpha + \beta_1 x_{1,i} + \beta_2 x_{2,i} + \beta_3 x_{3,i} + \cdots + \beta_k x_{k,i})}.$$

After the application of the method of maximum likelihood, it also holds that

$$\frac{b_j - \beta_j}{s_j} \sim N(0, 1).$$

A simple way to interpret the parameters in the logit regression is the following. When one has estimates of the parameters, then one can compute the estimated probabilities by plugging in various values of x_i. That is, one computes

$$\hat{F}(a + bx_i) = \frac{\exp(a + bx_i)}{1 + \exp(a + bx_i)}.$$

For specific values of x_i, this gives the probability that $y_i = 1$.

5   Postage Stamps and Banknotes

Designs in connection with postage stamps and coinage may be described,
I think, as the silent ambassadors on national taste.

—William Butler Yeats

AT A GLANCE

This chapter is about collectibles. There are many types of collectibles,
like early or rare bootleg records of the Rolling Stones, rare books and
prints, and what have you, and sometimes certain collectibles can
become very expensive. In particular, art, like paintings, can be very
expensive, and also postage stamps and coins and banknotes, especially
when they are rare, may become of interest to investors. For example,
the banknote of Australia[1] in Figure 5.1 may cost you at present more
than 200,000 USD at an auction. So, you might come to think that some
collectibles could be a good investment for the future and perhaps
might even be better in terms of returns than corporate bonds or real
estate.[2]

   This chapter deals with collectibles like stamps and paper
money and examines to what extent they have properties that are
similar to financial assets. At the same time, I focus on what may
cause that collectibles are scarce. I begin with postage stamps.[3] One
often-found feature for financial products is that they experience price
bubbles. Therefore, based on a large sample of prices of a range of
Dutch postage stamps, I examine whether postal stamp prices also
experience or have experienced such bubbles. Now, here is a data
feature that we have to tackle, and that is that there is no precise
definition of what a bubble is. So, I first have to define "bubble," and
then I need to summarize the available data such that the data-based

FIGURE 5.1 The first official banknote of Australia, which is very much in demand by collectors and apparently worth more than 200,000 USD (when in excellent condition).

bubble can be explained by various features of the stamps. The main idea of my method to detect such bubbles is based on comparing the price changes in turn with changes in those price changes. The emerging definition seems to work, but of course one could also think of other definitions. This shows that measurement of variables is an important feature before you can apply econometric methods and techniques.

If there are any price bubbles in the stamps, are these bubbles then the same across the stamps? That is, do scarce or high-valued stamps experience similar bubble patterns as more common and widely distributed stamps? We will see that scarcity matters, and this is of course interesting from an economic point of view. In fact, we will learn that it is the average type of postage stamp that increases most in price during a bubble, but this average type of stamp also lands faster and harder. Scarcer stamps, on the other hand, keep their high values even after the bubble has burst.

The next two questions in this chapter also deal with scarcity, which as we know is a key concept in economics. The first of the two questions deals with banknotes.[4] Scarce banknotes could be those with very high denominations, like the one from Hungary we saw in Figure 3.1 in Chapter 3. Ideally, exceptionally high inflation periods last only briefly, at least usually, and hence the very high denominations may have been necessary or useful only for a short while and after that high inflation period quickly become useless and in turn may become scarce when people simply throw them away. So, a first and natural question that comes to mind is whether the denominational range of banknotes goes hand in hand with inflation, or whether perhaps one is leading the other. That is, does high inflation lead to banknotes with more zeroes, or does the introduction of more zeroes lead to more inflation? To examine such potential causality can then also be useful to predict and quantify future scarcity, and for the individual investor it may be clever not to throw away those high-valued banknotes.

The second question on scarcity goes back to stamps, and again stamps from the Netherlands. Would it be possible to estimate which stamps are relatively scarce? The initial price of a postage stamp is of course printed on the stamp itself, and usually it is known (and reported in catalogs) how many were issued. When the current collector's price is known, it might be possible to estimate how many stamps are left, assuming that the price that collectors quote reflects the scarcity.

The appendix to this chapter introduces three new econometric methods and models. The first is what is called a recursive residual. It allows one to monitor if one-period-ahead forecasts somehow stay on track, and this is particularly useful in bubble times. When the price is in a tornado-like bubble, then one-step-ahead forecasts are most likely too low each time, which is because the price grows explosively. The second method involves a correction of the standard errors, which is useful in case one has noisy data. The third technical novelty is a new model, and it is a model not with one equation linking a dependent variable with the own past and the past of another variable but with a second equation where the roles of the two variables are switched. This is important for the inflation question, as we want to know whether the denominational range predicts inflation or it is the other way around.

The key takeaway of this chapter is that we may not always use econometric methods on raw data but first have to think about transformations of the data or alternative measurement. In real life, this is more the standard than otherwise. Any firm or institution that collects business or governmental data in its databases must think about what it is that it wants to explain or predict. Only in textbooks does the spreadsheet contain the dependent variable in the first column and the explanatory variables in the adjacent columns. In the real world, this (almost) never happens!

CAN WE PREDICT PRICE BUBBLES IN COLLECTIBLE POSTAL STAMPS?

Prices may experience bubbles. This may be reflected by short periods in which prices go up very fast, seemingly explosively, and then the bubble bursts and the prices fall and land.[5] Such bubbles appear in stock markets and housing prices but also in products like art, postage stamps, and collectibles. It is interesting to see how these products experience those bubbles, that is, which products in a sense survive and keep on having high prices after the bubble bursts and which products helped to inflate the bubble but, once the hype is over, turn out to be almost worthless.

Before I come to an analysis of stamp prices, we first have to settle on how to measure a bubble. Indeed, it is about price changes, which are positive, and about quickly increasing price changes, which suggest that the changes of the price changes, which are something like acceleration, are also positive, at least for a short while.

A change for a time series variable y_t can be measured as

$$\Delta y_t = y_t - y_{t-1}$$

with the Greek capital letter Δ referring to difference or change. Note that where I previously used y_i for individuals, we now switch to y_t to indicate that we are talking about observations measured over time. Acceleration in a time series y_t can be defined as the change of the change, so

$$\Delta\Delta y_t = y_t - y_{t-1} - (y_{t-1} - y_{t-2}) = y_t - 2y_{t-1} + y_{t-2}.$$

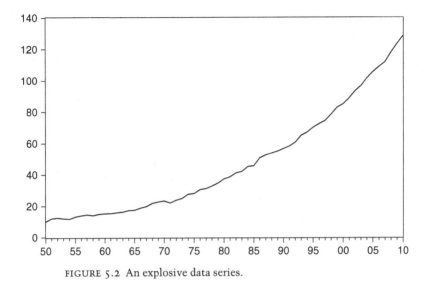

FIGURE 5.2 An explosive data series.

When both change and acceleration are positive, then the data show explosive behavior. For example, if the data can be described by

$$y_t = 1.05 y_{t-1}$$

and assume that the observations are all positively valued. Then it is easy to see that $\Delta y_t = 0.05\, y_{t-1} > 0$ and $\Delta\Delta y_t = 0.05\, y_{t-1} - (0.05\, y_{t-2}) = 0.05\, \Delta y_{t-1} = 0.05$ times $0.05\, y_{t-1} > 0$. In a picture it would look like the data in Figure 5.2.

The graph in Figure 5.2 looks familiar, doesn't it? Take a look at Figure 5.3, which presents the nominal gross domestic product (GDP) in China (in 100 millions of yuan), where the data run from 1992 Q1 to and including 2013 Q4.

Note that the sawtooth pattern in the graph is caused by the fact that the National Bureau of Statistics of China aggregates the quarterly data over time. So, the first observation in a year concerns quarter 1; the second observation is the sum of quarters 1 and 2; the third observation is the sum of quarters 1, 2, and 3; and the Q4 observation measures the entire year. Clearly, the economy of China is experiencing explosive growth. It is not to say that it is a bubble, and it is also

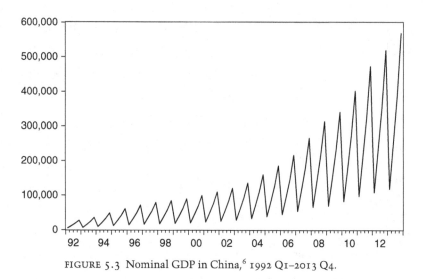

FIGURE 5.3 Nominal GDP in China,[6] 1992 Q1–2013 Q4.

unclear at the moment whether there will be some landing in the future, but evidently, China's economy was on the rise until the end of 2013.

Usually, explosive growth is not something that is continuous forever. At some moment, there may come a hard landing. Think about a Formula One car increasing its speed. At one moment, either the engine blows up, or the driver loses control of the car and crashes. So, for stability you would want growth and acceleration to be in balance, and increasing speed forever seems predictive of problems. Again, like the car, where speed increases and decreases and where these increases and decreases in turn can also increase or decrease, there must be a subtle balance such that the car stays on track and the engine does not blow up.

A good example of a hard landing in the recent history of stock markets (and later in the national economy of Japan) concerns the Nikkei index. Figure 5.4 shows that the index went up and up in the 1980s and tumbled downward since 1990.

Perhaps one way to diagnose whether the data are stable and not in a bubble is related to the idea that during stable times change and acceleration are in balance.[7] One way to look at this is that in stable

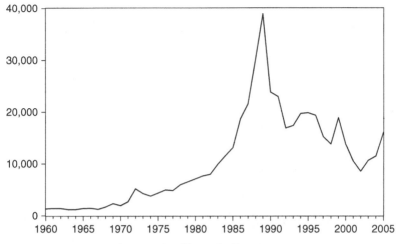

FIGURE 5.4 The annual Nikkei index for 1960–2005.

times $\Delta y_t + \Delta y_{t-1} = y_t - y_{t-2}$ has a stable mean. So, when you allow for some impact of past averaged increases, you can for example consider the simple regression

$$y_t - y_{t-2} = \alpha + \beta(y_{t-1} - y_{t-3}) + \varepsilon_t$$

and look at the forecast errors. Hence here you are not so much interested in the estimates a and b of α and β, respectively, but merely in the one-step-ahead forecasts

$$\hat{y}_{t+1} - y_{t-1} = a + b(y_t - y_{t-2})$$

as compared to the actual realizations. These numbers are called recursive residuals, and in the appendix to this chapter, I explain how these can be computed in the case of the one-variable regression model. An illustration of these residuals is given in Figure 5.5 for the Nikkei index, and it is clear that these forecast errors were too large in 1986 and 1988, as they then cross the boundaries. So, in these years, growth was too fast, and the Nikkei index could be considered to be "in a bubble."

So it seems that positive changes and positive increases in those changes can be instrumental in "defining" a bubble.

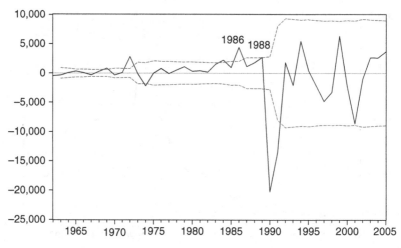

FIGURE 5.5 Recursive residuals for the Nikkei index.

Let us go back to the postal stamps. Each year, the Dutch Stamp Dealers' Association (with Dutch abbreviation NVPH) publishes a price catalog with the prices of all Dutch stamps. I will only consider the prices for stamps in mint condition. According to one of these dealers, located in the city center of Rotterdam, it is not possible to purchase past catalogs, as apparently these catalogs are simply thrown away after a few years. So I first had to collect the catalogs via various auction websites. It took quite some time to purchase all editions, but after two months (during the fall of 2012), I managed to acquire the catalogs of 1971 to and including 1999. These editions are relevant as they contain the price information in those specific years. I did not extend the sample beyond 1999, as a speculative bubble was already observed for this sample. I do not use auction prices but the (recommended) prices in the catalogs, as this allows me to study all stamps that were issued in a particular period and not only those that appeared at auctions.

Given the availability of the price catalogs since 1971, I focus on the post–World War II stamps issued in 1945 until 1970. One reason not to include data prior to 1945 is that many collectible stamps in

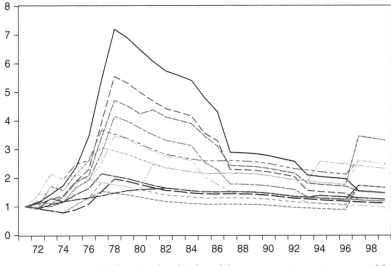

FIGURE 5.6 The price level index of the stamps 428 to 446, corrected for inflation.

that period have many varieties with different prints, colors, and misprints, and it is therefore not easy to retrieve various properties for many of these stamps. I thus consider the stamps with numbers NVPH 428 to 937. The prices in 1971 are scaled to 1, and since then all data are indexed against 1971. The price level in 1971 is in Dutch guilders (NLG), and so I use the relevant inflation data from Statistics Netherlands to create real price levels (indexes).

Figure 5.6 shows for 19 stamps how prices vary over time. Clearly, around 1978 several stamp prices peaked, and around 1994 many of them were back at their initial levels. In this small sample of stamps, stamp numbered 439 showed the sharpest increase in price around the late seventies. Figure 5.7 displays stamp 439.

In total I consider 500 stamps, which associate with the indicated NVPH numbers, where I took account of some renumbering as the numbers 821 to 826 and 864 to 867 ceased to be included in catalogs after 1973. This illustrates what practical data collection can involve. One has to meticulously scrutinize each and every single observation to see if everything is OK with the observation. Of course,

FIGURE 5.7 Liberation stamp with a portrait of Queen Wilhelmina, issued in 1946; amount issued is 1,489,300, and it is the 12th stamp in a series.

this takes time and effort, but it is my experience that this scrutinizing is better done before analysis than afterward if "strange" outcomes of the econometric analysis are obtained. Note that I am not saying that strange data should be deleted – no, it is best to take data analysis very seriously, as doing so can prevent unpleasant results in the end.

For most stamps I can collect various features like quantity issued, position within a series, whether there are any special charity features, and the like. These features will later on become the explanatory variables, as I want to examine whether specific features of the stamps have predictive value of bubbles and their aftermath. Also here, some features are not completely observable. For example, for 33 of the 500 stamps, information on issued quantities is missing. Hence, I sometimes analyze 500 data on stamps, and sometimes I have a restricted sample with 467 data points.

When all prices are set equal to 1 for 1971, I can create 500 indexes (corrected for inflation). We start with an analysis of the average price index, which is depicted in Figure 5.8. Clearly, there is steep growth in the period from 1971 to 1978, then a constant level peak period from 1978 to around 1982, and then a decline toward a rather constant level from 1987 onward to 1999. The bubble is

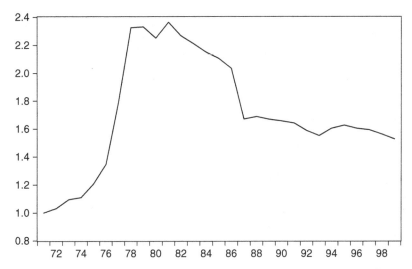

FIGURE 5.8 The average of the index values (across 500 stamps), after correction for inflation, 1971–1999.

clearly visible from the steep growth, that is, real prices on average increased from 1 to 2.3, which amounts to a return of 230% in just five to six years. Well, that is a serious return on investment, if I may say so.

Before I turn to the heterogeneity across the stamps and the potential predictive power of their features, I first see whether there are any features of the data that elicit properties of that bubble. Explosive patterns seem to associate with a tendency to divert from the mean, and each new observation exceeds its previous observation with a faster pace. Positive feedback, so it might be called, is then displayed by positive changes in price levels and at the same time also positive changes (increases) in these positive changes. So, positive feedback may be observed when prices increase and at the same time these increases increase too. In Table 5.1, I present the number of stamps (out of the 500) for which, in particular years, price increases are positive (second column) and when changes in changes were positive (last column). Clearly, in the years 1972 to 1978–1979, there are many stamps with positive price changes and with positive

Table 5.1 *Number of stamps (per year) with positive changes in price and with positive changes in the price changes.*

Year	$\Delta Price_t > 0$	$\Delta\Delta Price_t > 0$
1972	234	NA
1973	255	321
1974	227	145
1975	249	363
1976	292	364
1977	381	457
1978	343	354
1979	195	180
1980	89	49
1981	290	460
1982	63	191
1983	20	426
1984	51	43
1985	41	447
1986	2	378
1987	173	192
1988	43	343
1989	0	1
1990	60	61
1991	70	64
1992	24	417
1993	25	445
1994	135	157
1995	37	356
1996	13	27
1997	20	28
1998	0	480
1999	0	0

acceleration. In 1976, 1977, and 1978, the fraction of stamps with positive feedback in prices can be as large as 0.6 or 0.7. Such positive feedback may thus be an indicator of a current bubble. The bursting bubble is noticeable from a sharp drop in positive feedback in 1979

Table 5.2 *Characteristics of 500 postage stamps (the variable with an
* only has 467 observations).*

Variable	Mean	Median	Minimum	Maximum
Quantity issued*	14,054,509	1,545,392	205,700	9.36E+08
Series length	6.528	5	1	24
Additional price (in cents)	3.978	3	0	37.500
Children's benefit	0.26	0	0	1
Rank within series	3.766	3	1	24

and 1980, which is the period that prices did not change much on
average.

Now I turn to the potential explanatory variables. Table 5.2
presents the relevant characteristics of the 500 stamps. The minimum
quantity issued is just over 200,000, while the maximum number is
more than 900 million, and this range suggests quite some diversity
across the stamps. This can also be noted from the series lengths,
which ranges from 1 to 24, and from the added price value (usually
for charity reasons), which ranges from 0 to 37.5 cents. In most years,
the Dutch Postal Services issued so-called children's stamps, for
which the additional fee was used for childcare charities. So, the
data show quite some variation.

Table 5.3 presents various statistics on the price series over the
years, and here the differences across the stamps are illustrated even
further. The first row of Table 5.3 shows that there are substantial
differences across price levels. For example, in 1971 there were stamps
with price levels over 100 guilders, while the mean was just 1.985
guilders. To account for these skewed data, later on I will consider
these 1971 prices after using the natural logarithmic transformation.
To give an impression of the after-bubble prices, I present the price levels
of 1990. After correction for inflation, we can learn that price levels, on
average, seem to have dropped from 1.985 to 1.658, and it seems that in
particular the high-priced stamps showed most significant price landings.

Table 5.3 *Characteristics of the prices of 500 postage stamps in the sample 1971–1999 (the variable with an * only has 297 observations).*

Variable	Mean	Median	Minimum	Maximum
Value in 1971	1.985	0.750	0.050	120.00
Value in 1990	3.996	3.333	0.417	20.00
Corrected for inflation	1.658	1.383	0.173	8.297
Maximum price index	5.775	5	1	35
Corrected for inflation	2.796	2.332	1	12.599
Years to peak price index	14.348	11	0	26
Years from peak to lowest price	4.86	5	0	19
Years from 1971 to lowest price*	18.178	16	3	28

The bubble price index value is 5.775, on average, with a median value of five years. The maximum bubble price is 35, and this would involve a serious gain on one's investment. Corrected for inflation, the maximum price level is 2.796 on average, which suggests a return of close to 280% at the peak of the bubble.

Finally, Table 5.3 shows in the bottom panel that the median number of years for prices to peak is 11 years. This suggests that during the period after the burst of the bubble – that is, during 1979–1982 – there were various stamps that reached top price levels, while for other stamps this peak occurred earlier, and for many it occurred much later. The burst of the bubble seems to take only four to five years, as the average number of years from peak to the lowest price is 4.86 years.

Let us consider a regression model for the nominal price levels. Table 5.4 presents the estimation results to explain the (natural logs of) nominal maximum price index value by an intercept, the quantity issued (after natural logarithmic transformation), the year the stamp was issued, a dummy variable if there was some added children's benefit, the rank in the series and the size of the series, a variable with the additional surplus value in case there is one, and the price value of 1971 (after taking natural logarithms). The table contains

Table 5.4 *Regression of the (natural log of) nominal maximum price index value on various explanatory variables (estimated White-corrected standard errors in parentheses).*

Variable	Full model		Final model	
Intercept	**51.837**	**(8.627)**	**51.439**	**(8.324)**
Quantity issued (in logs)	**–0.085**	**(0.026)**	**–0.087**	**(0.023)**
Year	**–0.025**	**(0.004)**	**–0.025**	**(0.004)**
Children's benefit	**–0.154**	**(0.059)**	**–0.153**	**(0.058)**
Rank in series	–0.005	(0.015)		
Size of series	**0.030**	**(0.010)**	**0.028**	**(0.008)**
Additional price	0.129	(0.691)		
Value in 1971 (in logs)	**0.080**	**(0.027)**	**0.074**	**(0.024)**
Adjusted[8] R^2	0.254		0.257	

a panel with all estimated parameters and their associated White-corrected standard errors and a panel where all insignificant parameters (at the 5% level) are set at 0. These White-corrected standard errors, named after the very eminent econometrician Halbert White, are explained in the appendix. The deletion of irrelevant variables is carried out stepwise, where each time the least significant parameter is set at 0 (until 5% significance is achieved) and hence the associated variable is dismissed.

If we consider the rightmost column of Table 5.4, we can learn that stamps that were issued in larger quantities, were issued more recently, and have a surplus for children's charity have lower maximum price levels. At the same time, stamps in series with many items and higher initial price levels have higher maximum price levels. Otherwise put, more valuable, older, and scarce stamps reach higher maximum price levels (during a bubble).

Table 5.5 reports on the estimation results for a regression model for the number of years from the peak price to the lowest price. In other words, this is the time that it takes for the bubble to burst. A shorter time period means that price levels drop more rapidly.

Table 5.5 *Regression of the log of the number of years in between the year of the peak price and the year of the trough on various explanatory variables (estimated White-corrected standard errors in parentheses).*

Variable	Years + 1 (in logs)	
Intercept	–47.50	(14.01)
Quantity issued (in logs)	–0.119	(0.040)
Year	0.026	(0.007)
Children's benefit	–0.303	(0.100)
Rank in series	0.065	(0.032)
Size of series	–0.046	(0.017)
Additional price	3.977	(1.014)
Value in 1971 (in logs)	0.146	(0.053)
Adjusted R^2	0.223	

Zooming in on some of the key variables, we learn from Table 5.5 that higher-valued, scarce, and more recently issued stamps have a longer time in between peak and trough, while initially lower-valued and abundantly issued stamps witness rapid price drops after the bubble bursts. This is an indication that the latter type of stamps joins in the price bubble, but they are also the first to show sharp price landings. The rare and higher-valued stamps seem to suffer less from the price bubble.

Finally, for stamp prices to show a bubble, there must be a specific reason why such a bubble could occur. One such reason may be that the collection of stamps became very popular in the bubble years, and hence that demand for stamps suddenly increased. Perhaps the graph in Figure 5.9 supports this. In this graph, I depict the log of the numbers of issued new stamps since 1945, and it is clear that there is an upward trend from the mid-seventies to the beginning of the eighties. The Dutch postal services recognized the increasing popularity of collecting stamps and started to sell in larger quantities in the late 1970s. They also issued special themes and books, and many

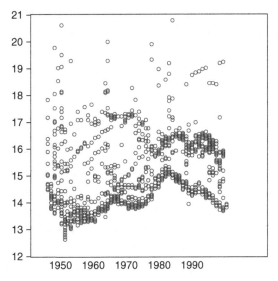

FIGURE 5.9 The natural logarithm of sales (in units) versus the year of issue.

stamp collectors could not keep up the pace, also in terms of money, and after around 1985 stamp collecting became much less popular.

To sum up, specific properties of the 500 stamps seemed informative for the bubble period and also for the period right after the burst of the bubble. Scarce and higher-priced (on the stamp) collectible stamps reach higher peak levels at the top of the bubble, whereas scarce stamps also reach this peak level faster, while the very same types of stamps witness a slower pace in times when price levels drop to trough values. For investment purposes, these stamps seem to be the best buy, although these stamps also show tremendous drops in value once the bubble is over.

At a more general level, we gained more insights on the data properties at the time of the price bubbles. We saw that during the bubble, the fraction of stamps with positive feedback is more than 50% or even higher, and this suggests that an analysis along these lines can be very informative about the current state of affairs. We could also note that properties of the stamps, like scarcity and initial price levels, mediate the positive feedback, that is, these types of stamps substantially contribute to the price bubble. Other stamps are taken along in the upswing of prices, but once the bubble bursts, these stamps quickly lose their value.

An important implication is that it pays off to look at the assets at a more detailed level when analyzing price level conditions. Individual characteristics of the assets had a mediating and signaling role. This insight might be useful when analyzing bubbles in other markets. Typically, one analyzes the top-level prices of artists' works, but the results suggest that analyzing all works of these artists can be beneficial. The same holds true for the dot-com bubble, where perhaps some companies did not suffer as much as others did due to some specific features of these companies. Similarly, not all stocks may peak at the same time, and the burst of a stock market bubble may be experienced differently for different stocks.

ARE BIGGER BANKNOTES DUE TO INFLATION?

Having seen that scarcity matters and that scarcer stamps keep their value even in the aftermath of a price bubble, it might now be interesting to see how scarcity can be addressed for banknotes.[9] Periods of hyperinflation usually do not last long,[10] so it may be that banknotes with high denominational value are issued only for a short while and hence may become scarce after such periods of hyperinflation. Thus, it would be interesting to see whether inflation and the numbers on the banknotes are somehow related. Monetary theory predicts that high inflation rates may imply the need for bigger banknotes.[11] At the same time, monetary authorities may fear that the introduction of higher-valued banknotes might reflect an expectation of upcoming inflation.

The inflation data (based on the consumer price index) were obtained from the Penn World Tables (version 6.1), and data collection took place in 2004. At that time, the largest sample ran from 1960 to 2000. Information on the banknote denominations was obtained from the web site www.banknotes.com, which contains data on the introduction of new banknotes for all countries in the world.

The span or width of the denominational range, denoted as $Range_{i,t}$, can be measured in various ways. I chose two methods. The first amounts to the mean value of the banknote range, which can increase over time due to the introduction of higher-valued notes. The second amounts to the relative difference between the largest and the smallest banknote. For example, for the current euro range with banknotes 5, 10, 20, 50, 100, 200, and 500, the first measure would yield

$$\frac{5 + 10 + 20 + 50 + 100 + 200 + 500}{7} = 126.4.$$

The second way to measure the range would be

$$\frac{500 - 5}{5} = 99.$$

Figures 5.10 and 5.11 give a graphical impression of how the data look for each of the investigated countries, where here the data for Argentina and Mozambique are presented. Clearly, and expectedly,

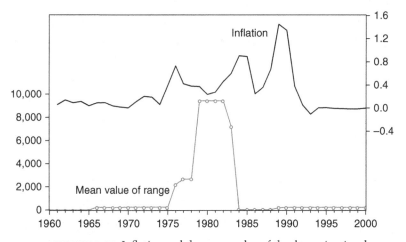

FIGURE 5.10 Inflation and the mean value of the denominational range: Argentina.

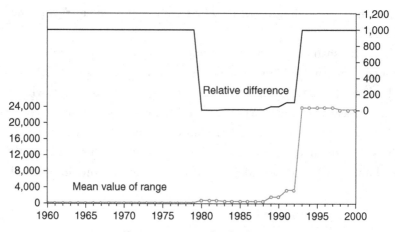

FIGURE 5.11 The two measures for the denominational range: Mozambique.

there is not that much variation in the data over time. Given the small amount of variation, it seems that a simple regression of a single country would not lead to much information. So, it seems wise to collect data for more countries and next to analyze all data jointly. Table 5.6 presents the countries for which full samples ranging from 1960 to 2000 could be collected. It is nice to see that all continents are represented. Also, there are various countries included that experienced periods of hyperinflation, like Argentina and some African countries.

At the same time, another property of the data, which is evidenced from Figure 5.12, is that there is substantial variation in the data on the ranges, so it is wise to take the natural logarithms of these range data.

The econometric method that I will use is called a vector autoregression, which here says that inflation can depend on past inflation and on past range and, at the same time, in a second equation, that the range can depend on the past range and on past inflation. Moreover, to "borrow" information from other countries, I set all slope parameters

Table 5.6 *The 59 countries involved in the empirical analysis.*

Africa	Asia	North America	South America	Europe	Australasia
Burundi	Bangladesh	Canada	Argentina	Austria	New Zealand
Burkina Faso	Hong Kong	Costa Rica	Colombia	Belgium	
Cameroon	India	Jamaica	Ecuador	Finland	
Cape Verde	Iran	Mexico	Paraguay	Greece	
Egypt	Israel	Nicaragua	Peru	Ireland	
Ethiopia	Jordan	El Salvador	Venezuela	Iceland	
Ghana	Japan	Trinidad and		Italy	
Guinea	Sri Lanka	Tobago		Netherlands	
Gambia	Nepal			Portugal	
Kenya	Pakistan			Romania	
Lesotho	Singapore			Sweden	
Madagascar	Syria				
Morocco	Thailand				
Mali					
Mozambique					
Niger					
Rwanda					
Senegal					
Seychelles					
Tanzania					
Zimbabwe					

as equal across the 59 models. The appendix tells you more about the details of this methodology.

When the range is measured by the mean value of the available banknotes, then the estimate of the slope is 0.001 for the past range variable in the equation for inflation with a t test value of 1.152. In contrast, the parameter estimate for lagged inflation in the equation for the range is 0.424 with a t test value of 4.402. Note that both parameters are now estimated using more than 2,300 data points. When the other measure of the range is used, that is, the range is measured by the width of the denominational range, the estimates

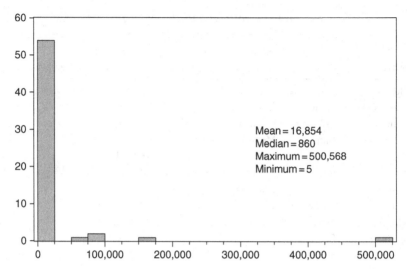

FIGURE 5.12 Statistics of the range (when measured as the average) for the 59 countries involved.

are –0.0004 with a t test value of –0.408 and 0.676 with a t test value 5.276, respectively.

These estimation results suggest that increasing inflation leads to bigger banknotes and not the other way around.[12] The implication from monetary theory is not invalidated, and at the same time, there is no evidence for monetary authorities to worry about the possibly unwanted effects of issuing higher-valued banknotes.

So, what do we learn from this? Equations can help each other. Parameters in one equation can be estimated with the help of information in the other equations.

WHICH STAMPS ARE SCARCE, AND WHY?

The final part of this chapter again deals with postage stamps, and again for the Netherlands, but now the data are not analyzed in a time-series format, like when I looked at bubbles, but in a cross-sectional format. Time-series data are longitudinal data that are sequentially observed over time. A cross section is a snapshot of the data at one given moment in time. You can also have panel data, which means that you observe the same individuals or entities over time. In fact, the data that we just used for the banknotes were panel data, that is, the same countries were monitored over the same years.

Now I will look at data that were collected in 2003, using the Netherlands stamp catalog of 2002, which concern numbers 428 to 1983,[13] for the year 1945 to and including 2001. As there are some numbers not used, I have data on 1,413 stamps. A couple of features of these stamps are relevant for the analysis. The first is the price of the stamp when it was issued. Conveniently, the price is printed on each postage stamp. At the time of issue, this price was the same for all people. Also, postal stamps can be used either for sending postage mail or for collection. Except for misprints, all issued stamps have the same quality, and preferences for certain stamps over others issued at the same time do not exist. The second feature is the amount of stamps that were issued. Often, stamps come in series with a certain theme (summer, anniversaries of royalty). Each series usually contains a stamp with a value that, at that time, equals the price for sending a regular letter. Usually, more of these particular stamps are issued, so within a series quantities can differ. The third feature is the current (in 2002) price of the stamps, either in mint condition (not used) or stamped (used). Each year the average current prices are reported in a catalog, which is available to the general public. These prices reflect a consensus value and are set by informed traders and collectors. These prices concern regular versions of these stamps, so misprints, rare prints, or special envelopes are not taken into account. Also, all stamps are assumed to be of good quality. This is a relevant feature of stamps, in contrast to products like old cars or early vinyl recordings, where quality might decrease over time due to their usage. Indeed, used stamps could have been used only once, although of course some used stamps are in better condition than others.

Table 5.7 presents some basic statistics of the variables that are useful to explain the price differences. These price differences can signal scarcity. If the original price is called $p_{i,0}$ and the current price is

Table 5.7 *Some statistics of features of 1,413 stamps (for the amount issued information is available for only 1,084 stamps). Prices are all in euros.*

	Mean	Median	Maximum	Minimum
Original price	0.253	0.250	4.538	0.005
Current price, used	0.871	0.35	38.6	0.09
Current price, mint	2.735	0.80	545	0.15
Amounts issued	16,571,308	3,494,858	1.1 Mio	318,257
Rank in series	3.363	2	24	1
Series length	5.713	4	24	1
Added surplus	0.030	0	0.363	0
Children's benefit	0.167	0	1	0

$p_{i,1}$, and if the amount issued is called $q_{i,0}$, then it might be reasonable to assume that

$$p_{i,1}q_{i,1} = p_{i,0}q_{i,0}.$$

This equality presents a simple expression to estimate the amount $q_{i,1}$, which would be the amount currently available. For 1,084 observations, these numbers can be computed, and the minimum numbers available are 544, based on used stamps and 486 based on mint-condition stamps. These numbers seem quite small and are most likely far from exactly correct, but it is possible to rank-order the data and determine that the most scarce stamps should be those depicted in Figures 5.13 and 5.14.

So, as scarcity can be measured by the difference in prices, it is interesting to examine whether there are any variables among those in Table 5.7 that can have explanatory value for these price differences. The estimation results are presented in Table 5.8. All variables are transformed by taking natural logarithms, except for children's benefit, which is a 1/0 dummy variable, and added surplus, which is very often equal to zero. The sample size in both regressions is equal to 1,083.

FIGURE 5.13 A scarce series, dating back to 1950.

FIGURE 5.14 Another scarce series, also issued in 1950.

The estimation results in Table 5.8 give a clear picture of what explains the price differences (and hence scarcity). Stamps with children's benefit do not show price increases. Older stamps are scarcer. Higher values with a series are now more expensive, the series length itself does not matter, added surplus has some positive effect in scarcity, and, most importantly, stamps with low initial values increase scarcity and, of course, those stamps with a limited number issued now have higher prices.

The fit of each of the two models is remarkably high, so I do have quite some confidence in the outcomes.

Table 5.8 *Estimation results for a multiple regression model explaining log(p$_{i,1}$) − log(p$_{i,0}$) by seven explanatory variables. The sample size is 1,083 as some information on amounts issued is unavailable. The standard errors are White-corrected.*

	Mint stamps		Used stamps	
Variable	Parameter	Standard error	Parameter	Standard error
Intercept	424.9	66.90	213.6	45.52
Children's benefit	−0.377	0.066	−0.238	0.058
Log year	−55.27	8.798	−27.11	5.975
Log rank in series	0.314	0.063	0.158	0.053
Log series length	0.131	0.073	−0.030	0.048
Added surplus	−2.510	0.482	−0.864	0.402
Log $p_{i,0}$	−0.581	0.076	−0.822	0.049
Log $q_{i,0}$	−0.318	0.025	−0.541	0.022
R^2	0.737		0.832	

As promised, the key takeaway of this chapter was that econometric methods are rarely applied to raw data. First, we have to think about the data format and perhaps transformations of data. For the last illustration, we saw that the dependent variable of interest was $\log(p_{i,1}) - \log(p_{i,0})$. In real life, data preparation is more the standard than otherwise.

APPENDIX: ECONOMETRIC METHODS

RECURSIVE RESIDUALS
Recursive residuals can be useful to monitor the forecasting abilities of the model. If the one-step-ahead forecast errors start to increase and become too large at one moment, then one may wonder whether the model is inadequate.

Consider the simple regression model

$$y_t = \beta x_t + \varepsilon_t,$$

where for simplicity of notation it is assumed that both variables have mean zero. If that is the case, then there is no need to include an intercept term with parameter α. Suppose that the data run from 1, 2,..., to N and the first $t - 1$ are used to estimate the slope parameter β. That is, the forecast for time t is then equal to

$$\hat{y}_t = b_{t-1}x_t,$$

where b_{t-1} is the least-squares-based estimate of β and where I assume for the moment that x_t is known at time t. The forecast error f_t at time t is

$$f_t = y_t - \hat{y}_t = y_t - b_{t-1}x_t.$$

For the variance of f_t, we can derive[14] that

$$\text{variance}(f_t) = \sigma^2 \left(1 + \frac{x_t^2}{\sum_{i=1}^{t-1} x_i^2} \right).$$

A recursive residual is now defined as

$$w_t = \frac{f_t}{\sqrt{1 + \frac{x_t^2}{\sum_{i=1}^{t-1} x_i^2}}} \sim N(0, \sigma^2).$$

And thus

$$\frac{w_t}{\sigma} \sim N(0, 1).$$

This scaled recursive residual can then be used to test whether the forecasts are off track.

WHITE-CORRECTED STANDARD ERRORS

Consider again the simple regression for two zero-mean variables

$$y_i = \beta x_i + \varepsilon_i.$$

The standard assumption (see Chapter 2) is that the variance of ε_i is the same for all observations, namely, σ^2. It could however be that the errors do not have a constant variance but that there is what is called heteroskedasticity. This could mean that the variance for each of the errors is σ_i^2. If there is no specific knowledge about the very nature of these varying variances, one can use the estimated residuals to correct the estimated standard errors for the estimated parameters. So, for the simple regression model

$$y_i = bx_i + e_i$$

and the assumption of the common variance σ^2, the variance of b equals

$$\text{Var}(b) = \frac{\sigma^2}{\sum_{i=1}^{n} x_i^2}.$$

When one suspects heteroskedasticity,[15] it is better to use

$$\text{Var}(b) = \frac{\sum_{i=1}^{n} e_i^2 x_i^2}{\left(\sum_{i=1}^{n} x_i^2\right)^2}.$$

A VECTOR AUTOREGRESSION OF ORDER I

In Chapter 2, I discussed a first-order autoregressive model for the marathon data. The model for the records in the marathon was given by

$$y_t = \alpha + \beta y_{t-1} + \varepsilon_t$$

(although, in Chapter 2, I used y_i instead of y_t because the observations are not equally spaced). Such a model was called a first-order autoregression, with acronym AR(1), as the values of y depend on their own past, just one period ago. As indicated, this model is very useful for forecasting into the future, as one can plug in the current observation y_t on the right-hand side to predict the next value. For example, if you have data y_t for January, February, and March of 2017, like (hypothetically) 100, 110, and 105, respectively, then y_{t-1} is 110, 100, and further back, where you use β times 105 to predict the observation for April 2017.

This AR(1) model is a univariate model, as it makes y_t dependent on its own past and not on the past of another variable. When one wants to do that, one may enlarge the model by introducing another variable x_t as follows (without the intercept for convenience):

$$y_t = \beta_1 y_{t-1} + \beta_2 x_{t-1} + \varepsilon_t$$

and at the same time

$$x_t = \beta_3 y_{t-1} + \beta_4 x_{t-1} + \omega_t.$$

So, y_t depends on the past of y_t and the past of x_t, and at the same time, x_t depends on its own past and the past of y_t. The past of the two variables helps to forecast the future of both variables. The two equations together are called a vector autoregression of order 1 or, in short, VAR(1). As the two equations have the same regressors, the parameters of each of the two equations can be estimated using the same least squares technique as before, even if the two associated error terms ε_t and ω_t have a covariance unequal to 0.[16]

The VAR(1) model is often called a reduced-form model. This originates from the notion that it associates with a so-called structural model in which it is allowed to have not just lagged impact but also contemporaneous correlation. Take a look at the following two equations, where now the current values (instead of the past) of the other variable are included, that is,

$$y_t = \alpha_1 y_{t-1} + \alpha_2 x_t + \varepsilon_t,$$
$$x_t = \alpha_3 y_t + \alpha_4 x_{t-1} + \omega_t.$$

This set of two equations is usually called a simultaneous equations model.

However, it is possible to show that this simultaneous equations model can be written as a VAR model.[17] The way to see this is to plug the second equation into the first one, like

$$y_t = \alpha_1 y_{t-1} + \alpha_2 \left(\alpha_3 y_t + \alpha_4 x_{t-1} + \omega_t \right) + \varepsilon_t.$$

Arranging the y_t terms on the left-hand side gives the following result:

$$y_t = \frac{\alpha_1}{1 - \alpha_2 \alpha_3} y_{t-1} + \frac{\alpha_2 \alpha_4}{1 - \alpha_2 \alpha_3} x_{t-1} + \frac{\alpha_2}{1 - \alpha_2 \alpha_3} \omega_t + \frac{1}{1 - \alpha_2 \alpha_3} \varepsilon_t.$$

Likewise, plugging in the first equation into the second gives

$$x_t = \alpha_3 \left(\alpha_1 y_{t-1} + \alpha_2 x_t + \varepsilon_t \right) + \alpha_4 x_{t-1} + \omega_t.$$

Rearranging like before gives

$$x_t = \frac{\alpha_1 \alpha_3}{1 - \alpha_2 \alpha_3} y_{t-1} + \frac{\alpha_4}{1 - \alpha_2 \alpha_3} x_{t-1} + \frac{1}{1 - \alpha_2 \alpha_3} \omega_t + \frac{\alpha_3}{1 - \alpha_2 \alpha_3} \varepsilon_t.$$

So, the two equations of the simultaneous equations model can be written as the two equations of a VAR model, where now the error terms are correlated because w_t and ε_t appear in both equations. For this specific case, by the way, it also holds that the parameters of the simultaneous equations model can be retrieved from the parameters in the VAR model because

$$\alpha_3 = \frac{\beta_3}{\beta_1}, \ \alpha_2 = \frac{\beta_2}{\beta_4}.$$

This makes

$$1 - \alpha_2 \alpha_3 = 1 - \frac{\beta_3 \beta_2}{\beta_1 \beta_4}.$$

And hence

$$\alpha_1 = \beta_1 \left(1 - \frac{\beta_3 \beta_2}{\beta_1 \beta_4} \right), \ \alpha_4 = \beta_4 \left(1 - \frac{\beta_3 \beta_2}{\beta_1 \beta_4} \right).$$

The model that is used for the N countries with T yearly observations reads as

$$\text{Inflation}_{i,t} = \mu_{1,i} + \beta_{1,i} \, \text{Inflation}_{i,t-1} + \beta_{2,i} \, \text{Range}_{i,t-1} + \varepsilon_{i,t}$$

and at the same time

$$\text{Range}_{i,t} = \mu_{2,i} + \beta_{3,i} \, \text{Inflation}_{i,t-1} + \beta_{4,i} \, \text{Range}_{i,t-1} + \omega_{i,t}.$$

So, there is a VAR(1) model for each country. Now, as the data variation is not very strong – see Figures 5.10 and 5.11 – there is not enough variation in the data to reliably estimate the individual parameters $\beta_{j,i}$

with j = 1, 2, 3, and 4. One simple solution now is to estimate the VAR (1) models while imposing that these parameters $\beta_{j,i}$ are the same across all N countries. Hence, one estimates the parameters in the same equations but now where the parameters $\beta_{j,i}$ are restricted to be the same, that is,

$$\text{Inflation}_{i,t} = \mu_{1,i} + \beta_1 \text{ Inflation}_{i,t-1} + \beta_2 \text{ Range}_{i,t-1} + \varepsilon_{i,t}$$
$$\text{Range}_{i,t} = \mu_{2,i} + \beta_3 \text{ Inflation}_{i,t-1} + \beta_4 \text{ Range}_{i,t-1} + \omega_{i,t}.$$

Note that the intercepts still are different across the countries but that the slope parameters are assumed to be the same across countries. In other words, per equation there is information – or, if you like, variation – "borrowed" from the other equations. Hence, variation in the other $N-1$ countries is helpful to estimate the parameters for each of the countries.

PREVENTING SPURIOUS CORRELATIONS AND RELATIONS USING A VAR

The VAR model is also useful to prevent having spurious correlations.[18] Let us have a look at the following two data-generating processes:

$$y_{1,t} = \beta_1 y_{1,t-1} + \varepsilon_{1,t},$$
$$y_{2,t} = \beta_2 y_{2,t-1} + \varepsilon_{2,t},$$

where the two variables $\varepsilon_{1,t}$ and $\varepsilon_{2,t}$ have mean zero and variances σ_1^2 and σ_2^2 and are otherwise completely uncorrelated. It can be shown for actual data that you can find spuriously relevant correlation between the two variables and that the size of that correlation depends on the values of the parameters β_1 and β_2.

To illustrate this, let us run some simulation experiments. I set the starting values of the two variables equal to 0 and assume a sample size of 25, 100, or 400. In Table 5A.1, I report on four features of correlations. The first feature is the percentage of cases (out of the 10,000 replications) in which the estimated slope parameter in the regression

$$y_{1,t} = a + b y_{2,t} + e_t$$

Table 5A.1 *A selection of results for three different samples sizes T.*

Feature	T	$\beta_1 = 0.7$ $\beta_2 = 0.7$	$\beta_1 = 0.8$ $\beta_2 = 0.8$	$\beta_1 = 0.9$ $\beta_2 = 0.9$	$\beta_1 = 1.0$ $\beta_2 = 1.0$
		\multicolumn{4}{c}{Parameters in the data-generating processes}			
Significant slope	25	23.0%	30.4%	38.4%	54.0%
	100	23.6%	34.5%	50.5%	75.2%
	400	23.8%	35.0%	51.9%	88.2%
Average correlation	25	−0.001	0.003	−0.002	0.002
	100	0.004	−0.001	0.001	−0.005
	400	0.000	0.001	0.000	−0.001
Average absolute	25	0.248	0.283	0.325	0.422
correlation	100	0.131	0.164	0.225	0.417
	400	0.068	0.084	0.121	0.424
Standard deviation	25	0.302	0.341	0.388	0.491
	100	0.164	0.203	0.275	0.486
	400	0.084	0.105	0.149	0.493

is found as statistically significantly different from 0 (at a 5% level). The second feature is the average correlation coefficient between $y_{1,t}$ and $y_{2,t}$. The third feature is the average of the absolute values of these correlation coefficients. Finally, the fourth feature is the sample standard deviation of all the 10,000 estimated correlation coefficients.

The results in this table give a few insights. The first is that, as expected, the average correlation is 0. And the larger is the sample, the closer it gets to the true value of 0. In contrast, the average absolute correlation (so negative numbers are turned into positive ones) is not equal to 0, although it gets closer to 0 with increasing sample size, except for the case where both parameters are equal to 1.[19] This is also noticeable from the standard deviation of the correlations. If there would be a symmetric distribution around 0 with those standard deviations, then a correlation of more than 0.4 is already likely if T is 25 and the parameters each have value 0.7. Finally, the fraction of cases when one finds a significant slope in a simple regression model where two completely uncorrelated variables are regressed on one another is quite high, and does not decrease when the sample size increases. For the cases where $\beta_1 = 1$, $\beta_2 = 1$, the fraction goes to 100%.[20]

Now, how can you prevent spurious correlations? The answer is simple and can be understood when we become aware of why these spurious correlations occur in the first place. It is now relevant to separate the cases with $\beta_1 = \beta_2 = 1$ from the other cases. Indeed, this $\beta_1 = \beta_2 = 1$ is special as the usual statistical theory does not work in the first place (more on that in Chapter 8). In the other situations, it works as follows. Take for example the case of $\beta_1 = \beta_2 = 0.9$. If observations at time n of both $y_{1,n}$ and $y_{2,n}$ have a positive value, then with these parameters the next observations of $y_{1,n+1}$ and of $y_{2,n+1}$ are likely to be smaller (but still positive) than $y_{1,n}$ and $y_{2,n}$, respectively, because of the multiplication by 0.9 (given symmetrically distributed errors). So, at that moment, the two variables tend to stay above their mean for a longer period. When both $y_{1,n}$ and of $y_{2,n}$ are negative, this happens too. And, due to the value 0.9 of the parameters, there are sequences of positive- and negative-valued observations. So, the two series show common periods when the data are above or below their mean.

To prevent such correlations is very simple, and the method is called pre-whitening. If you want to study the correlation between $y_{1,t}$ and $y_{2,t}$, you first have to get rid of the influence of the own past of each of the variables. So, you run two regressions:

$$y_{1,t} = b_1 y_{1,t-1} + e_{1,t}$$

and

$$y_{2,t} = b_2 y_{2,t-1} + e_{2,t}.$$

In the next step, you compute the correlation between $e_{1,t}$ and $e_{2,t}$. When the two variables have nothing to do with each other, you will find that the correlation between the two estimated residuals is 0. For the regression, you should replace

$$y_{1,t} = a + by_{2,t} + e_t$$

by

$$y_{1,t} = a + by_{2,t} + cy_{1,t-1} + e_t.$$

Then it will quickly become clear that b is not statistically significant anymore.

6   Fashion, Art, and Music

Style is a simple way of saying complicated things.

—Jean Cocteau

Information is not knowledge. Knowledge is not wisdom. Wisdom is not truth. Truth is not beauty. Beauty is not love. Love is not music. Music is THE BEST.

—Frank Zappa

AT A GLANCE

The previous chapters dealt with money, financial values like stamps and coins, and people's understanding of financial products. Now it is time for something completely different. This chapter will show that econometric methods like correlation and regression can also deliver insights into questions about other aspects of life, the aspects that some would say make us humans differ from animals. This chapter will deal with questions concerning fashion (although, admittedly, somewhat in relation to the economy), art, and music. At the same time, I will introduce a novel econometric technique, and again I will relegate a discussion of this method to the appendix.

An important takeaway from this chapter will be that the outcomes of econometric methods and models can be used again in a second round, so to speak. Let me explain what I mean with that. The third and last question of this chapter will ask whether music from the sixties and seventies of the previous century was better than present-day popular music. So, were Led Zeppelin, Pink Floyd, and the Eagles the real giants of popular music, and are Amy Winehouse and Drake perhaps just passengers? Is it like the old quote "In the past, everything was better"? Now, to answer this question, I will analyze

149

various Top2000 rankings of songs over a range of years. The database is very large and contains many dimensions, which by the way could also lead one to ask many other questions. We will see that the data can be described by a certain (new for you – and therefore an explanation is given in the appendix) econometric model and that the estimated parameters in turn are again modeled to answer the question. So, here we have an example of a case where not only the raw data need to be prepared properly prior to analysis but also this preparation itself already involves econometric methodology. That is, the final data to be analyzed are the outcome of the application of econometric methods, and these data are then analyzed again using (other) econometric methods. By the way, the answer to the question will be that "not everything in the past was better," but that will become clear later on.

First, I address two other questions, of which the first one deals with fashion. Back in 2010, I became aware (it was mentioned somewhere in a newspaper by then) that a popular French fashion magazine was digitalizing its entire history. This meant that all the previous issues of that magazine would become publicly available and that one could scroll through the magazines, even those that came out as early as the late 1920s. Now, at the same time, the 2008–2009 economic crisis was still going on, and people wondered whether there would already be any signals of some recovery. And, as is usual in uncertain times, people do not always look at scientifically proven indicators. Sometimes they even resort to urban legends (even in the professional financial press), and one urban legend is called the hemline index. This urban legend says that in economically prosperous times, women's skirts get shorter (where one tends to think of the roaring twenties and hippie sixties of the previous century), and when the economy gets gloomy, women's skirts start to hit the floor. Together with my student Marjolein van Baardwijk, I decided to examine this urban legend using the data from the magazine, and we wrote a report on which the first part of this chapter is based. We also gave some forecasts, and oh wonder, oh luck, these forecasts turned out to be pretty accurate, as was also noted by the popular press in those days.

The middle question in this chapter goes back to data on creativity of artists, where I now also use data on painters, writers, and classic composers. The question here is whether older artists peak later in terms of creativity. This would correlate with the notion that an artist first needs some experience, and perhaps to experience some failures, before creating a masterpiece. We will see.

ARE HEMLINES INFORMATIVE FOR THE BUSINESS CYCLE?

Urban legend has it that the hemline is correlated with the economy. In times of decline, the hemline moves toward the floor (decreases), and when the economy is booming, skirts get shorter and the hemline increases. We collected monthly data on the hemline, for 1921–2009, and evaluated these against the NBER chronology of the economic cycle.[1]

In 1926, an economist named George Taylor introduced a "theory" that is called the hemline index.[2] This theory says that hemlines on women's dresses fluctuate with the economy, measured by stock prices or gross domestic product. When the economy is flourishing, hemlines increase, that is, skirts go up, meaning one would see more miniskirts, and when the economic situation is deteriorating, the hemlines drop. Figure 6.1 displays three distinct hemlines.

A Google search (June 2010) on the hemline index (or its Dutch translation) gives a range of articles in fashion magazines and newspapers. Interestingly, observations made to the contrary of the hemline theory are also reported in magazines and newspapers. Indeed, in June 2010, women's skirts were rather short, while the economy still had not yet recovered from the 2008–2009 recession.

Let us put the hemline index ("theory") to an empirical test to see if there is any validity in this urban legend. We collected monthly data on the hemline, for the sample 1921 to 2009. These data are correlated with an economic cyclical chronology, in this case the NBER dates. Because today's fashion was designed one or more years ago and also as it takes time for new fashion to become "ready to

FIGURE 6.1 Three distinct dress lengths.

wear," we will explicitly incorporate leads and lag effects. So, it may be found that it is not today's economic condition that dictates the hemline but perhaps the condition a few years earlier.

Urban legends are interesting to read and discuss, but it can be challenging to determine whether they can be falsified. The so-called hemline index theory provides a unique opportunity as actual data on the hemline can be collected. We look at the website of the French publications, which appear under the header of "Jalou." This involves a range of publications, and among them is the magazine *L'Officiel*,[3] which still exists. This magazine published its first issue in 1921. The editors have put all past magazines[4] on the Internet, so it is possible to scroll through all past magazines and compile a database.

For many years, the magazine had 12 monthly editions. In some years, there were just 10, and there were years with only five editions.

At first, we decided to collect the monthly data. When data are missing, we entered the value of the most recent issue.[5] So, when there were 10 editions per year, we gave the months 11 and 12 the same value as that of the month 10.

There are five distinct dress lengths. We distinguish mini (1), ballerina length (above-the-knee cocktail) (2), below the knee (3), full-length (ankle) (4), and floor-length (5). The actual data that we compiled are presented in Figure 6.2. We obtained these by scrolling page by page through the historic magazines and based on our own judgment providing a score for each month.

It is clear from Figure 6.2 that over the years the hemlines seem to increase, which means that dresses seem to get shorter over the years. Second, there seems to be quite some variation, certainly in more recent years. Anyway, the overall trend is downward, although of course it cannot go below 1. Oh, right, let us assume that skirt lengths as obtained from the French magazine hold for the (Western) world.

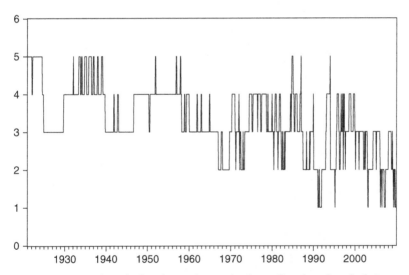

FIGURE 6.2 The hemline index, with 5 being floor-length and 1 being mini. The data run from January 1921 to December 2009.

We now aim to correlate this variable with "the world econ-omy," but this is of course not well defined, and certainly not for such a long period of time. We could look at all kinds of countries and variables, but this could lead to a diversity of outcomes, and hence we decided to just look at the NBER[6] business chronology and take that as a kind of "world business cycle." The monthly data appear, as far as they were known in November 2016, in Table 6.1.

In the analysis, we will code a month with a recession as 1, and we code it with 0 if there is an expansion.

The data in Figure 6.2 are rather noisy, and there are also many, so to begin with, we aggregate the data to annual data. We simply aggregate the monthly hemline data into annual data (by averaging), and these are presented in Figure 6.3.

Now the data are less noisy, and at the same time, they can also take any value between 1 and 5. We also aggregate the monthly

Table 6.1 *NBER chronology with recession periods.*

1920M01–1921M07
1923M05–1924M07
1926M10–1927M11
1929M08–1933M03
1937M05–1938M06
1945M02–1945M10
1948M11–1949M10
1953M07–1954M05
1957M08–1958M04
1960M04–1961M02
1969M12–1970M11
1973M11–1975M03
1980M01–1980M07
1981M07–1982M11
1990M07–1991M03
2001M03–2001M11
2007M12–2009M06

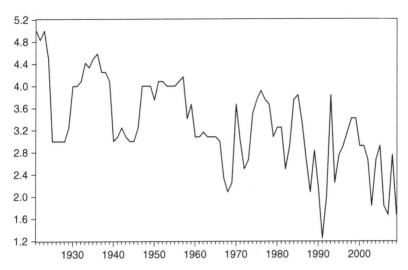

FIGURE 6.3 The hemline index, when the data in Figure 6.2 are aggregated to annual data for 1921–2009.

chronology in Table 6.1 into annual data. This is done by assigning a value of 0 to a year with zero or one month with a recession; a value of 0.25 when a year has two, three, or four months with a recession; a value of 0.5 when there are five, six, or seven months with a recession; a value of 0.75 when there are eight, nine, or ten months with a recession; and a value of 1 when there are eleven or twelve months with a recession. The resultant annual data appear in Figure 6.4. In the Appendix to this chapter, I give the two annual time series.

Let us analyze the annual data. The variable to be explained is the length, as it is given in Figure 6.3. It is not unexpected that there is some time dependence in the data on skirt lengths, so the model will contain the length in the previous year. Given the slow pattern downwards, it also seem reasonable to include a trend term, but this trend term should not be a straight trend line. Rather, it should be something that levels off. In sum, a reasonable model seems to be

$$\text{Length}_t = \alpha + \beta_1 \, \text{Length}_{t-1} + \beta_2 \log \left(\text{trend}_t \right) + \beta_3 \, \text{NBER}_{t-k} + \varepsilon_t.$$

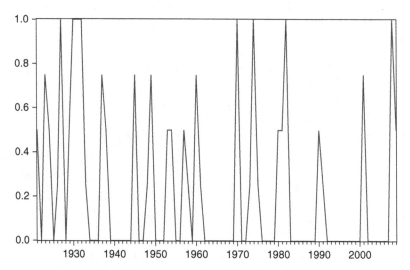

FIGURE 6.4 NBER recession chronology when the data are compressed to annual data.

The variable trend$_t$ is simply 1, 2, 3, and so on. Table 6.2 reports on some estimation results for various values of k, with a focus on the parameter β_3.

We experiment with values 0, 1, 2, 3, and 4 for k and also with values –1, –2, –3, and –4 to see if there are any lead effects. The only model where the NBER dates *do* result in a significant parameter estimate is when $k = 3$. The R^2 of this model is 0.555. So, we would conclude here that the economic cycle precedes the hemline by three years, and this effect is positive, which means that an economic recession correlates with the three-year ahead hemline (meaning that women's dresses get longer). Future recessions do not associate at all with the hemlines. By the way, one could now try to model the NBER dates where the skirt lengths would be the explanatory variable, but this model would raise quite some eyebrows. Women's fashion is of course important, but it can hardly be believed to be the cause of recessions, right?

Table 6.2 *Highlights of estimation results.*

k	b_3	(Standard error of b_3)	R^2 of model	Sample size
4	0.236	(0.185)	0.517	85
3	**0.421**	**(0.174)**	0.555	86
2	0.162	(0.177)	0.555	87
1	–0.117	(0.169)	0.574	88
0	0.211	(0.167)	0.580	88
–1	0062	(0.171)	0.575	87
–2	–0.268	(0.165)	0.593	86
–3	–0.161	(0.165)	0.567	85
–4	0.145	(0.166)	0.570	84

The effective sample size to estimate the parameters using least squares varies with k. A positive value of k associates with the past of NBER, while a negative value associates with the future.

I take the result for the annual data back to the monthly data, where now the model could read as

$$\text{Length}_t = \sum_{s=1}^{12} a_s D_{s,t} + \beta_{1,1}\text{Length}_{t-1}$$

$$+ \beta_{1,2}\text{Length}_{t-2} + \beta_2 \log(\text{trend}_t)$$

$$+ \beta_3 \text{NBER}_{t-36} + \varepsilon_t$$

where $t - 36$ for the NBER variable means that I take the three-year lag seriously. The 12 $D_{s,t}$ variables are called seasonal dummy variables. They take a value 1 in a particular season s (month here) and then 0 in other seasons; see the appendix to the present chapter on econometric methods. The model with two lags and 12 seasonal dummies and a log trend provides an adequate fit. The seasonal dummies indicate that the hemline dips in wintertime, which is of course not unexpected.

Again the log trend variable is relevant, and so is the NBER 1/0 dummy variable. The parameter estimate b_3 is equal to 0.073 with an estimated standard error of 0.031. So, also at the monthly level we see a three-year lag in the effect of the economy on the hemline.

In sum, based on the analysis of actual data on hemlines that go back to January 1921, I find that the economy precedes the hemline by about three years. Somewhat supporting the urban legend, we find that poor economic times are associated with a decrease in hemlines, which means that women's skirts get closer to the floor, and that prosperity is correlated with an increased hemline (more miniskirts). At the same time, and this is not exactly what the urban legend in its original format entails, we find that there is a time lag of about three years. This explains why in 2009–2010, in an economic downturn, the skirts were short – the economy was in a boom about three years before (2007–2008).

In our report in the spring of 2010, we concluded with the observation that the current (read: June 2010) short skirts would be due to the booming economy in 2007. We also predicted that due to the recession in 2008, we would see ankle-length skirts in the winter of 2011–2012.

Our study was later on covered on CNBC, and the author of the relevant article (www.cnbc.com/id/46414411), John Carney, stated, "Hence, the current economic crisis predicts ankle length shirts around 2011 and 2012, they [that is, Marjolein and I] wrote in 2010. And, sure enough, hemlines are falling right on schedule, if not yet all the way to the ankle." So, this time economists (that is: us) apparently made the right prediction!

DO OLDER ARTISTS PEAK LATER?

In Chapter 2, I presented a histogram that could be understood and analyzed in its own right. It gave data on the relative age at which 34 best-selling authors composed their best work, given the knowledge that they had already died. Indeed, it is unknown for an artist who still lives whether he or she could still create a masterpiece in the years to come. It might be conceivable that older people have more experience and thus are perhaps more likely to create a masterpiece toward the end of their lives. If I plot the ratio of the fraction of a lifetime in which the top work was created versus the age at which the author died, again for these 34 authors, I get the scatter diagram in Figure 6.5.

Clearly, Figure 6.5 suggests a link between the two, where the slope of a potentially useful regression model would be negative. This by the way suggests that authors who became old peaked earlier! This is in contrast with what one could have conjectured in advance. The outcome of applying least squares to a simple regression model gives

$$\text{Fraction}_i = 1.097 - 0.007 \text{ Age at death}_i$$

with an R^2 equal to 0.467.

As mentioned in the endnotes of Chapter 2, I have looked at various categories of creative individuals, like painters, Nobel

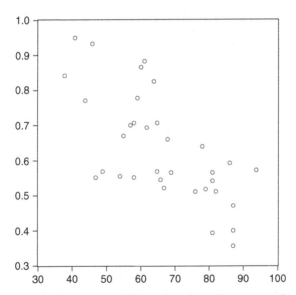

FIGURE 6.5 Fraction of life with peak work versus number of years eventually lived, 34 best-selling authors.

Prize–winning authors, and classic composers. Figure 6.6 gives a similar scatterplot as Figure 6.5, but now for those 189 painters who are known to have died. For these 189 data points,[7] the outcome of applying least squares to a simple regression model gives

$$\text{Fraction}_i = 1.173 - 0.008 \text{ Age at death}_i$$

with an R^2 equal to 0.297. These estimation results are remarkably close to those obtained for the 34 best-selling authors. The second column of Table 6.3 reinforces this impression, where I should note that the –0.008 is short for –0.007721, the number that is used for the computations in the table. Table 6.3 computes fractions given six selected ages at death.

Figure 6.7 gives the same type of scatterplot for 89 Nobel Prize laureates in literature.

The regression line for the Nobel laureates is

$$\text{Fraction}_i = 0.711 - 0.002 \text{ Age at death}_i$$

where –0.002 is short for –0.001792. The R^2 is equal to 0.014, and the standard error of the slope parameter is 0.001614, making it only significant at the 27% level. This irrelevance of the explanatory variable is also visible from the third column of Table 6.3, as the percentages are roughly the same. So, here we have a case where there is apparently no link between fraction and age at death.

Finally, I have the data on 100 classic composers visualized in Figure 6.8.

For this group of creative individuals the estimated regression line is

$$\text{Fraction}_i = 1.019 - 0.006 \text{ Age at death}_i$$

where –0.006 is short for –0.006214 and the R^2 is 0.227. The penultimate column of Table 6.3 shows that the predicted fractions are somewhere in between the numbers in the other columns. When you look back again at Figures 6.5–6.8, you see that

Table 6.3 *Age at peak creativity given age at death.*

Age at death	Fraction of life with peak creativity				
	Best-selling authors	Painters	Nobel laureates	Composers	All
80	53.7%	55.5%	56.8%	52.2%	55.4%
70	60.7%	63.3%	58.6%	58.4%	61.6%
60	67.7%	71.0%	60.4%	64.7%	67.9%
50	74.7%	78.7%	62.1%	70.9%	74.1%
40	81.7%	86.4%	63.9%	77.1%	80.4%
30	88.7%	94.1%	65.7%	83.3%	86.7%

Predicted fractions based on the regression models in the text.

you could have had a first hint how successful a regression model would be.

There are two more issues that might be mentioned. The first is that even though the estimation results seem very similar, the predicted percentages in Table 6.3 vary a lot. So, for interpretation of regression results, tables like Table 6.3 come in quite handy. The second, perhaps more interesting issue is what we would learn if we would pool all data together in one big sample of 34 + 189 + 89 + 100 = 412 observations. What would you think in advance?

Remember again that we have four regression models, and these are

$$\text{Fraction}_{c,i} = \alpha_c + \beta_c \text{ Age at death}_{c,i} + \varepsilon_{c,i},$$
$$\text{var}(\varepsilon_{c,i}) = \sigma_c^2,$$

where the subscript c refers to one of the four creative categories. Now, there are various ways to pool the data or, better, to make assumptions about the parameters α_c, β_c, and σ_c^2. Suppose I impose that the parameters across the categories are all the same, that is, $\alpha_c = \alpha, \beta_c = \beta, \sigma_c^2 = \sigma^2$; then the final regression model for all data inclusive is

$$\text{Fraction}_i = 1.054 - 0.006 \text{ Age at death}_i$$

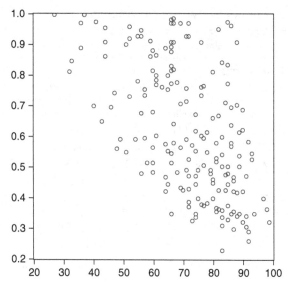

FIGURE 6.6 Fraction of life with peak work versus number of years eventually lived, 189 painters.

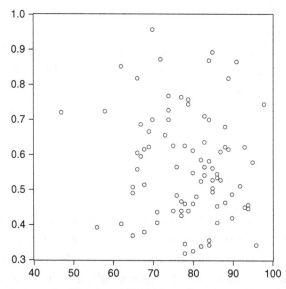

FIGURE 6.7 Fraction of life with peak work versus number of years eventually lived, 89 Nobel Prize laureates in literature.

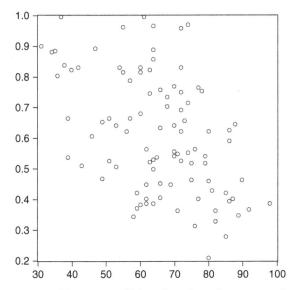

FIGURE 6.8 Fraction of life with peak work versus number of years eventually lived, 100 classic composers.

with an R^2 equal to 0.232. The predicted fractions for all data are presented in the last column of Table 6.3, and you can see that these numbers are somewhere in between the numbers in the other columns but not necessarily some kind of average. With pooling you can include information from the other samples to learn more about your own individual sample. Note, however, that the R^2 of the models for subsamples can be higher than for the model for the total sample. Here we have an illustration of the notion that "bigger is not more beautiful." The reason is that adding the samples also implies adding variation.

The overall conclusion is that, across a large sample of creative individuals, it holds that artists who die young peak relatively late in their active life whereas those artists who die at an old age live a long time after their peak success. So, for peak creativity and young artists, could it be as Neil Young once said, that it is "better to burn out than to fade away"?

WAS THE MUSIC IN THE SIXTIES AND SEVENTIES BETTER?

When you get older, you may come to believe that past times were better than current times. Technology has changed much in the past few decades, and our cognitive skills also decline with our age.[8] Our first encounters with popular music are usually in our adolescent years, and you grew up with the Beatles or the Rolling Stones if you are around 65 now, with Led Zeppelin and Pink Floyd if you are around 55 now, with Madonna and Prince if you are 45 now, and so on. Having grown up with such music might make one feel and believe that older music is better than today's music.

This is the kind of argument one can hear when radio stations play the songs from lists like the Netherlands-based station Radio 2's Top2000 best songs ever. These lists typically contain the same set of songs that have always been on those lists. Look at Table 6.4, and you can see that for 16 years, "Hotel California" by the Eagles topped the charts.

A usual complaint filed against this Top2000 list is that the charts are based on votes and that perhaps many middle-aged people vote repeatedly, which can also perhaps explain why all-male, all-white rock bands are at the top.[9] Now, to see if it is indeed true that newer music has less chance to make it to the top, we should have a closer look at the data. The data on the charts from 1999 to and including 2014 are publicly available. Each year the list has 2,000 entries, but over the years, songs can enter or leave the charts. In total, there are 3,906 different songs that at least once made it onto one of these 16 Top2000 charts.

There are various ways to visualize the data, but as I am interested in the trends over time, we look at time-series data. Figure 6.11 presents the time-series observations on the number of songs per year since 1924 in the charts of 1999 to 2014. Although the exact numbers are not very visible, an eyeball impression is that songs from around 1960 appear 10 to 20 times in the charts. Further, around the late 1960s, there is a peak, with around 80 to 100 songs in the charts, and

Table 6.4 *Ranks of various songs in the years 1999, 2004, and 2009, given that they were in the top 10 of 2014, in Netherlands-based Radio 2's Top2000 charts.*

			Rank in year			
Artist	Song title	Year	1999	2004	2009	2014
Eagles	Hotel California	1977	2	2	2	1
Queen	Bohemian Rhapsody	1975	1	1	1	2
Led Zeppelin	Stairway to Heaven	1971	4	4	4	3
Deep Purple	Child in Time	1972	3	3	5	4
Boudewijn de Groot[10]	Avond	1997	428	5	3	5
Pink Floyd	Wish You Were Here	1975	–	21	9	6
Billy Joel	Piano Man	1974	121	66	45	7
Pink Floyd	Comfortably Numb	1979	–	53	15	8
Pink Floyd	Shine On You Crazy Diamond	1975	–	25	13	9
Guns N' Roses	November Rain	1992	–	7	16	10

then there seems to be a period with a bit of a downward trend until the late 1980s. A dip seems to occur around the 1990s with around 20 songs in the charts, with a slight increase toward the end of the sample.

At the same time, there seems to be a strong variation over time. The range or spread of the frequencies can be as large as 50, meaning that from one year to another you can find 50 more or less songs of the same year in the charts. This implies that it does not seem wise to look at averages over time but that we had better analyze all rankings across the years 1999 to 2014 individually.

FIGURE 6.9 The Californian rock band the Eagles.

FIGURE 6.10 The British rock band Pink Floyd.

Table 6.5 presents some features of the rankings. The second column presents the years that have the most songs in the charts. Clearly, the years 1969 and 1979 dominate. You might now conclude that as later charts have more songs from 1979 than from 1969 that more recent music did become more popular, but this is not a very sophisticated analysis of the potential wealth of information. The third column of Table 6.5 reports the median of the data – that is, if you arrange all 2,000 songs per chart according to the year of the song, and you take the average of the observations 1,000 and 1,001, then you have the median. Again, there is tendency upward that the median increases with the years, even stronger than the peak years. So, a first impression is that the Top2000 charts are not very constant over time, and even though perhaps a few songs are always at the top, there is much movement in and across the lists.

Table 6.5 *Various features of the rankings.*

Year	Year with most songs	Median year	Inflection years
1999	1969	1975	1968
2000	1967	1975	1967
2001	1979	1976	1968
2002	1969	1976	1967
2003	1969	1976	1968
2004	1969	1976	1968
2005	1967	1976	1968
2006	1969	1977	1968
2007	1969	1977	1970
2008	1969	1977	1969
2009	1979	1979	1971
2010	1969	1979	1971
2011	1979	1980	1973
2012	1979	1982	1974
2013	1977, 1979	1982	1974
2014	1979	1984	1975

To add to the numbers in Table 6.5, I estimate the parameters of an econometric model that allows for the description of data patterns like those in Figure 6.11. More details on this model appear in the appendix, but a key expression of this model is

$$X_t = pm + (q - p)N_{t-1} - \frac{q}{m}N_{t-1}^2 + \varepsilon_t.$$

The variable X_t is, say, the frequency in a year, while N_{t-1} is the cumulative range of frequencies until and including year $t - 1$. This expression contains three key parameters – m, p, and q – and two variables. An example of a cumulative frequency is displayed in Figure 6.12 for the year 2010. Of course, the last observation of N_{t-1} is 2000, as there are 2,000 songs in the charts. The pattern in this graph reflects an S-shaped curve, which is frequently observed for the cumulative number of sales of, for example, durable products.

This curve has another feature: there is a point of inflection. That is the moment when the speed at which growth occurs reaches its top, and after that growth levels off to some final, the so-called maturity

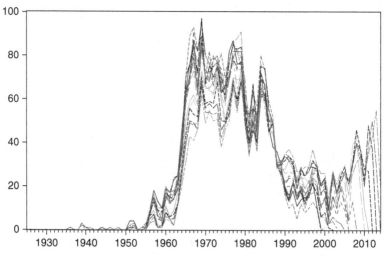

FIGURE 6.11 Number of songs per year since 1924 in the charts of 1999 to 2014.

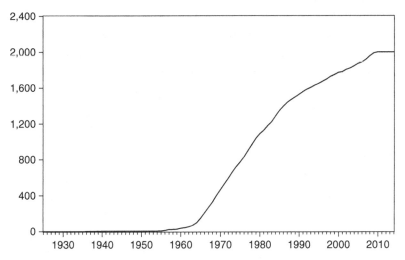

FIGURE 6.12 Cumulates of the frequency of songs per year in the Top2000 chart of 2010.

level (hence the letter m in the equation for one of the parameters). This inflection point should be associated with the peak level of the frequency of songs or of the average ranking. That is, with this model, one can estimate that peak level instead of just taking the maximum value or median, as I did in Table 6.5. The parameters p and q and m in the econometric model can be retrieved using least squares, where I let the samples start in 1945, and what is more, it is also possible to have an explicit expression of the estimated peak moment, which is

$$\text{Peak} = \frac{1}{p+q}\log\left(\frac{q}{p}\right).$$

The last column of Table 6.5 provides the thus obtained estimates of the peak years for the 16 different charts. We see some subtle variation in the estimates, and again, we can also see an upward tendency in the years, thereby supporting the earlier impressions that songs in later years become more prominent in the Top2000 charts.

Can we do more? Yes, of course, but now we should read the table with the raw data in a different format. That is, let us now arrange the time series observations such that we have a 16-observation sample ranging from 1999 to and including 2014 that contains the number of songs from each of the years. Figures 6.13 and 6.14 give examples of such alternative time series variables for the songs from the years 1970 and 1985, respectively.

Figure 6.13 shows that there were around 75 songs from 1970 in the first set of charts, but in the later charts only around 50 are still there. Hence, and also visually, there is a downward trend for the 1970 songs. We can analyze such trends using a simple regression model, which reads as

$$\text{Frequency}_t = \alpha + \beta \text{Trend}_t + \varepsilon_t,$$

where $\text{Trend}_t = 1,2,3, \ldots, 16$. To ensure that there are enough nonzero observations, I only consider this regression model for the songs from 1960 to 2014. The estimates b are presented in Figure 6.15. Now, here we see something interesting. Until around 1987, the estimated slope is negative, while after those years the slope becomes positive. Hence songs from more recent years appear more and more in the Top2000 charts.

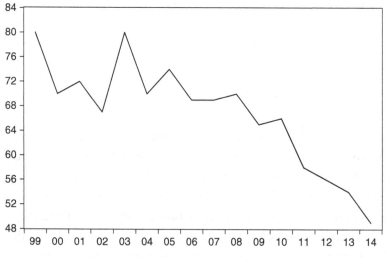

FIGURE 6.13 Number of songs from 1970 in the charts from 1999 to 2014.

WAS THE MUSIC IN THE SIXTIES AND SEVENTIES BETTER? 171

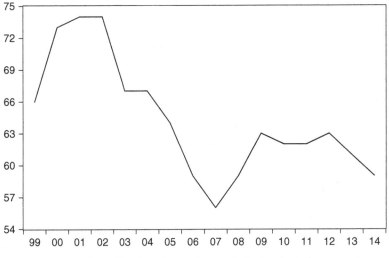

FIGURE 6.14 Number of songs from 1985 in the charts from 1999 to 2014.

This eyeball impression can be further substantiated using the regression result

$$b_t = -1.821 + 0.029 \text{ Trend}_t + 0.697 \ b_{t-1},$$

where b_t are the numbers in Figure 6.15 for each of the years. The standard error[11] for the trend parameter is 0.012, which makes it significantly different from 0, and the R^2 = 0.897, which is very high. The conclusion from this regression is that older songs appear less and less frequently while newer songs appear more and more in the charts.

In sum, my analysis suggests that there is no evidence that songs of the 1960s and 1970s are perceived as better and therefore appear more often in the charts. Over time, we see that there is a tendency for more recent music to get higher rankings and more often appear in the Top2000. So, in the longer run, it might well be that we will not find Pink Floyd and the Eagles in the charts anymore.

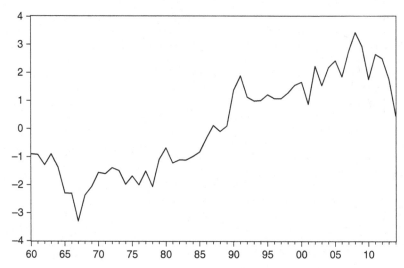

FIGURE 6.15 The estimated slope of the regression of the number of songs in a year on an intercept and a trend.

TO CONCLUDE

What are the main takeaways from this chapter? Well, first and most obvious is that econometric techniques and methods like means, median, correlations, and regression can be usefully considered for questions that have nothing to do with economics at all! Questions concerning fashion, art, and music can be addressed by those methods, and there may not be a need to make things overly complicated. Second, we could learn that some thinking about what exactly the data are that are relevant matters. Rearranging the Top2000 charts in a different way quickly provided the relevant insights and a simple answer to the research question. This last aspect is a common phenomenon in the practice of companies who collect and store many data on their customers and their behavior. This so-called Big Data provides us with a potential wealth of information, but I should stress that those data rarely appear in a format that is ready to use or even in a format that comes close to the format you want to have to answer the research question. So, some thinking about how the data can best be arranged prior to analysis is very relevant.

APPENDIX: ECONOMETRIC METHODS AND DATA

SEASONAL DUMMY VARIABLES

Seasonal dummy variables take care of qualitative features that could be associated with the seasons without having to specify explicitly what these qualitative features are. For women's skirts, one may expect that the temperature would relate to skirt length, as in the winter one would perhaps prefer longer length against the cold. In other situations, the seasonal dummy variables may be associated with sunlight, habits (like going on holidays in certain seasons more than in other seasons), or economic activity. The 1/0 values are thus just a numeric proxy for what actually happens, and that is why they are called "dummies." Suppose there is a variable that is observed quarterly; one can estimate the average values of each of the quarters by running a regression

$$y_t = \alpha_1 D_{1,t} + \alpha_2 D_{2,t} + \alpha_3 D_{3,t} + \alpha_4 D_{4,t} + \varepsilon_t,$$

where the four columns with the dummy variables have the repetitive data format

$$
\begin{array}{cccc}
1 & 0 & 0 & 0 \\
0 & 1 & 0 & 0 \\
0 & 0 & 1 & 0 \\
0 & 0 & 0 & 1 \\
1 & 0 & 0 & 0. \\
0 & 1 & 0 & 0 \\
0 & 0 & 1 & 0 \\
0 & 0 & 0 & 1 \\
1 & 0 & 0 & 0
\end{array}
$$

These four columns immediately show that

$$D_{1,t} + D_{2,t} + D_{3,t} + D_{4,t} = \begin{array}{c} 1 \\ 1 \\ 1 \\ 1 \\ 1 \\ 1 \end{array}$$

and so on. When it is of interest to see if the seasonal parameters matter, relative to a constant pattern, then one can test whether

$$\alpha_1 = \alpha_2 = \alpha_3 = \alpha_4.$$

Alternatively, one can consider the regression model

$$y_t = \alpha + \alpha_2 D_{2,t} + \alpha_3 D_{3,t} + \alpha_4 D_{4,t} + \varepsilon_t$$

and test whether

$$\alpha_2 = \alpha_3 = \alpha_4 = 0.$$

The two routes lead to the same test result and conclusion.

A MODEL FOR S-SHAPED DATA (THE BASS MODEL)

Suppose that, for a new product, there is a population of m potential adopters. For each of these adopters, there is a random time to adoption with distribution function $F(t)$ and density function $f(t)$ and a hazard rate satisfying

$$\frac{f(t)}{1 - F(t)} = p + qF(t),$$

where p is called the innovation parameter and q is the imitation parameter. The hazard rate can be interpreted as the probability to adopt given that you did not adopt as of yet. The cumulative number of adopters at time t is a random variable $N(t)$ with $\overline{N}(t)$ satisfying

$$\overline{n}(t) = \frac{d\overline{N}(t)}{dt} = p\left(m - \overline{N}(t)\right) + \frac{q}{m}\overline{N}(t)\left(m - \overline{N}(t)\right).$$

The solution[12] is

$$\overline{N}(t) = mF(t) = m\left[\frac{1 - e^{-(p+q)t}}{1 + \frac{q}{p}e^{-(p+q)t}}\right]$$

for the cumulative adopters and

$$\overline{n}(t) = mf(t) = m\left[\frac{p(p + q)^2 e^{-(p+q)t}}{(p + qe^{-(p+q)t})^2}\right]$$

for the adopters. Graphs of $F(t)$ and $f(t)$ are presented in Figures 6A.1 and 6A.2.

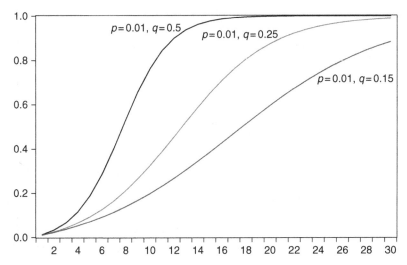

FIGURE 6A.1 Various shapes of the pattern of cumulative adopters, given different values of p and q, while $m = 1$.

The inflection point is the moment when the number of new adopters starts to decrease and is located at

$$T_{\text{inflection}} = \frac{1}{p+q}\log\left(\frac{q}{p}\right).$$

In practice, there are no observations in continuous time, and then one has to estimate the parameters for this Bass model for discretely observed data. Write X_t for the adopters in period t and the cumulative number of adopters at the end of time t as N_t, and then a regression model to estimate the parameters is

$$
\begin{aligned}
X_t &= p(m - N_{t-1}) + \frac{q}{m}N_{t-1}(m - N_{t-1}) + \varepsilon_t \\
&= pm + (q - p)N_{t-1} - \frac{q}{m}N_{t-1}^2 + \varepsilon_t \\
&= \alpha + \beta_1 N_{t-1} + \beta_2 N_{t-1}^2 + \varepsilon_t.
\end{aligned}
$$

Applying least squares to the bottom equation gives the estimates a, b_1, and b_2, and with these one can retrieve estimates for m, p, and q. If one also wants to have standard errors for m, p, and q, then one can apply the technique called nonlinear least squares.[13–15]

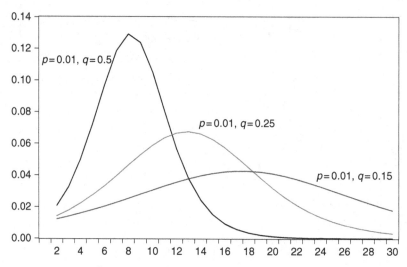

FIGURE 6A.2 Various shapes of the pattern of adopters, given different values of p and q, while $m = 1$.

The Annual Data on the Hemlines and Recessions

Year	Hemline	Recession
1921	5	0.5
1922	4.833333	0
1923	5	0.75
1924	4.5	0.5
1925	3	0
1926	3	0.25
1927	3	1
1928	3	0
1929	3.25	0.5
1930	4	1
1931	4	1
1932	4.083333	1
1933	4.416667	0.25
1934	4.333333	0

(*cont.*)

Year	Hemline	Recession
1935	4.5	0
1936	4.583333	0
1937	4.25	0.75
1938	4.25	0.5
1939	4.083333	0
1940	3	0
1941	3.083333	0
1942	3.25	0
1943	3.083333	0
1944	3	0
1945	3	0.75
1946	3.25	0
1947	4	0
1948	4	0.25
1949	4	0.75
1950	3.75	0
1951	4.083333	0
1952	4.083333	0
1953	4	0.5
1954	4	0.5
1955	4	0
1956	4.083333	0
1957	4.166667	0.5
1958	3.416667	0.25
1959	3.666667	0
1960	3.083333	0.75
1961	3.083333	0.25
1962	3.166667	0
1963	3.083333	0
1964	3.083333	0
1965	3.083333	0
1966	3	0
1967	2.333333	0
1968	2.083333	0

(cont.)

Year	Hemline	Recession
1969	2.25	0
1970	3.666667	1
1971	3	0
1972	2.5	0
1973	2.666667	0.25
1974	3.5	1
1975	3.75	0.25
1976	3.916667	0
1977	3.75	0
1978	3.666667	0
1979	3.083333	0
1980	3.25	0.5
1981	3.25	0.5
1982	2.5	1
1983	2.916667	0
1984	3.75	0
1985	3.833333	0
1986	3.333333	0
1987	2.666667	0
1988	2.083333	0
1989	2.833333	0
1990	2.166667	0.5
1991	1.25	0.25
1992	2	0
1993	3.833333	0
1994	2.25	0
1995	2.75	0
1996	2.916667	0
1997	3.166667	0
1998	3.416667	0
1999	3.416667	0
2000	2.916667	0
2001	2.916667	0.75
2002	2.666667	0

(cont.)

Year	Hemline	Recession
2003	1.833333	0
2004	2.666667	0
2005	2.916667	0
2006	1.833333	0
2007	1.666667	0
2008	2.75	1
2009	1.666667	0.5

7   Academic Publications

> A person who publishes a book willfully appears before the populace with his pants down. If it is a good book, nothing can hurt him. If it is a bad book nothing can help him.

—Edna St. Vincent Millay

> One can measure the importance of a scientific work by the number of earlier publications rendered superfluous by it.

—David Hilbert

AT A GLANCE

Whenever measurement is relevant, econometric methods and techniques can be helpful to summarize the data and to make statements about the data. An area where measurement is key is the scientific publication process. Academics like me are supposed to not only do research but also publish about it in international journals. The research should preferably be groundbreaking (as, for example, the European Research Council wants all grant proposals to be), and the journals should be top level.

The number of real top journals in economics and econometrics is small, whereas the number of academics who want to publish in those top journals is large. This means that there is ample room for a range of lesser-quality journals and, needless to say, also a range of lesser-quality articles. The scarcity implies that one sometimes may feel that academic work is some kind of a rat race, which is usually described as "publish or perish."

Having a paper published in a good journal is one thing; to have a paper being read and cited is another one. If no one has ever cited your piece, then the only one who enjoyed reading it was you yourself.

Later on in this chapter, you will come to know that about one-fourth of my own published papers have never been cited even once. With something like 300 journal publications on my track record and with each paper average 20 pages in Word, this means that I wrote something like $\frac{1}{4}$ times 300 times 20, or 1,500 pages, for no good reason, other than perhaps I got more experience with writing papers and my typing skills improved.

Anyway, this chapter deals with scientific publications. First, I will briefly outline how the publication and citation process works. I only have experience with economics, econometrics, marketing, and finance journals, so my overview will not cover all disciplines, but broadly speaking, I believe there are many similarities across disciplines. Then I will provide some statistics on the publication process. How long do parts of the process last? How many reviewers do you typically encounter? Then I move on to the first question, which is whether more productivity also leads to more citations. That is, suppose the goal is to obtain a better reputation through citations; does it then help to be prolific? In contrast, you may also believe that one killer piece with tons of citations would also lead to success, but then you have to bear in mind that very few of us ever write such a killer piece.

If it is not perhaps productivity, are there any typical ingredients of a very successful paper? Here again I dig into my own archive, quantify the ingredients, and see if some ingredients matter more than others do. Interestingly, I will find that papers that test an economic theory are most successful in acquiring attention.

Another question that might be relevant is whether the reviewing and subsequent revisions process makes the product better. That is, does the incorporation of all kinds of (mandatory) "suggestions" of the reviewers cause the paper to be cited more often?

Then, as an intermezzo, I will address a few famous articles in econometrics. There is no econometric analysis here, but this serves as a tribute to various leading econometricians. At the same time, it also shows with what size of modesty I have to live. I will also show that some papers can have a second life, that is, first citations go up, then they go down, but after a while, they go up again.

As usual, there will be new techniques introduced in this chapter, and a discussion of these is relegated to the technical appendix to this chapter.

HOW DOES THE PUBLICATION PROCESS WORK?

At the start of this chapter, I will first briefly outline how it works in the academic world, at least in the one where econometricians work.[1]

An important activity of academic researchers concerns the publication of their research findings in scientific journals. There are many researchers who work at universities and research institutes (think of central banks and statistical agencies), and their research interests are reflected by the existence of a large number of scientific journals. By now, each scientific discipline seems to have established a set of journals that are considered its highest-quality journals but a larger set of journals that are second best or of lesser quality. The top journal in econometrics is called *Econometrica*; see Figure 7.1 for a sample cover. Figure 7.2 shows the cover of a good (but not top) journal. It is widely accepted that academic researchers should regularly publish their findings in these journals. This is viewed as a measure of scientific achievement, and it is usually met with respect. This holds in particular for young academics, like graduate students, postdoctoral researchers, and assistant professors on a tenure track, whose subsequent academic careers often depend on their publications in good or high-quality journals. Whether this is good or bad is beyond my realm of influence, although some of the descriptive statistics that follow may shed some light on the period within which one can evaluate junior faculty. For example, the period between first submission and eventual publication (at least for the cases at hand) appears to cover two years on average.[2]

As the publication process is key to the careers of academic researchers, it is no surprise that there are many theoretical and empirical studies on this matter and that there are also topical

ECONOMETRICA

JOURNAL OF THE ECONOMETRIC SOCIETY

*An International Society for the Advancement of Economic
Theory in its Relation to Statistics and Mathematics*

CONTENTS

VOL. 79, NO. 3 — May, 2011

FIGURE 7.1 Cover of the top journal *Econometrica*.

journals, like the journal called *Scientometrics*. A quick scan of the relevant literature shows that there are mainly two types of studies here. Those of the first type consider the process starting with the conception of the paper until final acceptance. For example, it might be interesting to see how classic papers (when these turn out to be so, after many years or even decades) proceeded through the editorial process.[3] Another frequently encountered research issue concerns the editorial process and the decisions involved.[4] Many journals publish editorial statements, and some journals also evaluate their editorial behavior, often to see if there has been some bias.[5]

The second type of studies is concerned with what happens with the academic results after publication. One way to measure the quality of scientific output amounts to measuring the number of times other academics cite a paper and perhaps build their research activity

statistica neerlandica

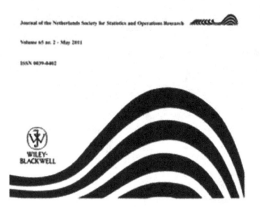

Journal of the Netherlands Society for Statistics and Operations Research

Volume 65 no. 2 - May 2011

ISSN 0039-0402

WILEY-BLACKWELL

FIGURE 7.2 Cover of the good journal *Statistica Neerlandica*.

on its content.[6] Very successful papers in economics and econometrics can get something like 150 citations per year for a period or a decade, as we will see later. However, for nonexceptional research, an average of five citations per author per year is a more common number. These citations are of importance not only for authors but also for the journals. Indeed, when a journal publishes papers that are cited more often, the journal gets a higher rating and in turn may attract better manuscripts in the future. There are by now various rankings of journals, and in several countries, there are lists that rate (economic) departments and researchers on their scientific output based on these rankings.

Studies that follow the full life cycle of individual papers over time are scarce. If journals report on their editorial policy and investigate the trajectories of papers in their journals, they of course do not analyze the trajectories of the papers they effectively rejected. This is indeed rather difficult, also as papers might get different names, other (co)authors or even other topics. Additionally, if one studies citations, then usually there is no information available on how the paper eventually was published. Hence, it may be that it was rejected first by many other journals.

Before I had to throw away much of my archives in 2001 when I moved to another office, I could analyze my own files, which contained information on various relevant variables, like dates of submission, revision and acceptance (or previous rejection), and, later on as well, annual citations. It concerns 66 (of my own) published papers for the period of 1990–1999. Of course, this database concerns just me, and it is not at all representative. In some dimensions, there is some representativeness, as the files concern different journals, topics, and journal ratings, and they cover 10 years. The papers were published in a wide range of journals, although these all related to economics, statistics, and econometrics. I will give them in a minute.

From First Submission to Acceptance

The first stage concerns the submission of a manuscript to a journal, the receipt of a letter (email) from the editor with attached referee reports, and an associated decision to reject or an allowance to revise and resubmit. Naturally, before one can submit a paper for possible publication, there should be a paper in the first place. In some areas, one can shape the paper beforehand toward the guidelines of the target journal. This means that one follows the style files, but it can also mean that one explicitly aims to contribute to a range of papers that have already appeared in the same journal on the very same topic. This strategy implies that the author is up-to-date with the published literature and with the unpublished working papers from other academics who happen to have the same strategy. This strategy seems to occur in disciplines such as marketing and finance, where the number of top-quality journals is very limited.

In other scientific disciplines, one first thinks about an issue or a problem, collects data, designs a new theory, evaluates related theories, or perhaps derives a new methodological tool, and after that, one considers which journal could perhaps be the best outlet. This strategy is more often followed in econometrics and statistics, where there are quite a number of good-quality journals. Indeed, if a manuscript is rejected by one journal, one can always send it to another journal.

Before an author (team) sends a manuscript to a journal, the author usually gives a presentation of his or her work at departmental seminars or international conferences. In most disciplines, there are many of these conferences. Smaller-scale seminars can be more fruitful in terms of feedback, as there is an opportunity to have closer contact with colleagues, and hence there is perhaps more room for discussion. By presenting, the author also gets to know his or her own work better, and this can be fruitful in the process of writing the final draft of the paper. First rough drafts usually appear in working paper series. Usually, these working papers serve as a kind of patent, implying that the author's rights are claimed.[7]

Key features of a manuscript that can be measured are its length (in number of pages), the number of references, and the number of coauthors. The quality and the topic are difficult to measure. It can happen that a manuscript is submitted to a special issue of a journal, and hence this usually implies that the topic of the paper matches with the interest of the (special issue) editors. At one moment the author is confident enough to submit the manuscript and to undergo the scrutiny of fellow researchers in the area. After submission, the most uncertain period commences, that is, the author has to await the response from the editorial team, whose judgment is usually based on what the referees have to say. At present, many editors work with desk reject, which means that they immediately make a decision in case they believe that the manuscript does match with the journal's aims and scope. The first row of Table 7.1 shows that, for my 66 papers under scrutiny, the period between submission and the receipt of reviewers' reports is on

Table 7.1 *Descriptive statistics concerning the editorial process: Time in months.*

Variable	Mean	Median	Maximum	Minimum
Submission-first response	5.545	5	15	1
Revision-decision	5.182	4	21	0
With journal	10.727	10	27	1
Decision-publication	8.606	9	24	0

average 5.545 months. It also happened that I had to wait for 15 months to hear from the editor for the first time.

The response of the editor can involve a few decisions. The first is the recommendation that the manuscript should be sent to another journal, which thus implies a rejection. The second is that the editor invites the submission of a revised manuscript, where this revision should take the comments made by the referees into account. This can involve additional work. In case one feels able to respond adequately, the revision is sent back to the editor, with a set of accompanying replies to the referees outlining how their comments were handled.

Then a second uncertain period commences. The second row of Table 7.1 shows that this period can be about equally long as the first period, that is, on average 5.182 months. The total time that a manuscript can be with a journal is on average 10.727 months, with in my case a maximum of 27 months. The second letter of the editor can involve a decision of acceptance, of rejection (meaning one has to start all over again by sending the paper to another journal), or of a request for a further round of revision. There are journals that have a policy that one round of revision should suffice, while there are also journals that ask you to revise perhaps four or even more times. Most certainly, it rarely happens that a paper is accepted outright. Finally, the time it can take between a positive decision and eventual publication (in print) is on average 8.606 months, and we can see a peak at 24 months.[8]

A special issue of a journal usually concerns a specific theme, and the special issue editors invite certain colleagues to submit while sometimes also allowing interested individuals to submit. Hence, some form of reputation plays a role. It may be that only researchers who are expected to have their paper be cited well receive invitations to submit. Also, it may be that the editorial process is different, in the sense that there are more concise referee reports, a faster response, a smaller number of referees, and so on.

Once a paper has been accepted, it will be put in line for eventual publishing. And, once it is published, people can access it, read it, use it, cite it, apply it, and so on.

As rankings of academic researchers are based on their published papers, the timing of the actual publication is not unimportant. The line for publication can be rather long. This may be due to an a priori allocated special issue or simply to a large number of papers in the pipeline of the journal. The latter may be due to a high acceptance rate of the editorial board and to a large number of submitted manuscripts. At present, many journals make the accepted papers available through their websites, and corrected proofs can be downloaded ahead of publication. Even so, one should take the time between acceptance and publication into account when evaluating résumés of young faculty.

In many cases, the working paper version and the final published version differ substantially, which is simply because the author has tried to meet the comments from the reviewers. So, once a paper is published, it is better to discard the working paper version.

Once a paper has been published, it is uncommon to present it again at seminars and conferences, and hence, the paper has to attract attention itself. A key measure of attraction is the number of citations. When a paper is cited often, it can be considered more relevant. Of course, there are various reasons why in exceptional situations this suggested relevance may not hold (the author's students are obliged to cite the work of their supervisor – and this does happen! – or the paper is so wrong that everybody wants to stress that), but in general the citation score is believed to be a rather reliable measure of quality.

A final interesting feature is the time it takes between the first and last citation of a paper. It seems that the citation curve mimics the diffusion process of durable products, as you will see later on. That is, first it increases, then there is an inflection point, and finally the total citations level off to some maturity level.

DOES MORE PRODUCTIVITY PRECEDE MORE CITATIONS?[9]

To evaluate the performance of scientists, the evaluators need to strike a balance between the quantity and the quality of the output. The quantity can be measured by (functions of) the number of publications.[10] The ISI database and Google Scholar (using tools like Harzing's Publish or Perish methodology) allow for comparing scientists. Rankings can then be based on publications in international journals and books. Such rankings are important as prospective students apparently incorporate the rankings of university programs in their choices, and there is also evidence that universities design explicit policies to increase their rankings in the various charts.[11] At the same time, the discussion of the quality of scientists' performance usually seems to focus on (functions of) citations.[12]

Let us have a look at the productivity rankings of 236 Dutch economists, and let us link the ranks in a certain year with citations in later years. The research question is "Are highly ranked economists according to output also the most often cited in later years?"

The data concern 29 annual rankings, which concern the top 40 (or 20) most productive economists in the Netherlands. Productivity is based on weighted scores assigned to publications in international journals. The weights are a function of the quality of the journal, the number of pages, and the number of coauthors.

This historical dataset[13] concerning no fewer than 236 Dutch economists lends itself well to generating a reasonably objective measure of productivity, which in turn can be linked to citations in the years thereafter. A nice feature of the dataset is that it involves rankings instead of actual output numbers, and this makes it rather robust to methodological changes concerning the ranking. Hence, we have

Table 7.2 *Some statistics on the productivity variables.*

Variable	Sample	Mean	Median	Maximum	Minimum
Rank at first entrance	195	25.54	28	40	1
Average ranking	155	22.72	23	40	2
Number of years in list after entrance	190	2.34	1	18	0

the following data on productivity: (1) the position in the charts when an economist makes his or her first appearance, (2) the average ranking during the time that people appear multiple years in the charts, and (3) the number of years in the charts. As the first ranking cannot be used to measure (1) and also since there are a few missing observations, the sample size for these characteristics can vary, as can also be seen from the second column of Table 7.2.

Table 7.2 provides some data characteristics of the three productivity measures. There are economists who entered directly at position 1, but on average the mean entrance rank is around 25 (out of the 40). Over the years, the average ranking of 155 economists is around 23. And many economists appear in the ranks for only one year, while some are there for as long as 18 years.

For each of the 236 economists, I consult the Web of Science records to obtain their annual citations for the years 1981–2012.

Figures 7.3 and 7.4 give examples for economists Arnoud Boot and Herman Bierens, respectively, of what these data can look like. The patterns of these citations (and of many other economists) seem to obey an *S*-shaped pattern, and hence I decide to fit logistic curves to the actual citations. Note that I thus assume that toward a later stage in their career, people are cited with a constant amount, and we for the moment thus ignore that people's reputations eventually die out. Due to data limitations and also due to estimation problems in cases when the data cannot be adequately described by a logistic curve, I am able to fit the model to the citations data for 180 economists.

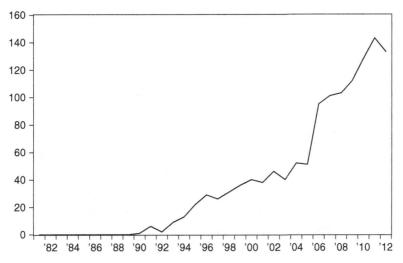

FIGURE 7.3 Annual citations to (single- or coauthored) articles written by Arnoud Boot.

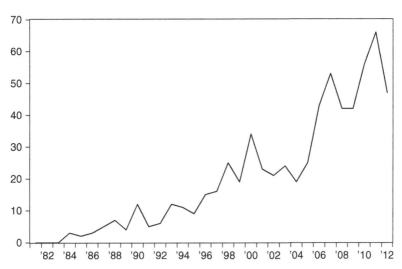

FIGURE 7.4 Annual citations to (single- or coauthored) articles written by Herman Bierens.

The logistic curve reads as

$$Citations = \frac{\alpha}{1 + \exp\left(-\beta(t - \gamma)\right)},$$

where $t = 1,2,\ldots$, α is the level toward which the total yearly citations eventually converge, and β is the parameter that measures the speed at which the high growth before the inflection point at time γ changes into lower growth after that inflection point. These three parameters are all useful features of the citations process. The maturity level α measures the cumulative total citations to be acquired per year. The higher α is, the more often the economist's work is cited. The inflection point γ measures when an economist attains half of his or her ultimate yearly citations. Why half? Because when $t = \gamma$, the denominator becomes $1 + \exp(-\beta(\gamma - \gamma)) = 1 + \exp(0) = 2$. Hence, the smaller γ is, the more rapidly an economist reaches success. The parameter β measures the intensity of that success. The larger that β, the more suddenly an economist becomes well cited.

The logistic curve has two more noticeable stages, and they are associated with the moment of takeoff and the moment of slowdown; see the graph in the technical appendix to this chapter. The moment of takeoff is when the increase in growth before the inflection point is at its peak, and its counterpart is the slowdown when the decrease in growth peaks. The derivations, which amount to the computation of the third-order derivative of the logistic function, appear in the appendix, and the end result is that

$$\text{takeoff} = \gamma - \frac{1}{\beta}\log(2 + \sqrt{3}),$$

$$\text{slowdown} = \gamma + \frac{1}{\beta}\log(2 + \sqrt{3}).$$

A faster takeoff means an earlier boost in citations, and a later slowdown entails a longer-lasting popularity of the work of an economist.

In Table 7.3, I report various statistics on the estimated key properties of the 180 logistic curves. The total maturity level of annual

Table 7.3 *Some statistics on the estimated characteristics of the citation curves (sample is 180).*[14]

Variable	Mean	Median	Max.	Min.
α	197.0	119.0	1,806	1.254
β	0.445	0.329	5.192	0.065
γ	25.46	26.62	37.74	3.333
γ – year of entrance	7.942	6.164	31.56	−9.915

The estimation method is nonlinear least squares.

citations α is highly skewed to the left. There is one economist who may expect annual citations of about 1,800, while the number of economists with a rather small number of citations is large. The average value of the inflection point γ is around 26 years, but the more interesting variable is the inflection point minus the year of entrance; its average value is around eight years. So, on average it takes eight years after the first signal of top productivity before the impact via citations starts to grow. Note from the last column of Table 7.3 that there are also economists who were already cited before they entered the rankings. These economists apparently are later hired at universities, and in fact they most likely were hired by the economics departments *because* they would appear on the rankings. Figures 7.5 and 7.6 summarize some statistics on the estimated moments of takeoff and slowdown, which average around 20 and 30, which is five years on each side of the average of γ in Table 7.3. The histograms give an impression of substantial variation with quite a number of observations appearing in the tails.

A priori, I guess we would associate more productivity with a higher rank at the first entrance into the charts, with a higher average rank throughout the years and with more years in the rankings. One would think that more productivity would lead to more citations in the end, that is, a larger value of α and that an economist is cited more rapidly. In the latter case, more productivity means that γ minus

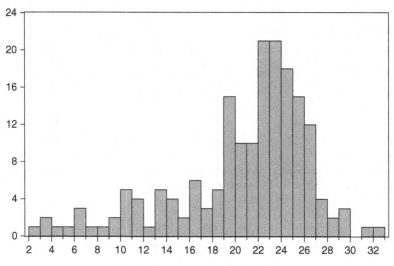

FIGURE 7.5 Sample characteristics of takeoff.

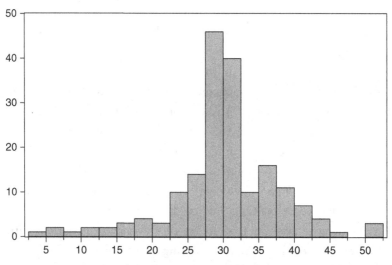

FIGURE 7.6 Sample characteristics of slowdown.

the year of entrance is smaller and also that the takeoff year minus year of entrance is smaller. More productivity would then also lead to a quicker arrival at the level of maturity, which means a larger value of β.

Table 7.4 *Estimation results for the natural logarithm of the estimated values of* α.

Explanatory variable	Full model		Reduced model	
Intercept	**7.141**	**(0.605)**	**6.740**	**(0.419)**
Log of rank at first entrance	0.020	(0.476)		
Log of average rank	**–1.019**	**(0.550)**	**–1.072**	**(0.174)**
Log of years in list +1	–0.490	(0.292)		
Year of first entrance times				
Log of rank at first entrance	–0.003	(0.028)		
Log of average rank	**0.019**	**(0.028)**	**0.025**	**(0.004)**
Log of years in list +1	0.024	(0.015)		
Sample size	119		119	
R^2	0.361		0.337	

The included cases are only those for which γ – year of entrance > 1. Parameter estimates with White-heteroskedasticity-corrected standard errors.

Additionally, as I have data covering the past three decades, we also have to consider potential changes in publication and citation habits. In the past decades, we have witnessed increases in productivity, perhaps due to the very fact that there are such rankings and people want to show off by being mentioned in those rankings, and we have also seen that academic journals have increasingly focused on acquiring higher citation levels. Hence, in the models that follow, I will include a mediating variable, which is the year of entrance of each of the economists involved. Indeed, as time goes by, more scientists and more journals strive to improve their reputation. So, it may have become more difficult to be cited and to improve a reputation.

In Table 7.4, I report the key estimation results for a regression model that includes the natural logarithm of the rank at first entrance, the natural logarithm of the average rank, and the natural logarithm of the number of years that an economist appears in the rankings (with 1 added to avoid observations with value 0) as explanatory variables. In addition to these three variables, I include the same three variables but then multiplied with the year of first entrance (measured as a variable taking values 0, 1, 2, and so on). So, the initial regression model contains an intercept and six variables. Once I have estimated the six relevant parameters using least squares, I delete all variables that have parameters, that are not significant at the 5% level, and in the last column of the table, I present the estimation results for this reduced model.

In Table 7.4, the dependent variable is estimated maturity level α. Note that I only include the cases where the entrance into the charts preceded the start of the citations. In a sense, this means that one can only be cited once one has appeared in the charts. As the log of average rank has a significant negative effect and the year of first entrance times the log of average rank has a significant positive effect (0.025), I conclude that these results show that larger-valued average ranks (meaning lower positions in the rankings) give lower scores on total citations, where this negative effect has become smaller over the years.

In Table 7.5, I present the estimation results in case the estimated takeoff moment is the dependent variable. As the logarithm of the years in the list has a significant negative parameter (see the last column of that table), while this variable multiplied with the year of first entrance has a significant positive parameter, I conclude that more years in the list gives earlier moments of takeoff, where this effect has become smaller over the years.

Finally, in Table 7.6, I present the estimation results in cases where the estimated value of γ (minus the year of entrance) is the variable to be explained. Given that the log of the rank at first entrance has a significant positive parameter, while its multiplication with the year of first entrance has a significant negative parameter, I conclude that these results show that a higher first ranking gives a smaller difference between the citations' peak year and the year of entrance. So, higher-ranked economists are cited sooner than those with lower first rankings.

In sum, more productivity, which is measured by a high entrance in the charts, a longer stay in the charts, and a higher average

Table 7.5 *Estimation results for the estimated values of the takeoff time, takeoff* $= \gamma - \frac{1}{\beta}\log(2 + \sqrt{3})$.

Explanatory variable	Full model		Reduced model	
Intercept	19.87	(2.775)	21.50	(0.725)
Log of rank at first entrance	1.459	(2.466)		
Log of average rank	–2.200	(2.713)		
Log of years in list +1	–2.488	(1.445)	–4.497	(0.846)
Year of first entrance times				
Log of rank at first entrance	–0.017	(0.133)		
Log of average rank	0.100	(0.135)		
Log of years in list +1	0.126	(0.073)	0.267	(0.038)
Sample size	119		137	
R^2	0.398		0.296	

The included cases are only those for which γ – year of entrance > 1. Parameter estimates with White-heteroskedasticity-corrected standard errors.

Table 7.6 *Estimation results for the estimated values of* γ – *year of entrance.*

Explanatory variable	Full model		Reduced model	
Intercept	7.526	(3.177)	8.375	(2.290)
Log of rank at first entrance	2.597	(2.903)	3.923	(0.801)
Log of average rank	1.748	(3.290)		
Log of years in list +1	–0.004	(1.794)		
Year of first entrance times				
Log of rank at first entrance	–0.143	(0.163)	–0.209	(0.019)
Log of average rank	–0.068	(0.166)		
Log of years in list +1	–0.014	(0.091)		
Sample size	119		139	
R^2	0.539		0.544	

The included cases are only those for which γ – year of entrance > 1. Parameter estimates with White-heteroskedasticity-corrected standard errors.

rank while being in the charts, does seem to lead to a more successful citation track record. So, we might conclude that more productivity leads to more citations and also to being cited more quickly.

To sum up, there is a moderate positive correlation between productivity and citations. This support was obtained for Dutch economists who displayed high productivity during the past three decades and their citations' record of accomplishment (when summarized using a logistic curve). It is uncertain whether this would also hold for the economists who did not make it onto these charts. These results can also be interpreted to say that evaluators should look not only at quantity or at quality but better at both at the same time.

WHICH TYPES OF ECONOMETRICS PAPERS GET MOST CITATIONS?

An important measure of impact of scientific work is the number of citations. When colleagues cite your work, you can interpret this as saying that your work is relevant to theirs. There are various measures for citations, and one that combines both publication output and citations is the h (or Hirsch) index,[15] which is frequently used to evaluate and rank the performance of an individual scholar. The h index is the amount of h publications that are cited at least h times.

An issue of informal discussion among scholars concerns the specific features of an article that make it worthy to cite.[16] Let us see what happens if I analyze the properties of my own papers and see which of those are cited most and why. This is convenient as I do recall the attributes of my own papers. For example, one of the attributes will be whether the paper concerns the analysis of special data that were collected just for that particular paper and not more than that. Of course, the analysis here concerns a single author and is not at all representative.

The data are drawn from the ISI Web of Science database, and data collection took place on November 1, 2010 (as by then my total number of ISI-recorded publications equaled exactly 200). The publications

Table 7.7 *Some statistics of the papers.*

Variable	Mean	Median	Minimum	Maximum
Total citations	6.635	3	0	68
Average citations per year	0.684	0.365	0	7.56

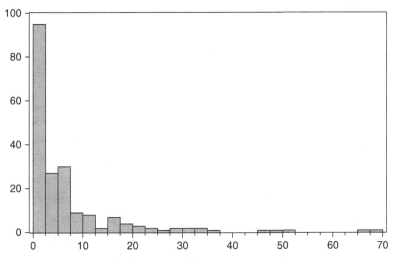

FIGURE 7.7 Total number of citations.

cover the period 1989 to and including 2010. Table 7.7 presents some key statistics. The minimum number of citations is 0, and this occurs for 51 of the 200 papers – hence the big spike on the left-hand side of the histogram in Figure 7.7. Hence, about one out of four of my papers has never been considered relevant enough to be cited. Such a finding is very good for character building.

Next, I characterize each of these papers on four attributes. The scores on these attributes are either 1 or 0 to keep matters simple. The first attribute is whether the paper focuses on an empirical test of an economic theory or hypothesis. This is taken in a broad sense, as some of the papers look at issues in marketing, and there one can test marketing theories. The second attribute is whether in the paper special data are collected and analyzed. By special data I mean that new survey

Table 7.8 *Attributes of the papers.*

Variable	Fraction
Test of theory	17.5%
New data	41%
New model	50.5%
Novel application	47.5%
Test of theory and new data	15.5%
Test of theory and new model	5.5%
New data and new model	20%
New model and novel application	18%

data are collected specifically for that paper, while nonspecial data are, for example, stock market data or GDP data, which can easily be retrieved from the Internet. The third attribute is whether the paper develops a new econometric model or a new econometric methodology. Finally, the fourth attribute is whether an already available econometric model (in the literature) is applied in an innovative way.

Table 7.8 summarizes the fractions of these four attributes and a few interactions (that is, the cases where one variable is 1 and another obtains the value 1, too). Clearly, most papers concern either a new econometric model or method or a new application of existing methods. Some papers contain both (18%). Note that a paper can have more than one feature at the same time, so the percentages do not sum to 1.

As 51 papers never received any citations, we may want to replace a regression model by a so-called censored regression model. This model contains two components, that is, a component that models whether a paper is cited (using a 1/0 variable to be explained) and a second component that models the number of citations given that the paper is cited (the case with 1 in the first component). In the technical appendix, I give some further details of this model.

The dependent variables are the natural log of the average citations per year (+1) and the natural log of the total citations (+1). By adding 1 each time and by taking the natural logs, I get 51 zeros

Table 7.9 *Estimation results of censored regression models.*

	Dependent variable			
Explanatory variables	Log(Average citations+1)		Log(Total citations+1)	
Intercept	–0.134	(0.109)	**–0.703**	**(0.264)**
Test of theory	**0.478**	**(0.115)**	**1.122**	**(0.242)**
New data	0.078	(0.080)	0.307	(0.194)
New model	**0.285**	**(0.081)**	**0.926**	**(0.194)**
Novel application	0.096	(0.096)	**0.498**	**(0.237)**
2010-year	**0.018**	**(0.009)**	**0.100**	**(0.022)**
Scale parameter	**0.503**	**(0.034)**	**1.217**	**(0.067)**

Sample size is 200 (White-corrected standard errors are in parentheses). Parameters significant at 5% are in boldface.

and 149 nonzero–valued observations for the variable to be explained. Table 7.9 presents the estimation results. The models also contain a time trend, as obviously papers that are more recent have had less of an opportunity to be cited.

As the explanatory variables only take values 1 or 0, it is easy to compare the parameter values. So, for example, a paper published in 2000 that tests a theory using a new model gives

$$\exp\left(-0.703 + \frac{0.964}{2}\right)\exp(1.122)\exp(0.926)$$
$$\exp\left((2010 - 2000)^*0.100\right) \approx 17$$

citations (where 0.964 is the estimated variance of the errors), whereas a paper from 2005 that tests a theory with standard methods using already available data receives

$$\exp\left(-0.703 + \frac{0.964}{2}\right)\exp(1.122)\exp\left((2010 - 2005)^*0.100\right) \approx 5$$

citations. When the significance and the size of the estimated parameters are evaluated, it is clear that the most relevant attributes for

202   ACADEMIC PUBLICATIONS

Table 7.10 *Attributes of typical articles in six econometric journals, fully based on my own judgment and a few of my colleagues here at the Econometric Institute.*

	Attributes			
Journal	Theory	Data	Model	Application
Econometric Theory	0	0	1	0
Journal of Applied Econometrics	0	1	1	1
Journal of Econometrics	0	0	1	1
Journal of Business and Economic Statistics	0	1	1	1
Review of Economics and Statistics	1	1	0	1
Econometric Reviews	0	0	1	1

more citations are a test of a theory or hypothesis and the introduction of a new econometric model or methodology.

To examine whether the estimation results in Table 7.9 have any external validity, I consider six academic journals that usually publish econometric articles. Table 7.10 gives the scores on the attributes of typical articles in these journals based on my own judgment and experience (and with the help of various colleagues). Table 7.11 gives the predicted average citations for an article published in, say, 2009 using the estimates of Table 7.9, and additionally I give the actual impact factor in 2009. The correlation between the numbers in the two columns in Table 7.11 is 0.822. So, it seems that the estimation results in Table 7.9 based on my own paper do have some external validity.

The main conclusion is that papers that put an economic hypothesis to an empirical test using a newly developed econometric model or econometric methodology seem to have the most impact in terms of citations. Newly collected data and a novel angle to an existing method also have positive effects, but much less than the first two attributes.

Table 7.11 *Estimated average citations for a 2009 article, based on the regression model of Table 7.9 and the actual impact factor in 2009.*

Journal	Average citations	Impact factor
Econometric Theory	0.514	0.743
Journal of Applied Econometrics	0.879	1.635
Journal of Econometrics	0.750	1.902
Journal of Business and Economic Statistics	0.879	1.562
Review of Economics and Statistics	0.953	2.555
Econometric Reviews	0.750	1.745

DO MORE REVISIONS LEAD TO PAPERS BEING CITED MORE OFTEN?

In many economic and social sciences disciplines, a paper is submitted to the editor of a journal and either is rejected immediately or begins the editorial process. This process typically involves the opinions of one, two, and sometimes even four referees, and they tend to hand in their reports to the editor after three to six months if everything goes well. The editor then decides whether the paper should be rejected based on these reports and his or her own insights or the author is invited to revise and resubmit. Usually, the author or author team carries out the revision, taking account of the referees' comments, and then there is a resubmission. Based on this revision, in many cases the editor decides to accept or to have one shorter round of revision with only minor modifications.

In the academic marketing discipline, the process is similar, expect for one major difference, at least in my perception. The number of revisions can be quite large, and authors and referees already tend to anticipate this phenomenon. For example, my personal experience includes statements of referees who say, "These are my comments for this round."

A natural question now is whether this extensive editorial process serves its purpose. That is, do more revisions lead to better

FIGURE 7.8 A cover of one of the leading journals in the marketing discipline.

papers? Let us have a look at a range of articles that were published in a top marketing journal called *Marketing Science* in the period 1988–1997; see Figure 7.8 for an example cover.

A way to characterize the quality of an article is the number of citations it receives after publication. For this purpose, the Thomson Reuters' *Social Science Citation Index* is very helpful. Of course, the citations need to be standardized by the number of years in which they could have been cited. In Figure 7.9, I display the citation scores of 212 articles. There are four articles that were never cited, there are a few that were cited many times, and clearly, the distribution is skewed to the right.

Citations can perhaps depend on the size of the article, the number of authors, and other features. In Table 7.12, I display the main descriptive measures of these potential explanatory variables.

Table 7.12 *Descriptive statistics concerning the 212 articles.*

Variable	Mean	Median	Maximum	Minimum
Citations	16.594	11	145	0
log(Citations), standardized*	0.271	0.336	2.412	−2.303
Authors	1.976	2	5	1
Pages	18.184	18	35	3
References	32.561	31	92	5
Revisions	2.349	2	4	1

* Cases with 0 are deleted.

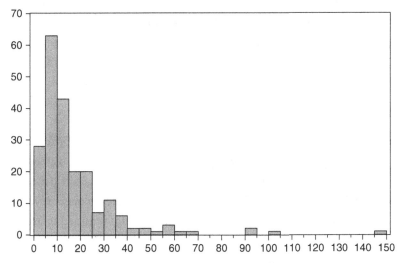

FIGURE 7.9 Frequency (vertical axis) of number of citations, cumulative up to December 2001 (horizontal axis).

Quite conveniently, *Marketing Science* reports the number of revisions at the end of each article, so that is how I was able to acquire these numbers. Of the 212 articles, there are 19 with one revision, 113 with two revisions, 67 with three revisions, and 13 with no fewer than four revisions.

To see whether the number of revisions and the control variables explain citations, I run a simple regression. The dependent variable is the natural logarithm of citations divided by the number of years between publication and 2002. The explanatory variables are the number of authors, the year, the issue number, the number of pages, the number of references, and the number of revisions. Deleting three insignificant variables, I obtain the final (significant at 5%) estimation results as

log (citations) = –1.358 + 0.048 Pages + 0.009 References + 0.199 Revisions.

The sample size is 208 due to four articles that were never cited and that I decided not to consider. The final model contains only those variables with parameters that are significant at the 5% level. Given the significance of the number of revisions, we see that more revisions seem to correspond with more citations (0.199 is the estimated parameter), and apparently, revisions lead to better papers.

OUTLIERS IN ECONOMETRICS

As stated previously, the leading academic journal in economics and econometrics is *Econometrica*.[17] A key reason for this top position in the rankings is that the most cited economics and econometric papers have appeared in *Econometrica*. A closer look at these papers reveals that they all have appeared around 1978–1987. I am tempted to argue that this is not a coincidence but in fact in part due to PC and software developments around that period.[18]

As measured in December 2016, Table 7.12 gives the number of citations of the most cited economics and econometric papers that have appeared in *Econometrica*. Note that these numbers put the ones discussed before (mine) in proper perspective.

Interestingly, all these top-cited studies have appeared in approximately a 10-year interval covering 1978 to 1987. Even though papers are cited more over time, and more recent studies naturally are cited less frequently, it still is remarkable that there are nine outlier publications all published in about the same period.

Table 7.13 *Top-cited articles published in* Econometrica.

Author[19]	Year	Google Scholar citations (December 2016)
Robert F. Engle and Clive W. J. Granger	1987	30,447
James J. Heckman	1979	24,118
Halbert S. White	1980	23,660
Robert F. Engle	1982	21,163
Whitney Newey and Kenneth D. West	1987	14,531
Jerry A. Hausman	1978	13,921
David A. Dickey and Wayne A. Fuller	1981	11,987
Christopher A. Sims	1980	11,035
Lars Peter Hansen	1982	11,987

In his 2008 book *Outliers*, Malcolm Gladwell describes how the Beatles and Bill Gates, among others, became so successful. A first reason is associated with the so-called 10,000 hours of practice. Successful individuals simply practice much and much more than others do or would be willing to do. A second key to success is luck, in the sense that successful individuals seize the opportunities once they recognize them. Bill Gates was able to develop into such a powerful individual because he entered the computer industry at exactly the right time.

Would such arguments also hold for the publications in Table 7.13? By the time the authors of those papers published their most cited work, they were all already established econometricians with a substantial record of accomplishment. All 11 academics had already written about a variety of topics. Additionally, all authors wrote their papers such that their new methods should be useful in practice. In fact, all papers give detailed illustrations of the methods in such a way that students could replicate them (which turned out to be relevant!). Therefore, we can safely assume that the 10,000 hours of practice holds for the 11 authors in Table 7.13.

The second success factor, I would argue, is that, as suggested, students and other academics could replicate the empirical results in

FIGURE 7.10 The IBM5150 personal computer.

the papers. This situation happened exactly at the time around the end of the seventies and the beginning of the eighties in the previous century, which is due to three developments in those days. The first development concerns of course the personal computer, like the one in Figure 7.10. Students and academics could have computations done in their own office with great speed. This was followed by a second development: students began to use programs such as Gauss and Matlab (developed around that time; see Table 7.14) in order to do the computations. A third development was that statistical packages were also developed at that time, which included pre-programmed routines to do the very same calculations (like RATS and MicroTSP; see again Table 7.14).

In other words, by the time the important publications appeared in *Econometrica*, anyone could replicate the reported empirical results and, of course, run their own computations for their own data. Hence, the papers that appeared around these developments in

Table 7.14 *Software development (still available).*[20]

Period	Econometric and statistical software
1975–1979	Shazam
	Limdep
	RATS
	Autoreg (became Give and later PcGive)
1980–1985	MicroTSP (became Eviews around 1990)
	Gauss
	Stata
	Matlab

econometric software had an enormous advantage. Not only are these papers of high quality, addressing very relevant econometric methodology, they also appeared just at the right moment.

Outlier publications in econometrics do exist, and all seem to have appeared in the same decade. In addition to the exceptional skills of the authors and the methodological relevance of the papers, these papers also appeared at just the right time. Suddenly every student and academic could compute what these authors did, thanks to fast developments in computing power and econometric software.

An implication of the preceding discussion is that it will take new exceptional moments for citation classics to emerge. Without a doubt, many current academics have their 10,000 hours of skills already. However, we may have to wait for a new period with exceptional circumstances. As is usual with outliers, the timing of this period can unfortunately not be predicted.

CAN PAPERS HAVE A SECOND LIFE?

Classic academic articles can have a "career" like those of a rock band. In the beginning, an article can attract much attention because the authors continue to work on the topic and the authors have PhD students who work on the same topic too. Then there can be a slowdown where interest fades away, and then, due to inclusion in

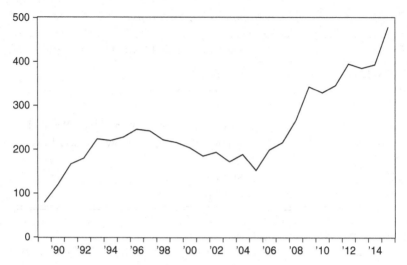

FIGURE 7.11   Yearly citations to the key paper on cointegration (based on the *Social Science Citation Index*, consulted December 2016).

statistical programs or a widespread dissemination through empirical work, an article can have a revived interest. Take a look at Figure 7.11 showing the yearly citations to Robert F. Engle and Clive W. J. Granger's masterpiece on cointegration, which appeared in *Econometrica* in 1987.

The cumulative observations in Figure 7.12 show that around 2004 the data seem to level off to some level of maturity. However, right after that the trend starts to go up again. In terms of the model for S-shaped data we looked at in Chapter 6, it seems that we can consider a model like

$$X_t = pm_1 + (q - p)N_{t-1} - \frac{q}{m_1}N_{t-1}^2 + \varepsilon_t,$$

for the data before 2004 and

$$X_t = pm_2 + (q - p)N_{t-1} - \frac{q}{m_2}N_{t-1}^2 + \varepsilon_t.$$

(Nonlinear) Least squares estimation (with the restriction that p and q are the same across the two periods) result in p is 0.026 (with

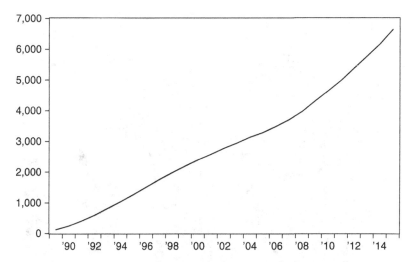

FIGURE 7.12 Cumulative yearly citations to the key paper on cointegration (based on the *Social Science Citation Index*). Sample is 1988–2015.

standard error 0.001), $q = 0.235$ (0.019), but more importantly, that m_1 is 3,546 (139) and m_2 is 5,171 (305). Clearly, the total number of citations in the second life of the paper outnumbers the number in the first stage.

EPILOGUE

Clive W. J. Granger is perhaps the most well-known and most often cited econometrician ever encountered in our discipline. Wikipedia correctly writes: "Sir Clive William John Granger (4 September 1934–27 May 2009) was a British economist, who taught in Britain at the University of Nottingham and in the United States at the University of California, San Diego. In 2003, Granger was awarded the Nobel Memorial Prize in Economic Sciences, in recognition that he and his co-winner, Robert F. Engle, had made contributions to the analysis of time series data that had changed fundamentally the way in which economists analyse financial and macroeconomic data."

FIGURE 7.13 Clive Granger presents his speech at the honorary doctorate ceremony.

In 2006, Clive W.J. Granger was awarded an honorary doctorate at the Econometric Institute, Erasmus University Rotterdam.

It was my great personal pleasure to be Clive Granger's honorary professor, and as such I spoke the following laudation:

One of the first conferences I attended as a recent graduate of the Econometric Institute was the Econometric Society European Meeting in Cambridge UK in 1992. It must have been the hot weather (and lack of showers at St. Catherine's College) or the fact that I managed to finish my PhD thesis within four years (something that had never happened before to my supervisor Teun Kloek), but my confidence when giving my presentation about periodic cointegration was sky-high. After my talk, someone in the audience asked me whether I could also have done something so and so, and I could not resist answering that I would not as that would be a bad idea. Until that moment the audience had a friendly shine, but after my answer this attitude changed and people looked shocked. Later, my friend Niels Haldrup kindly informed me that "that was

Clive W.J. Granger," leaving me in a panic. One hour later, I met with Professor Granger, and to my total surprise he told me that he liked my talk and that he agreed with me that his question was not a sensible one indeed.

This encounter with, as I strongly believe, "the greatest econometrician on earth" did make an everlasting impression. I could spell out his articles; I lectured to undergraduate students about his inventions as causality, cointegration, and forecast combinations; I purchased and read all his books; and one day I thought I should press my luck and go to San Diego for a month or two. Those two months turned out to be the two most important months in my scientific career. Without these two months, I would be working in business now and be very rich.

Professor Granger is an exceptional man, both as an academic and as a colleague. As a colleague he showed me the surroundings of San Diego, desert, beach, and restaurants, and he seemed to have ample time to discuss any kind of topic, sometimes even concerning time-series econometrics. As an academic, his record of papers and books simply is incredible, and this is also due to the wide variety of topics that he has covered and still covers. To indicate his stature, Professor Granger can permit himself to say about his invention called "bilinear time series models" (a book with more than 200 citations) that perhaps this was not a very good idea after all.

I feel enormous honor and also pleasure to be here, at this stage, at this occasion, with Professor Granger and to be able to grant an honorary doctorate to the man who, without perhaps knowing, made me what I am today.

APPENDIX: ECONOMETRIC METHODS

THE LOGISTIC GROWTH CURVE

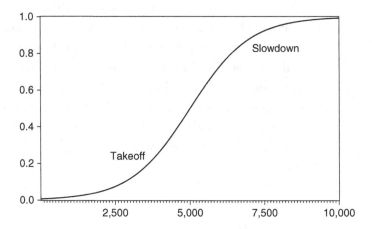

The moments of takeoff and slowdown are the moments where growth starts to grow rapidly and where the slowdown sets in rapidly, respectively. These two moments occur when the third-order derivative of the logistic curve equals 0.

Let us start with the simplest logistic curve ($\gamma = 0$, $\beta = 1$, $\alpha = 1$):

$$F(t) = \frac{1}{1 + \exp(-t)}.$$

The first derivative of $F(t)$ is

$$\frac{\partial F(t)}{\partial t} = F(t)\left(1 - F(t)\right).$$

Clearly, this first derivative is equal to 0 when $F(t) = 0$ or when $F(t) = 1$, the asymptotic values of the logistic function.

The second derivative of $F(t)$ is

$$\frac{\partial^2 F(t)}{\partial t \partial t} = \frac{\partial F(t)\left(1 - F(t)\right)}{\partial t} = \frac{\partial F(t)}{\partial t}\left(1 - 2F(t)\right).$$

As is well known, the second derivative is equal to 0 when $F(t) = \frac{1}{2}$, at the point of inflection.

The third-order derivative of $F(t)$ is

$$\frac{\partial^3 F(t)}{\partial t \partial t \partial t} = \frac{\partial F(t)\left(1 - F(t)\right)\left(1 - 2F(t)\right)}{\partial t} = \frac{\partial F(t)}{\partial t}\left(1 - 6F(t) + 6F(t)^2\right).$$

This third-order derivative is equal to 0 when

$$F(t) = \frac{1}{2} \pm \frac{1}{6}\sqrt{3}.$$

To find out at what value of t this $F(t)$ is obtained, consider the following:

$$F(t) = \frac{1}{1 + \exp(-t)}$$

then it can be solved for t as

$$t = \log\left(\frac{F(t)}{1 - F(t)}\right).$$

Substituting $F(t) = \frac{1}{2} \pm \frac{1}{6}\sqrt{3}$ gives that

$$t = \log(2 + \sqrt{3})$$

and

$$t = \log(2 - \sqrt{3}).$$

Note that

$$F(t) = \frac{1}{1 + \exp(-\beta(t - \gamma))}$$

gives

$$t = \frac{1}{\beta}\log\left(\frac{F(t)}{1 - F(t)}\right) + \gamma,$$

resulting in

$$\text{takeoff} = \gamma - \frac{1}{\beta}\log(2 + \sqrt{3}),$$

$$\text{slowdown} = \gamma + \frac{1}{\beta}\log(2 + \sqrt{3}).$$

A CENSORED REGRESSION MODEL

A censored regression model is a model for a variable for which the observations are censored. An example of left-censoring is that a paper has either 0 or some citations but never negative citations. One way to look at this is to introduce a latent (unobserved) variable y_i^*, which is only observed when it exceeds 0 and when it is not observed equals 0. In mathematical notation, one would then have

$$y_i^* = \alpha + \beta x_i + \sigma \varepsilon_i,$$

where

$$y_i = y_i^* = \alpha + \beta x_i + \sigma \varepsilon_i \text{ if } y_i^* > 0$$

and

$$y_i = 0 \text{ if } y_i^* \leq 0.$$

Simply now applying least squares only to the nonzero cases leads to bias. Various estimation methods are available, and the two-step estimation method developed by James Heckman in 1979 in Sample selection bias as a specification error, *Econometrica*, 47, 153–161, is frequently used.

8 Trends and Fads

Stocks have reached what looks like a permanently high plateau.

—Irving Fisher, October 17, 1929[1]

Picasso's prestige is rapidly waning, and the custodians of his fame – and his pictures – are fighting a losing battle to elevate him to a position among the immortals.

—Thomas Craven, November 15, 1934

AT A GLANCE

This penultimate chapter of this book deals with a key feature of many variables: a trend. A trend may be reflected by a steadily progressing upward pattern in the data, but of course, it can also be downward. Typically, macroeconomic variables show such a trending pattern, where gross domestic product (GDP) usually goes up year after year in good times, perhaps because of increasing numbers of inhabitants of a country, and where interest rates have gone down in the past few years. Indeed, a trend does not have to last forever; there may be a temporary dip – think of the 2008–2009 great economic crisis. Trends may also alternate. For example, unemployment usually goes down in economic good times, but when things go wrong with an economy, then unemployment can go up quite rapidly. There are also trending patterns, which seem to approach some final top level after a while. Think of the sales of durable products, which typically show an S-shaped pattern, meaning that in the end the full potential of eventual buyers has been reached. Or think of the citations to scientific articles in the previous chapter.

217

Naturally, an adequate understanding of a trend is very important for forecasting, in particular a few steps ahead. Look for example at the following simple regression model:

$$y_t = \alpha + \beta t + \varepsilon_t,$$

where $t = 1, 2, 3, \ldots, T$. After application of least squares to estimate the parameters, the one-step-ahead forecast, made at time T, is

$$\hat{y}_{T+1|T} = a + b(T+1),$$

and the 100-step-ahead forecast is

$$\hat{y}_{T+100|T} = a + b(T+100).$$

Put this in contrast to the regression model

$$y_t = \alpha + \beta y_{t-1} + \varepsilon_t$$

for which the one-step-ahead forecast is

$$\hat{y}_{T+1|T} = a + by_T$$

and the 100-step-ahead forecast is

$$\hat{y}_{T+100|T} \approx \frac{a}{1-b} + b^{100} y_T \approx \frac{a}{1-b},$$

at least when $|b| < 1$. Clearly, the second model does not create forecasts with a trend, while the first model does. Now, this is a key insight. That is, a trend in data is defined by the fact that a model, with which one can create data with a trend, can describe the data. It is a bit of a circular argument, but that is how it is. And, given that there are various trending patterns in many data, one can also expect that there are many models that can be considered. For example, there are dozens of mathematical expressions that can be associated with data that experience an S-shaped curve. The appendices to Chapters 5 and 7 gave two examples. There is also more than one way to describe data with a linear trend, like the preceding one.

In this chapter, I will consider five questions that all involve trends. The first question deals with climate and addresses whether it is perhaps only winters that are getting warmer. Here we deal with trends that can be described via the deterministic (as only depending on t) trend model noted previously. The second question deals with a trend in GDP data and its link with wealth. The twist here is that the focus is only on the wealth of the wealthiest, and hence the issue is whether already rich people get even richer when the economy grows. GDP is a variable that is not described by a deterministic trend model, and the reason is that there can be too many periods in which the data deviate from the overall trend line. In the appendix to this chapter on econometric methods, I will introduce an alternative trend model that allows for what is called a stochastic trend, and this suits GDP data better. The main takeaway from the appendix is that GDP-type data are better analyzed after transformation to growth rates. This makes sense for many reasons, one of them being that this allows for cross-country comparison, as growth rates are measurement-free percentage figures. This is why economic news is usually in terms of growth or change. You rarely hear people discussing the size of the US economy expressed in USD or the value of the Dow Jones index. In the latter case, discussion usually centers on the returns on the index. I do spend some time in the appendix explaining the differences between the two trend models because they correspond with the first decision one has to make when analyzing trending data: Do I stick to the levels of the data, or do I move to analyzing growth rates or returns? At the same, this discussion has been going on for the past few decades in academic research and has led to various classic articles in our top academic journals, so it is worth a mention!

Trends are everywhere, and sometimes one may wonder whether the trends are real or whether there will be an end to a trend. And, sometimes, a trend turns out to be a fad, which can happen in fashion but certainly also in actual business.

The third question in this chapter considers the top transfers in soccer. The 2016 move of Paul Pogba from Juventus to Manchester United for 89 million GBP, which was by then 105 million euros, marked a new record. It might be interesting to try to predict whether this trend of ever-increasing top transfer amounts will eventually level off to some value.

The fourth question deals with perhaps a bit of a disturbing trend: the diagnosis and treatment of attention deficit hyperactivity disorder (ADHD), with a particular focus on children.[2] I have data on medication levels for every age category, and for each year of data, a model can be fitted. The next step is to model the parameters over time, and there a trend is incorporated.

Finally, the last question in this book deals with a genuine fad in the world of business and economics. This fad is called the "New Economy," and its first appearance dates back to the time of the dot-com bubble and slightly before that. Promises were sky high, and all old problems in an economy would disappear. Now, as I will show, if there is anything that disappears, it is the use of the term and the citations to publications on this topic.

But, first, the focus is on the weather!

ARE ONLY WINTERS GETTING WARMER?

There is no doubt that present-day climate looks and feels different from climate a few centuries ago. There are signs of less ice in arctic areas, some of the permafrost has disappeared, glaciers seem to withdraw, and at the same time, we believe there are more and more hurricanes and other extreme weather conditions.[3] Given the relevance of potential outcomes of research on climate and the weather, it is important to have long series of data, preferably covering centuries, and the use of the proper econometric methods.

The reason for such care is that anecdotal evidence can quickly influence common ideas about the weather and may undermine a proper discussion on this important topic. Look, for example, at Figure 8.1.

Figure 8.1 gives a picture of what many in the Netherlands believe how winters looked like in the past: snow by Christmas, long periods with ice, and hence many skating events. Well, in my

FIGURE 8.1 A typical picture of the Netherlands in the winter (made a few centuries ago).

lifetime (since 1963), this happened only rarely. But suppose that temperatures really are on the rise; would that imply that we get warmer summers here in the Netherlands? Well, look at Figure 8.2. This is how many folks here would remember summertime in our own country.

So, a natural question, at least for a small-sized western European country like ours, would be: is it perhaps true that only winters are getting warmer?[4]

To see how we can get an answer to this question, it seems reasonable to consider the following 12 models, given that we can collect monthly data over the years:

$$\text{Temperature}_{\text{Month}, \, t} = \alpha_{\text{Month}} + \beta_{\text{Month}} t + \varepsilon_{\text{Month}, \, t},$$

where $t = 1, 2, 3, \ldots, T$ concern the years, and Month = January, February, ..., December. What you want is to use least squares to estimate the 24 parameters all at the same time. Next, one would want to test hypotheses like $\beta_{\text{Month}} = 0$, or hypotheses like $\beta_{\text{January}} = \beta_{\text{July}}$, for

FIGURE 8.2 Summertime in the Netherlands: rain, wind, and gray skies.

example. The tricky part here is that it is likely that there is correlation between $\varepsilon_{\text{Month},t}$ and $\varepsilon_{\text{Month},t-1}$ and also that there is potential nonzero correlation between $\varepsilon_{\text{January},t}$ and, say, $\varepsilon_{\text{July},t}$. It turns out[5] that if you take aboard all these potential correlations (and there can be many of them), then a proper expression for the standard errors and hence distributions of tests for hypotheses are not standard anymore. So, no 5% critical value equal to 2, but for a test for $\beta_{\text{Month}} = 0$, the 5% critical value becomes 5.222.[6] It is good to bear in mind when doing econometric analysis that sometimes the standard settings do not hold. And here it matters! When you get a t test value of 3, this means that there is no significant trend, while you could think there is one if you hold it against the (incorrect) benchmark value of 2.

Take a look at the estimates for the slope in the regression models with a trend, as summarized in Table 8.1; I report the figures for one and a half centuries for the Northern Hemisphere, for three and a half centuries for the United Kingdom data, and for close to three centuries for the Netherlands. Not in boldface are the t test statistics, which suggest insignificance of the slope at

Table 8.1 *Single equation estimation results for global monthly temperatures in the Northern Hemisphere (for the years 1856 to and including 1998)[7] and for the United Kingdom (1659–2000) and the Netherlands (1706–1993). The 5% critical value for the t test is 5.222.*

	NH		UK		Netherlands	
	b	t	b	t	b	t
January	0.0044	9.415	0.0044	7.391	0.0069	7.377
February	0.0052	9.631	0.0027	6.314	–0.0005	-1.073
March	0.0049	9.789	0.0038	10.83	0.0038	6.193
April	0.0039	7.683	0.0020	7.811	0.0003	0.850
May	0.0036	8.079	0.0011	3.310	0.0011	3.412
June	0.0024	4.159	–0.0002	–0.811	0.0005	1.359
July	0.0023	4.551	0.0010	3.421	0.0006	2.477
August	0.0029	6.577	0.0010	2.466	–0.0004	–1.282
September	0.0031	8.375	0.0016	3.388	–0.0019	–5.640
October	0.0046	13.08	0.0030	6.016	0.0004	0.817
November	0.0058	27.44	0.0030	5.300	0.0006	0.685
December	0.0050	12.56	0.0037	8.875	0.0028	3.104

the 5% level, when evaluated against the proper critical value of 5.222.

The results in Table 8.1 tell us that for the entire Northern Hemisphere, temperatures go up significantly, except for the months June and July. More specifically, for the United Kingdom, temperatures are on the rise from January to April and from October to December. Insignificant trend slopes are found for May to September, the spring and summer period. The last columns of Table 8.1 show that for the Netherlands matters are again different, as temperatures seem to increase only in January and March.

In sum, it seems that temperature increases seem to cluster around the winter months at least in this part of the world and that there is less evidence of warmer summers, at least for the data and period considered. What we learn from this exercise is that proper statistical analysis is very relevant, that even seemingly simple test regression models are associated with alternative statistical methods, and that these methods lead to other conclusions.

HOW DO THE WEALTHIEST FARE WHEN THE ECONOMY GROWS?

GDP is a kind of variable that is usually analyzed in terms of growth rates. One reason is that the levels of GDP depend on the currency of a particular country, so GDP of the United States is measured in USD, that of the United Kingdom in GBP, and that of various European countries in EUR. A second reason is that the size of GDP very much depends on the size of the country. The largest economies in the world are the United States, China, and Japan, and these are also large countries with many inhabitants. Of course, size is not the only factor, as the economies of India and Brazil do not similarly reflect their country sizes. This makes comparison of GDP values less useful. What you can do then is to scale GDP by the number of inhabitants and to put all GDP values into one currency using exchange rates. In that case, one ends up with GDP per capita in, say, USD.

An alternative way of scaling is to transform GDP into growth rates. These rates are in percentages, and this makes comparison possible. Growth rates are typically computed as

$$\text{Growth}_t = 100 * \frac{\text{GDP}_t - \text{GDP}_{t-1}}{\text{GDP}_{t-1}}.$$

They can also be approximated by

$$\text{Growth}_t = 100^* (\log \text{GDP}_t - \log \text{GDP}_{t-1}),$$

where log denotes the natural logarithmic transformation. Another reason is that GDP levels are typically associated with what is called a stochastic trend. That is, there is an overarching trend process, with say a 2% growth over a century, but there can be long or very long periods in which the data deviate from this trend. In the appendix to this chapter, I will present more details on a stochastic trend, and the reason for my doing so is that it seems that many economic time-series data obey such a trend.

Many studies in economics and econometrics address features of and relations with GDP growth. Do countries share the same growth rates? Do poorer countries grow such that they may catch up? Does more growth lead to more investments in research and development, or is the relationship perhaps the other way around? This last question illuminates an important issue when studying GDP, as it is not always clear if some variable is causing GDP to change or if it is the other way around – that is, that GDP grows because of changes in that variable. In econometrics' language, this is usually called simultaneity. In the notation of the regression model, we may have that

$$y_t = \alpha + \beta x_t + \varepsilon_t,$$

while at the same time

$$x_t = \gamma + \delta y_t + v_t.$$

To estimate the parameters in these two models jointly was a classic issue in the early development years of econometrics, in particular as in those times only annual data were available. So, even if in reality things do not happen at the same time, because of the low frequency of the data, it may seem so. Indeed, if one were to have minute-by-minute data on GDP and, say, inflation, then it is likely that one of these two variables is leading in time and then simultaneity disappears. In the appendix, I explain with some detail one of the often applied methods in econometrics to estimate the parameters in a simultaneous equations model.

To show how this works in practice, let us have a look at the question of what happens with wealth when the economy grows. More precisely, does the wealth of individuals grow when the economy grows? This question is of course addressed in many studies, and there usually the focus is on all people. Rightfully so – it is important to study whether economic prosperity propagates through all income classes of a country, or perhaps even better: Does economic growth make the poor less poor?

Here in this chapter, I focus on an alternative sample of people, and these are the 500 richest individuals in the Netherlands. Since 1998, the magazine *Quote* (following the ideas of *Forbes* and others) has reported on the wealth and relative ranking of the 500 wealthiest in the country. Annually there is a dropout of about 50 individuals, and hence each year there are also about 50 new entrants. This makes it a bit difficult to work with variance or standard deviations as measures of dispersion. At the same time, I also do not want to split the sample in groups, as there are zillions of ways to create such groups. Hence, I decide to use a scale-free approach, and this goes back to the law of Zipf (see Chapter 2).

As an example, take a look at the scatter diagram in Figure 8.3, which depicts the log of wealth (measured in the year 2000) against the

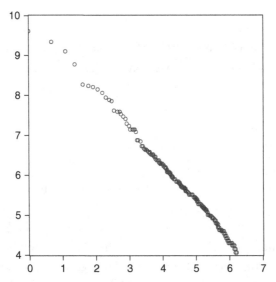

FIGURE 8.3 The 500 entries of the year 2000 edition of the *Quote* 500, with a scatter of the log of wealth (in billions of euros) against the log of the rank (1 to 500).

Table 8.2 *Three measures on wealth, 1997 to 2015, data for the Netherlands.*

Year	Inequality in wealth	Change in wealth	GDP growth
1997	NA	NA	4.3
1998	-1.038	NA	4.5
1999	-0.988	11.0	5.1
2000	-0.952	8.0	4.2
2001	-0.894	6.0	2.1
2002	-0.898	-2.0	0.1
2003	-0.894	6.0	0.3
2004	-0.879	4.0	2.0
2005	-0.899	4.0	2.2
2006	-0.980	5.0	3.5
2007	-0.926	6.0	3.7
2008	-0.908	5.0	1.7
2009	-0.899	-12.0	-3.8
2010	-0.896	6.7	1.4
2011	-0.880	4.7	1.7
2012	-0.842	0.0	-1.1
2013	-0.844	2.4	-0.2
2014	-0.851	0.0	1.4
2015	-0.861	3.2	2.0

log of the rank. Indeed, the left upper point associates with the log of 1 and hence is on the *y*-axis. There seems to be an almost perfect straight line across these points, and this is called a power law.[8] Note that the slope of the regression line can be interpreted as a measure of inequality. The steeper the line, and hence the more negative the slope, the more the inequality. Indeed, a horizontal line would mean that everyone has the same wealth.

As I have the data since 1998, it is possible to compute the slope using least squares for all these years, and the resultant "observations" are presented in the second column of Table 8.2. The years 1998, 1999, and 2006 showed the largest inequality, and indeed, if you look at the last column, these were also the years with substantial economic growth.

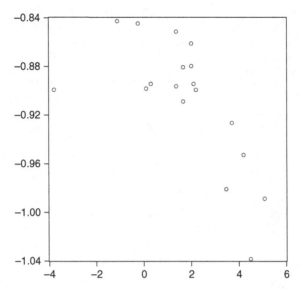

FIGURE 8.4 A scatter diagram of inequality versus GDP growth.

The third column gives the median of the percentage change in wealth across the individuals who are in the rankings in year T and $T-1$, so this is each time a different group of individuals, usually around 450 people.

An application of least squares for the regression model

$$\text{Inequality}_t = \alpha + \beta\text{GDPgrowth}_t + \varepsilon_t,$$

which seems a reasonable first guess given the data as they are pictured in Figure 8.4, results in $a = -0.880$ (0.012) and $b = -0.016$ (0.005), where the standard errors are given in parentheses, and $R^2 = 0.443$. So, positive GDP growth makes inequality increase, as b is significantly different from 0. Now here is a case where we may doubt whether there is some simultaneity. Using the method of instrumental variables, as explained in the appendix, where the instruments are the same two variables one-year lagged, results in $a = -0.857$ (0.019) and $b = -0.027$ (0.010). These estimation results do not differ much from the previous ones, so it seems that there is indeed a relation between GDP growth and inequality.

Encouraged by the data in Figure 8.5, the next regression model that I consider is

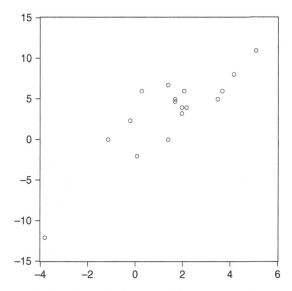

FIGURE 8.5 A scatter diagram of the percentage change in wealth versus GDP growth.

Change in wealth$_t$ = α + βGDPgrowth$_t$ + ε_t.

Least squares gives that a = 0.215 (0.792) and b = **2.067 (0.308)**, with an R^2 of 0.750. So, more economic growth also makes the wealth of the wealthiest increase. This suggests that economic prosperity makes the richest even richer. However, when I consider the instrumental variable method, where the same two variables when lagged with one year are again the instruments, then I get a = 0.820 (1.415) and b = 1.598 (0.922), where the latter result suggests that GDP growth is not statistically relevant, at least not at the 5% level.

In sum, we here have another example where the proper estimation method may make the difference. Simple and routine wise application of the least squares method may not always be the right thing to do. Indeed, and perhaps not unexpectedly, when GDP goes up, so goes the wealth of the wealthiest, on average. The first outcome on inequality, however, does show that the link between inequalities among the wealthiest does not change with the estimation method. This gives more confidence when drawing conclusions.

WILL TRANSFER PRICES OF SOCCER PLAYERS LEVEL OFF?

The trends in temperatures are observable visually, and they can also be quantified using an econometric model. So, it is beyond doubt that, at least for the samples considered, the temperatures seem to increase, although for the moment it seems that summer months do not get much warmer. Trends in economic prosperity also seem persistent, in the sense that many industrialized countries have experienced economic growth in the past decades; it seems that countries like China and India are catching up. So, in a sense, one may conclude that such trends make sense and have a connection with reality.

Sometimes, however, one may wonder whether trends have such a connection with reality. The last three questions of this book address such potentially disconnected trends, which some may call fads.

The first trend I address is what soccer clubs are willing to pay for a transfer of a player from one team to another. If we go back in time, in 1973, the most famous Dutch soccer player, Johan Cruijff (who unfortunately died in 2016), was once transferred from Ajax to Barcelona. The transfer amount was 922,000 GBP, which in those days was a stellar amount. Now, Cruijff was exceptionally good, and everybody felt happy for him to make such a splendid career move, although some would have said in those days that this amount would be the limit.

Well, by now we know that there does not seem to be a limit. The news of August 8, 2016, was that Paul Pogba would play for Manchester United for 89 million GBP, which is currently 105 million euro. If you look at the figures in Table 8.3, you can see that in just 20 years, the record transfer amount has increased fivefold.

One may now wonder: Where will this end? And, if it does not end, will there be a top transfer amount for the whole process? To answer this question, one can fit a logistic curve to the data, which is inspired by the shape of the data as in Figure 8.6.

We saw this curve already in Chapter 7, and it looks like

Table 8.3 *Development of record transfers in soccer, in millions of euros.*

Year	Player	From	To	Amount
1996	Alan Shearer	Blackburn Rovers	Newcastle United	21
1997	Ronaldo	Barcelona	Inter Milan	28
1998	Denilson	Sao Paulo	Real Betis	31.5
1999	Christian Vieri	Lazio Roma	Inter Milan	45
2000	Luis Figo	Barcelona	Real Madrid	60
2001	Zinedine Zidane	Juventus	Real Madrid	73.5
2009	Cristiano Ronaldo	Manchester United	Real Madrid	94
2013	Gareth Bale	Tottenham Hotspur	Real Madrid	101
2016	Paul Pogba	Juventus	Manchester United	105

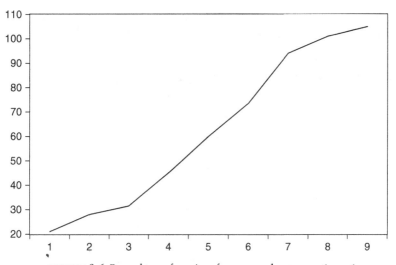

FIGURE 8.6 Record transfer prices for soccer players, 1996–2016.

$$\text{Transfer}_t = \frac{\mu}{1 + \exp(-\gamma(t - \delta))}.$$

The parameter δ measures the point of inflection, and the parameter γ measures the steepness of the curve. The parameter μ measures the maturity level. If you look at the data in Table 8.3, you can see that the first three transfer prices show a slow increase; after that it goes quickly to the 94 million euro for Cristiano Ronaldo, and then it seems to level off. Strictly speaking, the logistic curve does not apply as the data are not observed with equidistance. That is, we do not have an observation for each year.

But let us ignore this issue, and take t as 1,2,3, ..., 9. Estimating the parameters of the model

$$\text{Transfer}_t = \frac{\mu}{1 + \exp(-\gamma(t - \delta))} + \varepsilon_t$$

using the technique called nonlinear least squares, for the first eight observations (that is, leaving Pogba out), I get m = **158 (31.0)**, c = **0.379 (0.057)**, and d = **6.319 (1.109)**, with standard errors in parentheses, and with an R^2 of 0.992. A forecast for Pogba's transfer price is equal to 116. So, it seems that the last transfer price is not as high as it could have been given historical top transfers. This insight is reiterated when the model parameters are estimated for all nine observations, as then we get m = **129 (11.89)**, c = **0.437 (0.056)**, and d = **5.259 (0.528)**, with an R^2 of 0.989. So, these results show that increases in transfer prices are going down, and actually it is currently predicted that around 129 million euros will be the ultimate transfer price in the future.

DO TRENDS IN ADHD MEDICATION PERSIST?

The past few years have witnessed an important increase in the diagnosis of ADHD. This holds for children and for adults.[9] ADHD has positive associations with creativity and entrepreneurship[10] but also brings costs to society in terms of medical consultation and the issue of medication.

FIGURE 8.7 A visual perception of a child with ADHD.

Let us have a look at the data on the numbers of individuals who receive medication for ADHD.[11]

Let us analyze the numbers of individual users of methylpheni-date and atomoxetine in 2006–2011 (the full year) in the Netherlands per age, where age ranges from 4 to 85 years. The data were purchased in October 2012 from the "Stichting Farmaceutische Kengetallen" (Foundation for Pharmaceutical Statistics, www.sfk.nl/english), and at that time no full year data for 2012 were available. The data are depicted in Figure 8.8, and the actual numbers are given in the appendix. One can see from the graphs that each age category contains a positive number, meaning that also individuals of, say, 83 years can be prescribed ADHD medication.

The data have a typical shape, where the peak year appears to occur at age 11 in 2006 and 2011, while it is 10 in the inter-mediate years. Table 8.4 presents some basic statistics of these data per year and it is clear that there is an upward trend in the mean, median, and maximum values. In 2011, 13,025 children of age 11 were using ADHD medication, which on a total of 206,780 children of that age (http://statline.cbs.nl) amounts to 6.3% of this age category.

Table 8.4 *Basic statistics of the numbers of individual users of methylphenidate and atomoxetine in 2006–2011.*

Year	Mean	Median	Maximum	Minimum
2006	1,028	490	5,816	29
2007	1,295	638	6,877	23
2008	1,521	755	8,050	34
2009	1,773	947	9,652	25
2010	2,091	1,220	11,510	28
2011	2,368	1,393	13,025	24

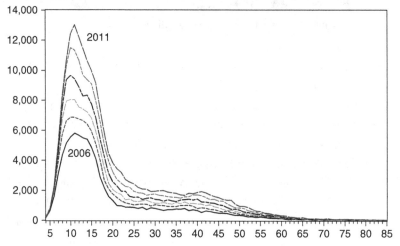

FIGURE 8.8 Numbers of individual users of methylphenidate and atomoxetine in 2006–2011 (the full year) per age.

As I have the data for each age category, it is possible to compute the percentage of new cases per age category. In Figure 8.9, these percentages are presented, and in Table 8.5, I report the basic statistics for these data. Table 8.5 shows that each year in between about 16% to 25% new cases per age category are diagnosed on average. The negative percentages typically associate with higher ages, and also the percentages over 100% correspond to the ages above 60.

Table 8.5 *Basic statistics of the percentages of new individual users of methylphenidate and atomoxetine in 2007–2011, for the same age category.*

Year	Mean	Median	Maximum	Minimum
2007	25.2	26.2	96.9	–21.0
2008	17.5	19.1	103	–33.3
2009	16.5	16.3	101	–44.4
2010	19.6	19.3	81.8	–17.6
2011	16.0	15.6	76.8	–31.4

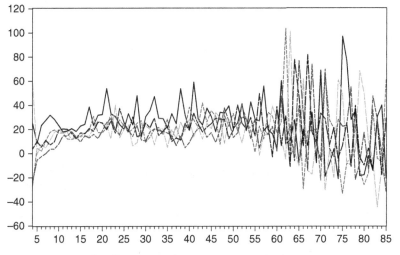

FIGURE 8.9 Percentage of new cases per age in the same age category, relative to one year before.

It might also be interesting to examine the percentage of new cases in each age category, relative to one age category lagged in the previous year. For example, if we assume that, say, eight-year-olds in 2009 maintain their prescription in 2010 (when they are age nine), how many new cases at age nine are diagnosed? These data are depicted in Figure 8.10, and the relevant basic characteristics are given in Table 8.6.

Table 8.6 *Basic statistics of the percentage of new individual users of methylphenidate and atomoxetine in 2007–2011, relative to the year before.*

Year	Mean	Median	Maximum	Minimum
2007	26.2	18.8	357	–26.5
2008	17.2	13.7	283	–22.7
2009	17.6	12.0	412	–49.0
2010	19.4	13.7	256	–30.4
2011	15.4	11.2	224	–23.0

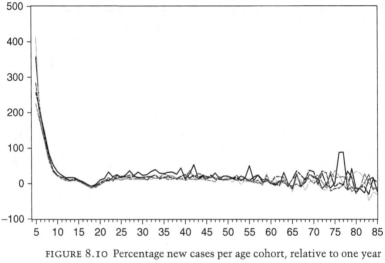

FIGURE 8.10 Percentage new cases per age cohort, relative to one year before.

Table 8.6 again shows that each year in between about 16% to 26% of new cases per age category are diagnosed on average. The negative percentages typically associate with higher ages, while now the percentages way over 100% (and sometimes even over 400%) correspond to the low ages like four, five, and six.

All in all, the numbers in the tables and the graphs clearly suggest the presence of trends in prescribing ADHD medication and that these trends are positive and even close to exponential.

Table 8.7 *Parameter estimates (and standard errors) of the model.*

Year	β_{year}		ρ_{Year}		R^2
2007	1.225	(0.012)	0.386	(0.105)	0.997
2008	1.153	(0.009)	0.451	(0. 101)	0.998
2009	1.155	(0.008)	0.283	(0.109)	0.998
2010	1.153	(0.011)	0.468	(0.101)	0.998
2011	1.098	(0.016)	0.688	(0.084)	0.998

To be able to forecast ADHD prescriptions for future years, I need a model to summarize the data. Given the strong similarities of the distributions across the years, it seems reasonable to incorporate the data for one year in a model to forecast the next year, and given the patterns in Figure 8.8 and 8.9, it seems reasonable to include per age category the data for the same category in the previous year.

For each year, the model for observations on ages 5 to 85 reads as

$$Y_{\text{Year, Age}} = \mu_{\text{Year}} + \beta_{\text{Year}} Y_{\text{Year Before, Age}} + \rho_{\text{Year}} \left(Y_{\text{Year, Age-1}} - \beta_{\text{Year}} \right.$$
$$\left. Y_{\text{Year before, Age-1}} \right) + \varepsilon_{\text{Age}},$$

where year = 2007, 2008, ..., 2011. The least squares estimates are reported in Table 8.7.

The fit of the models in Table 8.7 is very close to 1; see the values of R^2 in the last column. Also, the parameters β_{Year} are all estimated significantly in excess of 1, which emphasizes the exponential growth, although the acceleration over the years seems to slow down.

The next step is to obtain "future" parameter estimates for β_{Year} and ρ_{Year}. To obtain such estimates, I regress the parameter estimates in Table 8.7 on an intercept and a trend (1, 2, to 5), where the trend is natural log-transformed. That is, I consider

$$\beta_{\text{Year, }t} = \mu_{\beta} + \delta_{\beta} \log(\text{trend}_t) + \varepsilon_{\beta,t,}$$
$$\rho_{\text{Year,}t} = \mu_{\rho} + \delta_{\rho} \log(\text{trend}_t) + \varepsilon_{\rho,t,}$$

where each equation is fitted to one set of the five observations in Table 8.7, so $t = 1, 2, 3, 4, 5$. With estimated parameters in these two latter equations, I can extrapolate the values of β_{Year} and ρ_{Year} for the years 2012 to 2016. These values are 1.103, 1.093, 1.084, 1.076, and 1.070 for β_{Year}, which shows that growth seems to decrease over time, and for ρ_{Year} I obtain 0.559, 0.578, 0.594, 0.609, and 0.622 for the years 2012 to 2016, respectively.

When I assume that the number of prescriptions at age four remains the same as in 2011, that is, 184, and setting the intercept term μ_{Year} equal to zero (which by the way corresponds with the unreported parameter estimates and their standard errors for 2007–2011), I obtain the forecasts for 2012–2016 as they are displayed in Figure 8.11. Some basic statistics of these forecasts are presented in Table 8.8.

These numbers show that the forecast for 2016 is that there are close to 300,000 individuals in the Netherlands who will be prescribed ADHD medication. Also, when we assume that there will be about 200,000 children of age 11 in 2016, we see that close to 10% of these children will use such medication.

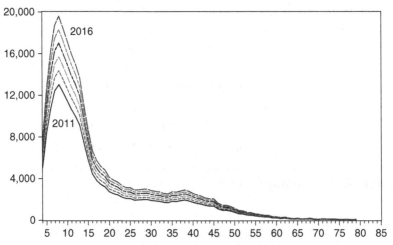

FIGURE 8.11 Forecasts for the numbers of individual users of methylphenidate and atomoxetine in 2012–2016 (2011 included for comparability purposes) per age.

Table 8.8 *Basic statistics of forecasts of individual users of methylphenidate and atomoxetine in 2012–2016.*

Year	Mean	Median	Maximum	Minimum
2012	2,640	1,567	14,362	26
2013	2,885	1,712	15,693	29
2014	3,127	1,856	17,013	31
2015	3,366	1,998	18,314	34
2016	3,600	2,137	19,588	36

An analysis of data on the ADHD medication prescriptions for 2006–2011 for the Netherlands reveals explosive growth. Extrapolating these data using a reliable econometric model suggests that this growth leads to an estimate for 2016 of about 1.8% of all Dutch citizens who would use such medication, with a peak around age 11 of 10%.

As of December 2016, the numbers for 2015 are available, and it turns out that 228,000 individuals used ADHD medication in 2015. And the growth in users was smallest for children ages 5 to 15. In a sense, this is good news, I would say, although less good news is that the model does not deliver very accurate forecasts.

THE END OF THE HYPE: NEW ECONOMY?

Now, one may dispute whether ADHD is a trend or a fad, and history will tell. I would like to conclude this chapter and this book with the last question, and this definitively concerns hype of a fad. The concept is called the "New Economy." The first time this concept appeared was on the cover of the *Time* magazine

The Wikipedia lemma says

The new economy is the result of the transition from
a manufacturing-based economy to a service-based economy. This
particular use of the term was popular during the dot-com bubble of
the late 1990s. The high growth, low inflation and high

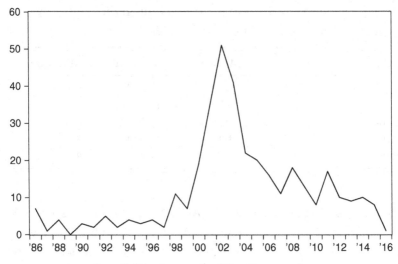

FIGURE 8.12 Publications on the "New Economy."

employment of this period led to overly optimistic predictions and many flawed business plans.

Now, the question is: Was it hype indeed,[12] and can we observe this with actual data? The answer is yes, as I will show you now.

Figure 8.12 shows the number of academic publications (per year) in the Social Sciences Database with the topic the "New Economy." In the period from 1985 to 1997, this number was about five to 10. But then, suddenly, there was a boom in the publications, with a peak around 2001 and 2002 with about 50 publications. Then, after the dot-com crisis, the number of publications slowed down, and at present (the data end in 2016), the level is back to about five. In the Appendix to this chapter, I give the relevant numbers. Figure 8.13 presents the cumulative number of publications, and here we see a by-now-familiar shape, where there seems to be some leveling off toward a maturity level.

When I consider the method outlined in Chapter 5, which was based on a balance between growth and acceleration for nonbubble data, the results are given in Figure 8.14. Evidently, it all went too fast in 1998, 2000, and 2001.

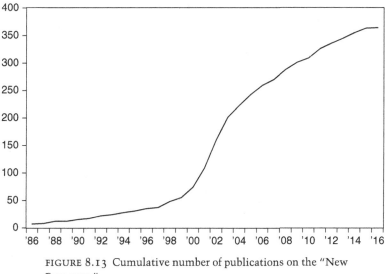

FIGURE 8.13 Cumulative number of publications on the "New Economy."

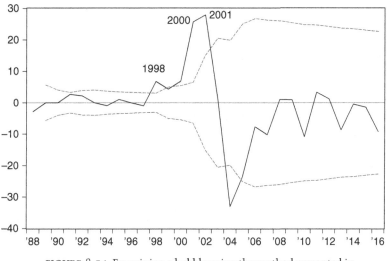

FIGURE 8.14 Examining a bubble using the method presented in Chapter 5.

Now, as we saw in Chapter 7, publications are one thing, citations are another. Figure 8.15 presents the number of studies that cite academic papers on the "New Economy," whereas

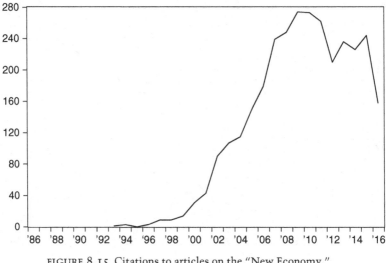

FIGURE 8.15 Citations to articles on the "New Economy."

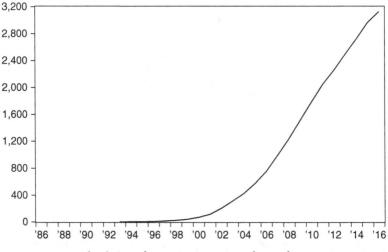

FIGURE 8.16 Cumulative citations to articles on the "New Economy."

Figure 8.16 presents the cumulative number. Does that look familiar?

As the data before 1995 are very close to zero, at least relative to the next observations, I discard those in my analysis

Table 8.9 *Parameter estimates (with estimated standard errors) for publications and citations.*

Parameter	Publications		Citations	
m	353	(24.9)	3566	(163)
p	0.020	(0.050)	0.008	(0.005)
q	0.300	(0.147)	0.297	(0.034)
r	0.670	(0.213)	0.556	(0.202)
R^2	0.689		0.958	

Sample is 1995 to 2016.

of publications and citations. Like earlier, I will consider the model for the growth process, but now with one modification: the error term has autocorrelation. Here it turns out to be relevant, and hence the model is

$$X_t = pm + (q - p)N_{t-1} - \frac{q}{m}N_{t-1}^2 + v_t$$

with

$$v_t = \rho v_{t-1} + \varepsilon_t.$$

The nonlinear least squares estimation results[13] are in Table 8.9.

Interestingly, in both cases the p is estimated insignificantly different from 0. As this parameter has the interpretation "innovation" and as the "imitation" parameter q is about 0.3 in both cases, one can suggest that the two processes concern imitation more than originality. The fit of the models is good, and what is interesting to see is that the cumulative number of publications in 2016 is 364, so the estimated m is too low, suggesting that this process has ended. At the same time, the cumulative number of citations in 2016 is 3,124. The estimated m is 3,566, and this means that in another two to three years, we will not hear nor read about the "New Economy" again.

APPENDIX: DATA AND ECONOMETRIC METHODS

Number of users of methylphenidate and atomoxetine per age category, sample 2006–2011

Age	2006	2007	2008	2009	2010	2011
4	158	197	146	231	240	184
5	666	722	755	748	823	779
6	1,604	1,979	2,014	2,165	2,281	2,225
7	3,086	3,939	4,347	4,536	5,034	5,032
8	4,354	5,742	6,760	7,509	8,044	8,334
9	5,170	6,641	7,951	9,372	10,294	10,670
10	5,573	6,877	8,050	9,652	11,510	12,420
11	5,816	6,865	8,048	9,416	11,349	13,025
12	5,678	6,749	7,559	8,903	10,702	12,261
13	5,502	6,643	7,415	8,283	9,682	11,456
14	5,410	6,404	7,216	8,338	9,364	10,643
15	4,844	5,955	6,818	7,759	9,097	9,975
16	4,091	5,084	5,945	6,836	7,966	9,141
17	2,887	4,001	4,770	5,457	6,594	7,446
18	2,163	2,667	3,490	4,232	5,017	5,820
19	1,598	2,106	2,475	3,146	3,962	4,453
20	128	1,757	2,058	2,568	3,222	3,825
21	985	1,515	1,841	2,281	2,733	3,436
22	982	1,305	1,735	1,948	2,477	3,198
23	893	1,167	1,390	1,947	2,276	2,731
24	897	1,114	1,427	1,613	2,217	2,560
25	872	1,047	1,290	1,548	1,946	2,435
26	809	1,076	1,264	1,563	1,849	2,212
27	891	1,103	1,326	1,407	1,834	2,095
28	736	1,089	1,363	1,485	1,693	2,087
29	857	976	1,241	1,512	1,742	1,937
30	811	1,058	1,155	1,416	1,774	1,955
31	747	1,013	1,151	1,385	1,681	1,984
32	679	999	1,199	1,284	1,660	1,998
33	733	946	1,152	1,387	1,595	1,898
34	735	948	1,098	1,321	1,564	1,852

(*cont.*)

Age	2006	2007	2008	2009	2010	2011
35	774	939	1,210	1,267	1,552	1,817
36	766	1,019	1,142	1,368	1,503	1,721
37	813	1,013	1,245	1,402	1,584	1,686
38	668	1,026	1,138	1,433	1,592	1,823
39	726	959	1,158	1,372	1,715	1,795
40	674	807	1,117	1,439	1,717	1,872
41	540	859	1,098	1,248	1,663	1,938
42	642	827	1,009	1,238	1,540	1,853
43	605	748	1,061	1,186	1,399	1,717
44	538	740	933	1,166	1,420	1,612
45	492	642	870	1,050	1,310	1,538
46	488	576	754	1,009	1,303	1,421
47	472	633	680	884	1,136	1,362
48	404	539	712	771	990	1,364
49	350	488	598	765	859	1,089
50	350	422	562	708	845	957
51	323	405	480	583	817	956
52	252	356	499	543	679	885
53	256	305	392	487	588	756
54	208	297	353	429	557	626
55	243	312	315	403	462	595
56	207	263	323	318	476	495
57	165	257	288	333	395	477
58	152	182	244	282	348	403
59	147	171	224	312	303	371
60	143	149	175	224	311	317
61	88	141	178	200	213	314
62	77	83	169	161	211	230
63	91	101	97	195	173	214
64	72	92	98	100	178	167
65	67	61	85	76	112	198
66	71	85	60	97	103	137
67	61	65	77	66	120	103
68	47	63	75	62	73	127

(*cont.*)

Age	2006	2007	2008	2009	2010	2011
69	64	59	71	78	85	92
70	45	76	59	78	104	98
71	63	51	85	59	76	129
72	59	54	69	71	76	79
73	56	58	70	56	68	66
74	62	49	46	74	71	91
75	32	63	42	63	67	82
76	34	60	55	51	64	79
77	50	64	58	55	49	76
78	31	42	52	53	74	58
79	54	44	38	64	62	57
80	56	46	34	51	46	54
81	49	48	40	44	46	40
82	42	36	49	46	40	59
83	36	47	45	25	32	41
84	30	42	39	34	28	28
85	29	23	37	27	35	24

Data on Publications on the "New Economy" and Their Citations

Year	Publications	Citations
1986	7	NA
1987	1	NA
1988	4	NA
1989	0	NA
1990	3	NA
1991	2	NA
1992	5	NA
1993	2	1
1994	4	3
1995	3	0
1996	4	3
1997	2	9

(cont.)

Year	Publications	Citations
1998	11	9
1999	7	14
2000	19	31
2001	35	43
2002	51	90
2003	41	107
2004	22	115
2005	20	150
2006	16	179
2007	11	239
2008	18	248
2009	13	274
2010	8	273
2011	17	262
2012	10	210
2013	9	236
2014	10	226
2015	8	244
2016	1	158

This final technical appendix of the book covers a brief discussion of so-called unit roots and stochastic trends and also briefly touches upon cointegration. The second topic deals with parameter estimation using the method of instrumental variables.

STOCHASTIC TRENDS

For econometricians, a trend in the data means that a model with an explicit expression for a trend can describe the data. The illustration earlier in this chapter is the regression model

$$y_t = \alpha + \beta t + \varepsilon_t,$$

where $t = 1, 2, 3, 4, \ldots, T$. Indeed, assume for ease of notation all ε_t are zero; then the first four observations of y_t are $\alpha + \beta$, $\alpha + 2\beta$, $\alpha + 3\beta$, $\alpha + 4\beta$, which clearly shows signs of an upward trend when β is positive.

Another model for a trend, with an implicit expression, is the following:

$$y_t = \beta + y_{t-1} + \varepsilon_t.$$

Assuming again that all ε_t are zero and letting the first observation be $y_1 = \alpha$, clearly the first four observations are also $\alpha + \beta, \alpha + 2\beta, \alpha + 3\beta, \alpha + 4\beta$. So, these two models can describe data with similar trends.

The key difference between the two models, however, is how the ε_t has an impact on future observations on y_t. For what is called the deterministic trend model,

$$y_t = \alpha + \beta t + \varepsilon_t,$$

the effect of ε_t only concerns the concurrent y_t. For what is called the stochastic trend model,

$$y_t = \beta + y_{t-1} + \varepsilon_t,$$

this is different. The difference is easiest seen by back substitution. This works as follows. For the stochastic trend model, we have

$$y_{t-1} = \beta + y_{t-2} + \varepsilon_{t-1}.$$

Plugging this into the first equation gives

$$y_t = \beta + \beta + y_{t-2} + \varepsilon_t + \varepsilon_{t-1}.$$

And if there is a y_0, then going on and on with this back substitution gives

$$y_t = \beta k + y_{t-k} + \varepsilon_t + \varepsilon_{t-1} + \ldots + \varepsilon_{t-(k-1)}$$
$$= y_0 + \beta t + \varepsilon_t + \varepsilon_{t-1} + \ldots + \varepsilon_1.$$

This shows that the current observation at time t still includes all past errors, all with unit weight. One also says that shocks or news from the past are still relevant, and hence that shocks are persistent. Another term for this stochastic trend model is that it is a random walk with drift. The best prediction for a model without such a drift, that is,

$$y_t = y_{t-1} + \varepsilon_t$$

is

$$\hat{y}_{t+1} = y_t.$$

The chances that the prediction is above or below y_t are equal, at least when ε_t has a symmetric distribution around 0; hence the term "random walk."

Now, why is this such a crucial case in (time-series) econometrics? This has to do with the mean and variance properties of the data, which depend on the model. For the model

$$y_t = \alpha + \beta t + \varepsilon_t,$$

the expected value of y_t is $\alpha + \beta t$, whereas the variance of $y_t - \alpha - \beta t$ is σ^2. For the model

$$y_t = \beta + y_{t-1} + \varepsilon_t$$

the expected value of y_t is $y_0 + \beta t$, but now the variance of $y_t - y_0 - \beta t$ is the sum of the variances of all the errors and hence is $t\sigma^2$. This means that with each new observation, there is another variance. This makes standard statistical analysis very difficult, as this suggests that each new observation corresponds with a new distribution.

This is also exemplified by the forecast errors. The, say, five-step-ahead forecast error for

$$y_t = \alpha + \beta t + \varepsilon_t$$

is

$$y_{t+5} - \hat{y}_{t+5} = a + b(t+5) + \varepsilon_{t+5} - \left(a + b(t+5) \right) = \varepsilon_{t+5}$$

with variance σ^2 (neglecting uncertainty in a and b). For

$$y_t = \beta + y_{t-1} + \varepsilon_t,$$

this five-step-ahead forecast error is

$$y_{t+5} - \hat{y}_{t+5} = y_0 + b(t+5) + \varepsilon_{t+5} + \varepsilon_{t+4} + \varepsilon_{t+3} + \varepsilon_{t+2}$$
$$+\varepsilon_{t+1} - \left(y_0 + b(t+5)\right) = \varepsilon_{t+5} + \varepsilon_{t+4} + \varepsilon_{t+3} + \varepsilon_{t+2} + \varepsilon_{t+1}$$

with variance $5\sigma^2$. So, for the random walk model we are much more uncertain about our forecasts than for the deterministic trend model, which is thus reflected by the word "deterministic."

Given that the two models describe data with a trend, it is common practice to test in a regression like

$$y_t = \alpha + \beta y_{t-1} + \gamma t + \varepsilon_t,$$

the null hypothesis that $\beta = 1$. The statistical theory behind this is not standard, as under the null hypothesis the model is a random walk model. In the econometrics literature, this topic is called "testing for unit roots."[14]

A further important issue in (time-series) econometrics is whether two or more time series that each have a stochastic trend perhaps have this trend in common. Having such a common trend is called cointegration.[15] To give some idea of this concept, consider again the first-order autoregression

$$y_t = \alpha + \beta y_{t-1} + \varepsilon_t$$

and write it as

$$y_t - \mu = \beta(y_{t-1} - \mu) + \varepsilon_t,$$

which makes uses of the notation

$$\alpha = (1 - \beta)\mu,$$

where μ is the unconditional mean of y_t. Now, write this last version of the model by subtracting from both sides $y_{t-1} - \mu$, that is,

$$y_t - y_{t-1} = (\beta - 1)(y_{t-1} - \mu) + \varepsilon_t.$$

On the left-hand side, you see increments (or differences) in y_t, and on the right-hand side, there is the difference between y_{t-1} and its unconditional mean. When $0 \leq \beta < 1$, then if $y_{t-1} > \mu$, there is a tendency (depending on the size of the concurrent ε_t) for $y_t - y_{t-1} < 0$, whereas when $y_{t-1} < \mu$, the tendency is for $y_t - y_{t-1} > 0$. So, when $0 \leq \beta < 1$, there is a tendency each time to move toward the mean μ. You may call this "error correction." Clearly, when $\beta = 1$, there is no such error correction at all, and there is the random walk.

This idea of error correction can also translate to two (or more) variables. Look again at the vector autoregression (in the appendix to Chapter 5), which reads as

$$y_t = \beta_1 y_{t-1} + \beta_2 x_{t-1} + \varepsilon_t,$$
$$x_t = \beta_3 y_{t-1} + \beta_4 x_{t-1} + \omega_t.$$

Assuming $\beta_1 \neq 1$, this two-equation model can be written as

$$y_t - y_{t-1} = (\beta_1 - 1)\left(y_{t-1} - \frac{\beta_2}{1 - \beta_1} x_{t-1}\right) + \varepsilon_t$$

$$x_t - x_{t-1} = -\beta_3\left(y_{t-1} - \frac{1 - \beta_4}{\beta_3} x_{t-1}\right) + \omega_t.$$

To make sure that there is only a single relationship between y_{t-1} and x_{t-1} that serves as an anchor point to which the series have a tendency to convert, the parameter restriction

$$\frac{\beta_2}{1 - \beta_1} = \frac{1 - \beta_4}{\beta_3} = \gamma$$

should hold, leading to

$$y_t - y_{t-1} = (\beta_1 - 1)(y_{t-1} - \gamma x_{t-1}) + \varepsilon_t,$$
$$x_t - x_{t-1} = \beta_3(y_{t-1} - \gamma x_{t-1}) + \omega_t.$$

So, cointegration is related to a parameter restriction. Taking the first equation, when $0 \leq \beta < 1$, if $y_{t-1} > \gamma x_{t-1}$, then there is tendency for $y_t - y_{t-1} < 0$, making the differences between y_t and γx_t smaller (which depends on the value of β_3). So, $y_t = \gamma x_t$ can be seen as some kind of equilibrium situation. When making forecasts for the two variables, under cointegration these forecasts have a tendency to stick together.

INSTRUMENTAL VARIABLES

Consider again the regression model

$$y_t = \alpha + \beta x_t + \varepsilon_t.$$

Now, one of the assumptions for the least squares technique to work well is that the x_t and ε_t are not correlated. Intuitively, if they would be correlated, then it is unclear what the estimator b for β is actually estimating. There are various approaches to solve this issue, and one simple method is the method of instrumental variables. What you need is an instrumental variable z_t that is uncorrelated with ε_t but that is correlated with x_t. Once you have this variable, and there are various ways to diagnose whether you have made the proper choice, then you consider the auxiliary regression model

$$x_t = \gamma + \delta z_t + v_t.$$

Apply least squares to this model to get the estimates c and d for γ and δ, respectively, and hence retrieve

$$\hat{x}_t = c + dz_t.$$

The original x_t is then replaced by $\hat{x}_t$ like

$$y_t = \alpha + \beta \hat{x}_t + \varepsilon_t.$$

Next, least squares is applied for this regression model.

9   The Takeaways

Tell me and I forget. Teach me and I remember. Involve me and I learn.

—Benjamin Franklin

In theory there is no difference between theory and practice. In practice there is.

—Yogi Berra

AT A GLANCE

Now that we have come to the end of this book, it is time to look at the main takeaways and attempt to wrap up. What did you learn – well, at least, in what was it that I tried to involve you?

Most prominently, I hope that by now you also feel, like me, that econometric methods and models can be useful in various dimensions. You can use them to interpret numbers, put these in position using benchmarks, and use them to say something about other numbers. You can tell if a certain number of cars means "many cars," and you can tell if aspects of soccer matches have anything to do with each other. You can make predictions on the future path of a variable given that you know the future path of another – or, at least, whether these two variables have something in common.

However, what I hope most is that you also feel, like me, that econometrics is a fascinating research area, which provides you with methods to answer all kinds of questions.

THE CHAPTERS

The key takeaway from the first chapter, as evidenced by a range of questions in subsequent chapters, is that any data analysis using econometric methods starts with a question. You might have seen that there is an enormous range of questions that can be addressed, and they could be of an economic nature, but they could also be very different. We talked about money; about collectibles; about art, music, and fashion; about sports records; about medication; and about what have you. But each time, the discussion started with a question. This is also why I do not have numbers next to the equations, nor do I have numbered sections; the only text that appears in the table of contents concerns the chapter titles.

Chapter 2 started with a very simple question: "Is four a lot?" This very basic question allows me to explain quite a few basic aspects of statistical or econometric analysis. The keyword here is "benchmark." We cannot say much about numbers if we do not have a benchmark. Benchmarks can be the average of similar data, where we have to know of course to what a number like four refers. Is it the number of children in a family or ownership of supercars? The average helps, the range a bit more, the variance of such data even more, and an empirical distribution most certainly. Sometimes questions can be answered using just these simple tools. With the histogram of the prices of products during the "three foolish days" in Chapter 4, you could immediately see that the actual prices were just fake. There was no discount, as there was no initial price to begin with. Most likely, it is the other way around. First, there is the final price, and then there is a random draw from a "distribution with discounts," which finally creates a hypothetical and random original price. This suggests that sometimes, simple methods can be very informative.

Textbooks on econometrics – and I coauthored one of them myself – usually start with a description of methods and models, and then later on these methods and models are applied to data to answer an illustrative question. This is all perfectly fine for textbooks, but it is good to know that in real life the sequence is reversed. First, there is a question, then we collect data, and then we see how we can use econometric methods to summarize the data such that an answer to the question can be given. Sometimes it can help to think about a model first prior to data collection. In the case of paying with cash money, some thinking about what the econometric model could be mattered for data collection, as the amount of data needed for reliable inference needed not be more than a few hundred (instead of ten thousands). So, basically, it is an interaction between question, data, and model. Professional econometricians approach this as chess players by phrasing a question such that they know that they can collect the data that later on would fit into a model. They think in advance before they start.

Chapter 2 also dealt with the key workhorse of econometrics: the regression model. This model will do in many situations, and I showed in various chapters that if you reshape the data somewhat, the model could come in handy, even if the data contain much detail. In many other situations, the simple regression model will not do, and extensions or modifications are in order. In the appendices to all chapters, I gave some examples of those variants, and of course, this is a very limited set of examples. The number of potential methods and models is sheer infinite, and no econometrician masters them all. In fact, at the very moment of my writing and your reading this sentence, someone somewhere is developing a new method or model. Usually such new methods are needed because of peculiar features of data or because the question requires a tediously formulated theoretical model, which in turn has to be translated to an expression useful for actual data. As a nice example, think of financial stock returns where the data in the tails, which are the more exceptional observations (think of booms and bursts), are of more interest than the data in the middle of the distribution. Well, even more so, it so happens that the observations in the tails are also connected and correlated. This means that the large positive and negative stock returns seem to occur in clusters. This has led to a Nobel Prize–worthy econometric model.[1]

Models can also become difficult because we often have to deal with nonexperimental data. That is, there is only a single observation on GDP for each quarter, and we cannot play around with other GDP values for that very same quarter. In contrast, in supermarkets one may try out various price levels across the weeks and then see how sales fare. The price levels are controlled by the manager, and then you can run "experiments." So, experimental data may allow for the application of simpler tools, as we also saw in Chapter 4, but then data collection could become more cumbersome.

Chapter 3 shows that careful data collection is important. Sometimes you can think of a model that you will need and then simulate how many observations you may need to collect to be able to make some reliable statements. Think of tossing a coin. To get a number close to 0.5 for the fraction of heads (or tails) when tossing a coin, you need maybe 30 or 40 tosses. Of course, millions of tosses will give you a number closer to 0.5, but with 30 or 40, it is already close enough to say that you have a proper coin.

A question that students often ask is "How many data should I collect?," and here you see that this question cannot be answered. You may need to know in advance the type of model that you have in mind. Also, variation is key, as is the number of questions and the number of answer categories in a questionnaire. For the Profit Bank case, we could interview just 50 people, as there were only four potential explanatory variables and each of them could take a value of 1 or 0. In such a setting, it may not be necessary to collect thousands of interviews.

What does help when using nonexperimental data is that there is something that happens from the outset. With the payment with cash studies, this was the introduction of the euro on January 1, 2002. Then you can analyze the data before and after to see if something has changed. Also, the change to rounding to 5 cents marked a moment in time to collect data before and after to see if things differ. So, when you foresee that something is going to change, then you may already want to start collecting data before that event happens.

In Chapter 4, I took you on a short tour on financial literacy. Interestingly enough, even though we have to make many numerical exercises per day when we do our shopping, when we have to take a bus on time, or when we purchase something on the Internet, it is often found that people may lack even the most basic skills. Also, it is not difficult to fool people. Simple experiments were set to highlight a few such notions. Of course, much more detailed experimental data should be collected to really "prove" matters, but here it turned out that some simple questions and well-designed hypothetical products could elicit how humans make all kinds of mistakes.

This chapter also alluded to a technique called conjoint analysis,[2] which allows you to collect data on people's preferences for hypothetical products. As such, you can control the attributes of these products, and you can create an experimental setting in which people can also quickly give answers, which allows for a potential wealth of information. The data are again quite easy to analyze.

A principle takeaway from Chapter 5 is that you may take some time to think about what the variables really are that you want to put into an econometric model. It is definitively not the case that all spreadsheets contain ready-to-copy-and-paste columns with nicely ordered dependent and explanatory variables. Sometimes you need the data to define new data, which are associated with the variables of interest. As was the case for the trends in Chapter 7, where trends only exist thanks to an econometric model that is designed to describe data with a trend, a price bubble also needs to be defined as such. This can be done in various ways, and one may think a bit on which definition could be useful for later modeling. So, it is better not to take the raw data for granted and start from there, but perhaps first explore the data themselves in more detail. Check the data, and find missing values, strange values, reporting errors, and the like. Next, you may think of transforming the data into another format, perhaps by taking natural logs or otherwise. It is better to do that first rather than after you have estimated any model parameters. Strange observations can mess up the entire analysis. Or, even worse, they can make outcomes look good while these outcomes only depend on typos.

Spurious correlations can also be found when the wrong model is used. The appendix to Chapter 5 indicated that it is not difficult to find suggestive links between otherwise completely independent variables. So, it is important to check the model and its quality and not just run out of your office yelling "Eureka!" before you have checked and double-checked again and again.

Chapter 6 illuminated that preparation of data sometimes already involves the use of econometric models. That is, econometric models and methods can be useful to arrange the data for further analysis, and in a next round the earlier obtained estimated data will be considered again using other methods and models.

One basic takeaway from the analysis of four samples with data on creative individuals is that adding the data into one big sample is not necessarily a good idea. You may be tempted to believe that more data are better, but if more data also introduce more variation or noise, then adding samples does a disservice. So, bigger (or more) is not always beautiful.

Chapter 7 talked about various ins and outs of the publication process. Academics like me are supposed to write papers and publish these as articles in international scientific journals. The number of top journals is small, and everyone wants to get in there, as this helps your career. The amount of academics is large, and hence there is quite a rat race going on to get into the premier league. There are even rankings of economists based on their output. With these rankings, I showed that those who publish more also acquire more citations faster. Those citations are a measure of impact, and university officials want to appoint academics who publish a lot and who have impact. Not everybody agrees with this attitude, but for the moment, this is how it is.

I felt like paying a tribute to various top econometricians by zooming in on a few articles that have thousands of citations. Showing some data on my own articles and citations provided a kind of benchmark; clearly, I have a long way to go, and I reluctantly have to admit that this road most likely will go nowhere. But, as Lao Tzu said, "A good traveler has no fixed plans, and is not intent on arriving."

Finally, Chapter 8 dealt with trends. Some trends will never come to end, some may converge to some final value, and some trends just disappear. When you deal with never-ending trends, you may want to collect data for long spans of time. Another takeaway is that sometimes the simple regression model seems to do while it does not. Correlation across errors in equations, or simultaneity, quickly call for alternative models and methods. Then conclusions can become quite different. So, it is important to look back at the basic assumptions of econometric methods to see if they plausibly hold for the data and question at hand. They may not, and then alternatives are warranted. Econometric textbooks will tell you what these alternatives are, and there are many.

And that brings me to the main takeaway of this book, and that is the following. If you liked what you have been reading so far, then now it is time to buy a real econometric textbook! Chapter 2 gave a list, and there are others too. I have tried to give you some flavor of what econometrics can do, but there is so much more.

Thanks for bearing with me throughout this book! I hope you enjoyed reading it as much as I did writing it.

Notes

2 CORRELATION AND REGRESSION

1. https://en.wikipedia.org/wiki/Variable
2. https://en.wikipedia.org/wiki/Zipf%27s_law provides a concise account of the law of Zipf
3. www.theguardian.com/books/2015/jan/13/is-there-an-ideal-age-to-write-a -masterpiece-infographic
4. Most computations in this book are performed using the software package Eviews. Other statistical software can be used as well as programming tools like Excel, R, and Matlab.
5. My similar investigation into peak creativity resulted in three published articles. These are (2013), When do painters make their best work?, *Creativity Research Journal*, 25, 457–462; (2014), When do Nobel Prize laureates in literature make their best work?, *Creativity Research Journal*, 26, 372–374; and (2016), When did classic composers make their best work?, *Creativity Research Journal*, 28, 219–221. For the 2013 article, I did similar calculations for 189 deceased painters, while the 2014 article deals with 89 deceased Nobel laureates in literature, and the 2016 article concerns 100 classic composers. The average ages of peak creativity turned out to be 41.9, 44.8, and 38.9, respectively. But what is more interesting is that these peaks occurred at the fractions 0.620, 0.570, and 0.613 of the lives of these creative individuals. Hence, there seems to be a remarkably constant factor in the link between age and peak creativity.
6. Note that Amy Winehouse, Kurt Cobain, and Jimi Hendrix died at the age of 27, and this might be considered as exceptionally young. Winehouse became most famous due to her album *Back to Black*, which appeared when she was 23. Cobain attained international fame with his band Nirvana and record *Nevermind* at age 24. And Hendrix's most successful record was *Are You Experienced?*, which was released in 1967 when he was 24. The average relative age of these successes is around 0.87, which is not at all close to 0.6.

7. A serious statistical analysis of when it is best to make such a foul is presented in Geert Ridder, J.S. (Mars) Cramer, and Peter Hopstaken (1994), Down to ten: Estimating the effects of a red card in soccer, *Journal of the American Statistical Association*, 89, 1124–1127.

8. Full derivations can be found in Chapter 2 in Christiaan Heij, Paul de Boer, Philip Hans Franses, Teun Kloek, and Herman van Dijk (2004), *Econometric Methods, with Applications in Business and Economics*, Oxford: Oxford University Press.

9. See again Chapter 2 in Christiaan Heij, Paul de Boer, Philip Hans Franses, Teun Kloek, and Herman van Dijk (2004), *Econometric Methods, with Applications in Business and Economics*, Oxford: Oxford University Press.

10. These data, as well as all data in this and the following chapters, are available from www.enjoyable-econometrics.com.

11. The law of Zipf says that there is a relation between the ranking and the scores. Call the ranks r_i and the scores z_i, then the law predicts that

$$\frac{r_i}{z_i^\gamma} = \delta.$$

Taking natural logs on both sides gives

$\log(r_i) - \gamma \log(z_i) = \delta.$

After rearranging, this becomes

$$\log(z_i) = -\frac{\delta}{\gamma} + \frac{1}{\gamma}\log r_i,$$

which is the linear relationship depicted in the scatter.

3 MONEY

1. www.bbc.com/news/business-36208146 (May 4, 2016): "The European Central Bank (ECB) says it will no longer produce the €500 (£400; $575) note because of concerns it could facilitate illegal activities. The decision comes in the wake of a European Commission inquiry in February into the way the notes are used. Senior ECB officials said at the time that they needed more evidence that the notes facilitated criminal activity. The UK asked banks to stop handling €500 notes in 2010 after a report found they were mainly used by criminals. The ECB says the €500 banknote remains legal tender and will always retain its value."

2. An interesting early study is Willem C. Boeschoten and Martin M. G. Fase (1989), The way we pay with money, *Journal of Business & Economics Statistics*, 7, 319–326.

3. See Jeanine Kippers, Erjen van Nierop, Richard Paap, and Philip Hans Franses (2003), An empirical study of cash payments, *Statistica Neerlandica*, 57, 484–508, for more details and also a statistical model to solve the key problem with the data, to be discussed next, and that was that the wallet contents were not observed.

4. There are several studies on the optimal range of denominations for coins and notes, and it can be argued that both the NLG denomination range and the EUR range are optimal in some dimension. See Lester Telser (1995), Optimal denominations for coins and currency, *Economics Letters*, 49, 425–427; and Mark A. Wynne (1997), More on the optimal denominations for coins and currency, *Economics Letters*, 55, 221–225, for two interesting accounts.

5. A very nice and alternative way of collecting data on money illusion is presented in Eldar Shafir, Peter A. Diamond, and Amos Tversky (1997), On money illusion, *Quarterly Journal of Economics*, 112(2), 341–374. This study is replicated in Heleen Mees and Philip Hans Franses (2014), Are individuals in China prone to money illusion?, *Journal of Behavioral and Experimental Economics*, 51, 38–46, for the case of China. This data collection method is based on survey questions. The method described in the current section is actually based on what people apparently do. Other relevant studies on money illusion are Amelie Gamble, Tommy Garling, John Charlton, and Rob Ranyard (2002), Euro-illusion: Psychological insights into price evaluations with a unitary currency, *European Psychologist*, 7, 302–311; Priya Raghubir and Joydeep Srivastava (2002), Effect of face value of product valuation in foreign currencies, *Journal of Consumer Research*, 29, 335–347; Markus K. Brunnermeier and Christian Julliard (2008), Money illusion and housing frenzies, *Review of Financial Studies*, 21, 135–180; Ernst Fehr and Jean-Robert Tyran (2001), Does money illusion matter? *American Economic Review*, 91, 1239–1262; Irving Fisher (1928), *The Money Illusion*, New York, NY: Adelphi Company; Charles N. Noussair, Gregers Richter, and Jean-Robert Tyran (2008), Money illusion and nominal inertia in experimental asset markets, http://papers.ssrn.com/sol3/papers.cfm?abstract_id=1307717; Don Patinkin (1965), *Money, Interest, and Prices*, New York, NY: Harper

and Row; Eldar Shafir and Richard H. Thaler (2006), Invest now, drink later, spend never: On the mental accounting of delayed consumption, *Journal of Economic Psychology*, 27, 694–712.

6. I am very grateful to my undergraduate students (in those days) – Tim Berretty, Sven Dijkshoorn, and Lotje Kruithof – for their help with collecting the data.

7. It could be that part of these differences can be explained by the notion that people, when making their NLG computations, ignored that a few years with inflation have occurred in the meantime.

8. The *t*-test is explained in the Appendix. It is a *t* test that compares two averages.

9. Finland created 1 and 2 EUR cent coins but opted to remove them from circulation at an early stage. A UNC (uncirculated) 1-cent Finnish coin costs around 7.50 EUR halfway through 2016.

10. https://en.wikipedia.org/wiki/Mars_Cramer says: "Jan Salomon (Mars) Cramer (28 April 1928–15 March 2014) was a Dutch economist, Professor of Statistics and Econometrics at the University of Amsterdam, known for his work of empirical econometrics."

11. J.S. (Mars) Cramer (1983), Currency by denomination, *Economics Letters*, 12, 299–303.

12. See Jeanine Kippers, Erjen van Nierop, Richard Paap, and Philip Hans Franses (2003), An empirical study of cash payments, *Statistica Neerlandica*, 57, 484–508, for the technical details.

13. As the data are counts, like 1, 2, 3, the regression model will rely not on a Gaussian (normal) distribution but on a Poisson distribution. The lemma https://en.wikipedia.org/wiki/Poisson_regression reads: "In statistics, Poisson regression is a generalized linear model form of regression analysis used to model count data and contingency tables. Poisson regression assumes the response variable Y has a Poisson distribution, and assumes the logarithm of its expected value can be modeled by a linear combination of unknown parameters. A Poisson regression model is sometimes known as a log-linear model, especially when used to model contingency tables."

14. Jeanine Kippers, Erjen van Nierop, Richard Paap, and Philip Hans Franses (2003), An empirical study of cash payments, *Statistica Neerlandica*, 57, 484–508.

15. Some people might argue that the NLG 50 note was so beautiful that
    individuals could have been hesitant to use it. However, no formal proof of
    this claim exists. Here is what the note looks like.

16. Philip Hans Franses and Jeanine Kippers (2007), An empirical analysis
    of euro cash payments, *European Economic Review*, 51, 1985–1997.
17. This theory part was circulated as Philip Hans Franses and Jeanine Kippers
    (2003), Do we need all euro denominations?, Econometric Institute Report
    2003-39, Erasmus University Rotterdam.
18. Philip Hans Franses and Jeanine Kippers (2010), How do we pay with euro
    notes when some notes are missing? Empirical evidence from Monopoly
    experiments, *Applied Financial Economics*, 20, 459–464.

19. This part of this chapter draws from Govert Bijwaard and Philip Hans Franses (2009), The effect of rounding on payment efficiency, *Computational Statistics and Data Analysis*, 53, 1449–1461.

4   FINANCIAL LITERACY AND NUMERACY

1. These prices were actually observed in August 2014 at one of the surf shops in Seignosse, France, which boasts one of the best beaches in Europe for surfing.
2. A milestone reading in this area is the classic John Allen Paulos (1988), *Innumeracy: Mathematical Illiteracy and Its Consequences*, New York, NY: Hill & Wang.
3. Interesting readings are Ariel Rubinstein (1998), *Modeling Bounded Rationality*. Cambridge, MA: Massachusetts Institute of Technology Press; and Herbert Simon (1991), Bounded rationality and organizational learning, *Organization Science*, 2, 125–134.
4. Dan Ariely (2010), *Predictably Irrational: The Hidden Forces That Shape Our Decisions*, New York, NY: HarperCollins Publishers.
5. Amos Tversky and Daniel Kahneman (1974), Judgment under uncertainty: Heuristics and biases, *Science*, 185 (4157), 1124–1131; and Amos Tversky and Daniel Kahneman (1981), The framing of decisions and the psychology of choice, *Science*, 211 (4481), 453–458.
6. A recent very readable account on this issue is George A. Akerlof and Robert J. Shiller (2015), *Phishing for Phools; The Economics of Manipulation and Deception*, Princeton, NJ: Princeton University Press.
7. The landmark piece on nudging is of course Richard H. Thaler and Cass R. Sunstein (2009), *Nudge; Improving Decisions about Health, Wealth and Happiness*, London: Penguin Books.
8. That consumers find it difficult to perform computations with interest rates is also documented in John Allen Paulos (1988), *Innumeracy: Mathematical Illiteracy and Its Consequences*, New York, NY: Hill & Wang; and in Haipeng Chen and Akshay R. Rao (2007), When two plus two is not equal to four: Errors in processing multiple percentage changes, *Journal of Consumer Research*, 34, 327–340.
9. Much of the material in this section draws upon the unpublished report Philip Hans Franses and Anita Vlam (2011a), Financial innumeracy: Consumers cannot deal with interest rates, Econometric Institute Report 2011-01, Erasmus University Rotterdam. Anita Vlam graduated as a PhD at

the Erasmus School of Economics in December 2011 with her dissertation titled "Customer first? The relationship between advisors and consumers of financial products."

10. Interesting studies are Subimal Chatterjee, Timothy Heath, Sandra Milberg, and Karen France (2000), The differential processing of price in gains and losses: The effect of frame and need for cognition, *Journal of Behavioral Decision Making*, 13, 61–75; Timothy Heath, Subimal Chatterjee, and Karen R. France (1995), Mental accounting and changes in price: The frame dependence of reference dependence, *Journal of Consumer Research*, 22, 90–97; Marianne Hilgert, Jeanne Hogarth, and Sondra Beverly (2003), Household financial management: The connection between knowledge and behavior, *Federal Reserve Bulletin*, 309–332; Annemaria Lusardi and Olivia S. Mitchell (2008), Planning and financial literacy: How do women fare?, *American Economic Review*, 98, 413–417; and Annemaria Lusardi and Peter Tufano (2009), Debt literacy, financial experiences, and overindebtedness, Working paper, Dartmouth College.

11. This material draws upon "Borrowing money costs money": Yes, but why not tell how much? by Philip Hans Franses and Anita Vlam, Econometric Institute Report 2011-02, Erasmus University Rotterdam.

12. A similar research design was implemented for couches. We chose this second product as we held the survey among undergraduate students at Erasmus School of Economics. Some prior experimentation showed that these two products were actually considered by students, where also the three different levels of payment methods were considered as realistic. In addition to the indicated choices, we also asked students to reveal their gender, age, and income level.

13. These experiments were carried out in Zsolt Sandor and Philip Hans Franses (2009), Consumer prices evaluation through choice experiments, *Journal of Applied Econometrics*, 24, 517–535.

14. Together with my then undergraduate student Siebe Versendaal, I published the outcomes of our experiments in the Dutch language magazine *Economisch Statistische Berichten*, 97, 633–634. The translated title of that article is "It is still possible to fool people using financial products."

15. Amos Tversky and Daniel Kahneman (1981), The framing of decisions and the psychology of choice, *Science*, 211(4481), 453–458.

16. For full derivations, see Chapter 3 of Christiaan Heij, Paul de Boer, Philip Hans Franses, Teun Kloek, and Herman van Dijk (2004), *Econometric Methods, with Applications in Business and Economics*, Oxford: Oxford University Press.

17. See Alexander M. Mood, Franklin A. Graybill, and Duane C. Boes (1974), *Introduction to the Theory of Statistics, Third Edition*, International Student Edition, McGraw Hill Publishers, page 540 (a book that I studied when I was an undergraduate student in between 1982 and 1987 at the University of Groningen).

18. See Chapter 6 in Christiaan Heij, Paul de Boer, Philip Hans Franses, Teun Kloek, and Herman van Dijk (2004), *Econometric Methods, with Applications in Business and Economics*, Oxford: Oxford University Press; or Chapter 4 of Philip Hans Franses and Richard Paap (2001), *Quantitative Models in Marketing Research*, Cambridge: Cambridge University Press.

19. I am indebted to my colleague and regular coauthor Richard Paap for making this marvelous picture.

5   POSTAGE STAMPS AND BANKNOTES

1. www.forstercoinsandcollectablesgroup.com.au/banknotes/

2. Recent interesting studies on the issue of whether it pays off to invest in art are Arthur Korteweg, Roman Kräussl, and Patrick Verwijmeren (2016), Does it pay to invest in art? A selection-corrected returns perspective, *Review of Financial Studies*, 29, 1007–1038; Bruno S. Frey and Reiner Eichenberger (1995), On the rate of return in the art market: Survey and evaluation, *European Economic Review*, 39, 528–537; Benjamin J. Burton and Joyce P. Jacobson (1999), Measuring returns on investments in collectibles, *Journal of Economic Perspectives*, 13, 193–212.

3. The first part of this chapter is based on Philip Hans Franses and Wouter Knecht (2016), The late 1970s bubble in Dutch collectible postage stamps, *Empirical Economics*, 50, 1215–1228.

4. Rare banknotes are expensive; see http://notes.bonnum.com/.

5. There is much ado about bubbles in the economic literature, and a few key references are Kenneth A. Froot and Maurice Obstfeld (1991), Intrinsic bubbles: The case of stock prices, *American Economic Review*, 81, 1189–1214; John Kenneth Galbraith (1993), *A Short History of Financial*

Euphoria, New York, NY: Viking; Peter M. Garber (1990), Famous first bubbles, *Journal of Economic Perspectives*, 4, 35–54; Stephen F. LeRoy (2004), Rational exuberance, *Journal of Economic Literature*, 42, 783–804; Vernon L. Smith, Gerry L. Suchanek, and Arlington W. Williams (1988), Bubbles, crashes, and endogenous expectations in experimental spot asset markets, *Econometrica*, 56, 1119–1151; and Kenneth D. West (1987), A specification test for speculative bubbles, *Quarterly Journal of Economics*, 102, 553–580.

6. A detailed analysis of the properties of China's GDP is provided in Philip Hans Franses, and Heleen Mees (2013), Approximating the DGP of China's quarterly GDP, *Applied Economics*, 45, 3469–3472.

7. The method is explained in more detail in my 2016 paper: A simple test for a bubble based on growth and acceleration, *Computational Statistics and Data Analysis*, 100, 160–169.

8. The R^2 automatically goes up when more variables are included. The adjusted R^2 takes account of that. It is computed as

$$\overline{R}^2 = 1 - \frac{n-1}{n-(k+1)}(1 - R^2),$$

where k is the number of variables in a multiple regression model.

9. The section draws upon my 2006 paper: Empirical causality between bigger banknotes and inflation, *Applied Economics Letters*, 13, 751–752. I must mention that I am (still) very grateful to Lotje Kruithof for her enormous efforts to collect the data.

10. For a list of the 50 main hyperinflation periods, see Steve H. Hanke and Nicholas Krus (2012), World Hyperinflations, Cato Working Paper no. 8, August 15, 2012, published in Randall Parker and Robert Whaples (eds.) (2013), *The Handbook of Major Events in Economic History*, London: Routledge Publishing.

11. Theoretical discussions on these matters appear in, for example, Chaunan Chen (1976), Currency denominations and the price level, *Journal of Political Economy*, 84, 179–183; and Willem C. Boeschoten and Martin M. G. Fase (1992), The demand for large banknotes, *Journal of Money, Credit and Banking*, 24, 319–337. A very readable book about monetary systems, payment with cash, and various historical events is Thomas J. Sargent and François R. Velde (2002), *The Big Problem of Small Change*, Princeton, NJ: Princeton University Press.

12. This type of examination – that is, to see if one lagged variable helps to forecast another variable – is commonly associated with a concept called Granger causality, named after Clive W.J. Granger, one of the most influential econometricians ever. More on his work appears in Chapter 7.

13. An alternative analysis of a subset of the data analyzed here appeared as my 2007 paper: Estimating the stock of postwar Dutch postal stamps, *Applied Economics*, 39, 943–946.

14. Full derivations can be found on page 311 in Christiaan Heij, Paul de Boer, Philip Hans Franses, Teun Kloek, and Herman van Dijk (2004), *Econometric Methods, with Applications in Business and Economics*, Oxford: Oxford University Press.

15. This result is attributed to the well-known econometrician Halbert White, although earlier results were available with similar thoughts; see https://en.wikipedia.org/wiki/Heteroscedasticity-consistent_standard_er rors. The Wikipedia lemma https://en.wikipedia.org/wiki/Halbert_White says: "Halbert Lynn White, Jr. (November 19, 1950–March 31, 2012) was the Chancellor's Associates Distinguished Professor of Economics at the University of California, San Diego, and a Fellow of the Econometric Society and the American Academy of Arts and Sciences. He earned his PhD in Economics at the Massachusetts Institute of Technology in 1976, and spent his first years as an assistant professor in the University of Rochester before moving to UCSD in 1979. He was well known in the field of econometrics for his 1980 paper on robust standard errors (which is the most-cited paper in economics since 1970), and for the heteroskedasticity-consistent estimator and the test for heteroskedasticity that are named after him."

16. This result goes back to Arnold Zellner (1962), An efficient method of estimating seemingly unrelated regression equations and tests for aggregation bias, *Journal of the American Statistical Association*, 57, 348–368. A first version of this article appeared as Econometric Institute Report EI-6114 in 1961, at what was then called the Netherlands School of Economics. Zellner was a regular visitor of the Rotterdam-based Econometric Institute in those days. Wikipedia says: "Arnold Zellner (January 2, 1927–August 11, 2010) was an American economist and statistician specializing in the fields of Bayesian probability and econometrics. Zellner contributed pioneering work in the field of Bayesian analysis and econometric modeling." In 2006, Arnold Zellner

was bestowed with an honorary doctorate at the Erasmus School of Economics on the occasion of the 50th anniversary of this Econometric Institute.

17. This is one of the ideas of the very influential article: Christopher A. Sims (1980), Macroeconomics and reality, *Econometrica*, 48, 1–48.

18. There are many studies on spurious relationships between time series variables. The classic pieces are G. Udny Yule (1926), Why do we sometimes get nonsense correlations between time-series? A study in sampling and the nature of time-series, *Journal of the Royal Statistical Society Series* A, 89, 1–69; and Edward Ames and Stanley Reiter (1961), Distributions of correlation coefficients in economic time series, *Journal of the American Statistical Association*, 56, 637–656. A recent humorous book is the one by Tyler Vigen (2015), *Spurious Correlations; Correlation Does Not Equal Causation*, New York, NY: Hachette Books, which essentially reiterates the exercises of Edward Ames and Stanley Reiter.

19. This is the familiar spurious correlation case noted by Clive W. J. Granger and Paul Newbold in their (1974) study: Spurious regressions in econometrics, *Journal of Econometrics*, 2, 111–120. Even when the sample gets larger, the correlation persists.

20. This empirical result was proved in theory by Peter C. B. Phillips in his 1986 article: Understanding spurious regressions in econometrics, *Journal of Econometrics*, 33, 311–340.

6   FASHION, ART, AND MUSIC

1. This part is largely based on Marjolein van Baardwijk and Philip Hans Franses (2010), The hemline and the economy: Is there any match? Econometric Institute Report 2010-40, Erasmus School of Economics. A condensed version of this report was published as Hemlines and the economy: Which goes down first?, *Foresight, The International Journal of Applied Forecasting*, 2012 (Summer), 27–28.

2. There is a lemma at Wikipedia, but unfortunately it is not very informative: https://en.wikipedia.org/wiki/Hemline_index.

3. www.lofficielmode.com/

4. http://partimoine.jalougallery.com/lofficiel-de-la-mode-sommairepatri moine-13.html

5. There is much to say about dealing with missing values, and I cannot deal with that issue in the current book. But a very useful reference is the 2002

book *Statistical Analysis with Missing Data* by Roderick J. A. Little and Donald B. Rubin, published by Wiley (New York, NY). If you hold a survey among respondents, and some of those forget to answer one or two questions, one may opt to delete the associated questionnaires, but that could mean quite a loss of information on the other questions that were answered. A sensible strategy could however be to replace the missing information by some kind of an average of the answers that other (perhaps similar) respondents gave. This strategy would only make sense if the missing data were, as we say, missing at random. Indeed, when the missing data would associate with unwillingness to answer questions on purpose, then matters become very different. One may then resort to include in the model a part that addresses the willingness to answer. So, part 1 of the model deals with "yes" or "no" provision of an answer (perhaps using a logit model as in Chapter 4) and next, if there is an answer, then part 2 of the model seeks to explain the answer, perhaps with a multiple regression model.

6. The National Bureau of Economic Research (NBER) provides the dates of recessions and expansions for the US economy (www.nber.org/cycles/rec essions.html). This is of course not the only economy in the world, but it is often found that the US economy plays a leading role in worldwide economic development.

7. The data for painters are given in my 2013 paper: When do painters make their best work?, *Creativity Research Journal*, 25, 457–462. When performing the analysis on the regression model in this chapter, I noticed a typing error in the dataset. The data for Georgia O'Keeffe should be that she was born 1887 and died in 1986.

8. There is some evidence that our cognitive skills decline after the age of 45; see Elizabeth L. Glisky (2007), Changes in cognitive function in human aging, in D.R. Riddle (ed.), *Brain Aging: Models, Methods, Mechanisms*, Boca Raton, FL: CRC Press, 1–15; and Archana Singh-Manoux, Mika Kivimaki, Maria Glymour, Alexis Elbaz, Claudine Berr, Klaus P. Ebmeier, Jane E. Ferrie, and Aline Dugravot (2012), Timing of onset of cognitive decline: Results from Whitehall II prospective cohort study, *British Medical Journal*, 344, d7622.

9. The Wikipedia page https://en.wikipedia.org/wiki/Top_2000 explains how the charts come about: "The Top 2000 is an annual marathon radio program, that plays the 2000 most popular songs of all time, from

Christmas through New Year's Eve. Hosted by Dutch national radio station Radio 2, over half of the population of the Netherlands listens to the broadcast each year. Starting in 1999, the Top 2000 was intended to be a one-time event, but due to the program's popularity, Radio 2 chose to make it an annual program, traditionally broadcast from midnight on Boxing Day and continuing until midnight of New Year's Eve. However, as of 2009, the show begins broadcasting at noon on December 25, Christmas Day. During the 6 to 7 day broadcast, the station broadcasts a set of 2000 songs that have been voted on by the show's audience via Internet voting to be the 'most popular songs of all time.'" This database provides a unique opportunity to examine trends over time.

10. From https://en.wikipedia.org/wiki/Boudewijn_de_Groot: "Boudewijn de Groot (Dutch pronunciation: [ˈbʌu̯dəʋɛi̯n də ˈɣroːt], born 20 May 1944) is a famous Dutch singer/songwriter. He is known for the songs 'Welterusten Meneer de President' (1966), 'Het Land van Maas en Waal (nl)' (1967), 'Jimmy (nl)' (1973) and 'Avond (nl)' (1996) among others. On 20 April 2015, he issued his latest album Achter glas (nl) (Behind glass)."

11. That the variable itself is an estimated variable is not a problem as that additional variation will be covered by ε. When X is an estimated variable, matters become different. This is associated with what is called the problem of generated regressors. Adrian Pagan wrote the key article on this topic: Econometric issues in the analysis of regressions with generated regressors, *International Economic Review*, 25(1984), 221–247.

12. See Frank M. Bass (1969), A new product growth model for consumer durables, *Management Science*, 15, 215–227, for a full derivation.

13. More on this method of nonlinear least squares in Chapter 4 of Christiaan Heij, Paul de Boer, Philip Hans Franses, Teun Kloek, and Herman K. van Dijk (2004), *Econometric Methods and Application in Business and Economics*, Oxford: Oxford University Press.

14. The lemma https://en.wikipedia.org/wiki/Frank_Bass says: "Frank M. Bass (1926–2006) was an American academic in the field of marketing research and marketing science. He was the creator of the Bass diffusion model that describes the adoption of new products and technologies by first-time buyers. He died on December 1, 2006."

15. Various relevant references of the Bass model are Frank M. Bass (1969), A new product growth model for consumer durables, *Management*

Science, 15, 215–227; H. Peter Boswijk and Philip Hans Franses (2005), On the econometrics of the Bass diffusion model, *Journal of Business and Economic Statistics*, 23, 255–268; William P. Putsis. and V. Srinivasan (2000), Estimation techniques for macro diffusion models, Chapter 11 in Vijay Mahajan, Eitan Muller, and Yoram Wind (eds.), *New-Product Diffusion Models*, Boston, MA: Kluwer, 263–291; V. Srinivasan and Charlotte H. Mason (1986), Nonlinear least squares estimation of new product diffusion models, *Marketing Science*, 5, 169–178; and Christophe Van den Bulte and Gary L. Lilien (1997), Bias and systematic change in the parameter estimates of macro-level diffusion models, *Marketing Science*, 16, 338–353.

7   ACADEMIC PUBLICATIONS

1. This part draws upon my paper that was published in 2002: From first submission to citation: An empirical analysis, *Statistica Neerlandica*, 56, 497–510. I have been the editor-in-chief of this journal for more than 10 years, and this paper was something like an editor's testimonial.
2. This matches with the findings of Glenn Ellison, reported in his 2002 study: The slowdown of the economics publishing, *Journal of Political Economy*, 105, 947–993.
3. The study of Joshua S. Gans and George B. Shepherd (1994), How are the mighty fallen: Rejected classic articles by leading economists, *Journal of Economic Perspectives*, 8, 165–179, is a nice and fascinating example of this.
4. Very readable accounts are Pravin Trivedi (1993), An analysis of publication lags in econometrics, *Journal of Applied Econometrics*, 8, 93–100; Daniel Hamermesh (1994), Facts and myths about refereeing, *Journal of Economic Perspectives*, 8, 153–163; and Marc D. Street, Dennis P. Bozeman, and J. Michael Whitfield (1998), Author perceptions of positive and negative editor behaviors in the manuscript review process, *Journal of Social Behavior and Personality*, 13, 1–22.
5. A nice example is the often-cited article by Janice M. Beyer, Roland G. Chanove, and William B. Fox (1995), The review process and the fates of manuscripts submitted to AMJ, *Academy of Management Journal*, 38, 1219–1260.
6. See, for example, Harry P. van Dalen and Kène Henkens (2001), What makes a scientific article influential?, *Scientometrics*, 50, 455–482. The journal

Scientometrics, by the way, is nowadays almost completely dedicated to the measurement of scientific quality and impact.

7. The notion of "patent" is quite important, in particular for younger researchers, as sometimes colleagues suddenly appear to have the same idea as you did. The ultimate case in which the notion of patent does not work out is when one finds out that one's paper has been copied to a large extent and published elsewhere. As an example, the paper of Weixian Wei (2002), Forecasting stock market volatility with non-linear GARCH models: A case for China, *Applied Economics Letters*, 9, 163–166, shows a remarkable overlap with my paper with Dick van Dijk in 1996, Forecasting stock market volatility using (non-linear) GARCH models, *Journal of Forecasting*, 15, 229–235.

8. The paper that took 24 months to be physically published in 1995 is my piece with Peter Boswijk titled Periodic cointegration – Representation and inference, *The Review of Economics and Statistics*, 77, 436–454. As of December 2016, it was cited 22 times.

9. I am very grateful to my student assistant (in 2015) Wouter Knecht for his help with collecting the data.

10. In the economic sciences, this has already been a common practice for years; see, for example, Badi H. Baltagi (2007), Worldwide econometrics rankings: 1989–2005, *Econometric Theory*, 23, 952–1012, for a worldwide ranking of econometricians; and Jan C. van Ours and Frederic M. P. Vermeulen (2007), Ranking Dutch economists, *De Economist*, 155, 469–487, for a ranking of Dutch economists. Recently, I compiled a historical overview of more than three decades of rankings of Dutch economists; see my 2014, paper: Trends in three decades of rankings of Dutch economists, *Scientometrics*, 98, 1257–1268.

11. See, for example, Institute for Higher Education Policy (IHEP) (2009), Impact of College Rankings on Institutional Decision Making: Four Country Case Studies, Issue Brief, IHEP, Washington, DC; and Giovanni Abramo, Tindaro Cicero, and Ciriaco Andrea D'Angelo (2013), The impact of unproductive and top researchers on overall university research performance, *Journal of Informetrics*, 7, 166–175.

12. The literature contains a range of studies that focus on the best choice for measurement criteria; see, for example, Chia-Lin Chang, Michael McAleer, and Les Oxley (2011), What makes a great journal great in the sciences? Which came first, the chicken or the egg?, *Scientometrics*,

87, 17–40; and Jang C. Jin and E. Kwan Choi (2014), Citations of most often cited economists: Do scholarly books matter more than quality journals? *Pacific Economic Review*, 19, 8–24.

13. I present the database in the 2014 paper: Trends in three decades of rankings of Dutch economists, *Scientometrics*, 98, 1257–1268.

14. Details are provided in Chapter 4 of Christiaan Heij, Paul de Boer, Philip Hans Franses, Teun Kloek, and Herman van Dijk (2004), *Econometric Methods, with Applications in Business and Economics*, Oxford: Oxford University Press.

15. https://en.wikipedia.org/wiki/H-index

16. Together with Dennis Fok, my former PhD student and now full professor at the Econometric Institute in Rotterdam, I modeled the diffusion of scientific publications (*Journal of Econometrics*, 139 [2007], 376–390). We correlated the characteristics of the diffusion with various features of the published articles, like number of references, number of authors, and the like. Our main findings were that survey-type papers and papers with more coauthors can have a longer-lasting track record of citations. However, we did not address the particular characteristics of the content of the papers and their potential impact. This is of course due to the difficulty of data collection, as it effectively means reading all papers and assigning values to attributes. For my own papers, this is of course easier to do, and hence thus I proceed.

17. An extended version of this part was coauthored by Peter Boswijk and Dick van Dijk and appeared as Cointegration in a historical perspective, *Journal of Econometrics*, 158(2010), 156–159.

18. This part is inspired by Malcolm Gladwell (2008), *Outliers: The Story of Success*, New York, NY: Little, Brown and Company.

19. The articles are David A. Dickey and Wayne A. Fuller (1979), Distribution of the estimators for autoregressive time series with a unit root, *Journal of the American Statistical Association*, 74, 427–431; David A. Dickey and Wayne A. Fuller (1981), Likelihood Ratio statistics for autoregressive time series with a unit root, *Econometrica*, 49, 1057–1072; Robert F. Engle (1982), Autoregressive conditional heteroskedasticity with estimates of the variance of U.K. inflation, *Econometrica*, 50, 987–1008; Robert F. Engle and Clive W. J. Granger (1987), Co-integration and error-correction: Representation, estimation, and testing, *Econometrica*, 55, 251–76; Lars Peter Hansen (1982), Large sample properties of

Generalized Method of Moments estimators, *Econometrica*, 50, 1029–1054; Jerry A. Hausman (1978), Specification tests in econometrics, *Econometrica*, 46, 1273–1291; James J. Heckman (1979), Sample selection bias as a specification error, *Econometrica*, 47, 153–161; Whitney K. Newey and Kenneth D. West (1987), A simple, positive semi-definite, heteroskedasticity and autocorrelation consistent covariance matrix, *Econometrica*, 55, 703–708; Christopher A. Sims (1980), Macroeconomics and reality, *Econometrica*, 48, 1–48; and Halbert White (1980), A heteroskedasticity-consistent covariance matrix estimator and a direct test for heteroskedasticity, *Econometrica*, 48, 817–838.

20. Source: Figure 1 in Marius Ooms and Jurgen A. Doornik (2006), Econometric software development: Past, present and future, *Statistica Neerlandica*, 60, 206–224.

8   TRENDS AND FADS

1. These quotes (and many more hilarious ones) can be found in the wonderful book of Christopher Cerf and Victor Navasky (1984), *The Experts Speak: The Definitive Compendium of Authoritative Misinformation*, New York, NY: Villard.

2. I do have some personal interest in this topic, in particular because of a remark made by a friend of our family who is a primary school teacher: "If you (which is I the author) would be a primary school pupil today, you would most certainly be prescribed Ritalin," which is one of the medications for ADHD.

3. In 2005, my Econometric Institute colleague Alex Koning and I published a paper in the *Journal of Climate* with the title Are precipitation levels getting higher? Statistical evidence for the Netherlands, 22, 4701–4714. One of the possible consequences of global warming is that that there will be more precipitation days throughout the year and the level of precipitation will be higher. We provided a detailed statistical analysis of a century of daily precipitation levels for the Netherlands. We showed that the often-considered gamma distribution does not fit well to the data. Next to that, we argue that its incorrect use can lead to spuriously high probabilities of extreme precipitation levels. Relying on a set of advanced nonparametric techniques, we documented that there is indeed more precipitation in the Netherlands, but that this involves only low levels. Second, we showed that the probability of having extremely high

levels had not changed over time. This shows how important it is to use proper statistical tools when analyzing weather data, in particular because the topic is so relevant to all of us.

4. This part is based on a joint paper with Timothy Vogelsang titled Are winters getting warmer? that was published in 2005 in *Environmental Modelling & Software*, 20, 1449–1455. For this empirical study, we used for the first time the newly developed tests in Timothy Vogelsang and Philip Hans Franses (2005), Testing for common deterministic trend slopes, *Journal of Econometrics*, 126, 1–24.

5. The methodology is developed in Timothy Vogelsang and Philip Hans Franses (2005), Testing for common deterministic trend slopes, *Journal of Econometrics*, 126, 1–24.

6. See Table 1 of Timothy Vogelsang and Philip Hans Franses (2005), Testing for common deterministic trend slopes, *Journal of Econometrics*, 126, 1–24.

7. Source: Tables 3 and 8 of Timothy Vogelsang and Philip Hans Franses (2005), Are winters getting warmer?, *Environmental Modelling & Software*, 20, 1449–1455.

8. In other studies where wealth data are analyzed empirically, it has been documented that such data can well be described by a Pareto distribution or, more generally, by a power law; see, for example, Joseph J. Persky (1992), Pareto's law, *Journal of Economic Perspectives*, 6, 181–192; and James B. Davies and Anthony F. Shorrocks (2000), The distribution of wealth, in A.B. Atkinson and F. Bourguignon (eds.), *Handbook of Income Distribution*, Amsterdam: Elsevier, 605–675. Carolina Castaldi and Mishael Milakovic (2007), Turnover activity in wealth portfolios, *Journal of Economic Behavior & Organization*, 63, 537–552, study the *Forbes* 400 list (which lists the 400 wealthiest American families and individuals), and they find supportive evidence for the presence of a power law; see also Moshe Levy and Sorin Solomon (1997), New evidence for the power law distribution of wealth, *Physica A*, 242, 90–94; and Eric Neumayer (2004), The super-rich in global perspective: A quantitative analysis of the Forbes list of billionaires, *Applied Economics Letters*, 11, 793–796. In brief, a power law implies that there is a link between the wealth value and the rank on the list. The (slightly more strict) law of Zipf states that the first ranked has twice as much wealth as the second ranked and that this second ranked has twice as much wealth as the number four on the

list. Mathematically, this implies that there is a linear link between the
(natural) logarithm of wealth and the (natural) logarithm of the rank.
A very readable survey of power laws is given in Mark E. J. Newman (2005),
Power laws, Pareto distributions and Zipf's law, *Contemporary Physics*,
46, 323–351.

9. See Thomas Spencer, Jospeh Biederman, Timothy E. Wilens, and Stephen
V. Faraone (1998), Adults with attention-deficit/hyperactivity:
A controversial diagnosis, *Journal of Clinical Psychiatry*, 59, 59–68.

10. Ingrid Verheul, Joern Block, Katrin Burmeister-Lamp, Roy Thurik,
Henning Tiemeier, and Roxana Turturea (2012), AD/HD symptoms and
entrepreneurship intentions, ERIM Research Paper 2012–09, Erasmus
University Rotterdam.

11. This next part builds on the study of Carlos Treceno, Luis H. Martin Arias,
Maria Sainz, Ines Salado, Pilar Garcia Ortega, Veronica Velasco,
Natalia Jimeno, Antonio Escudero, Alfonso Velasco, and Alfonso Carvajal
(2012), Trends in the consumption of attention deficit hyperactivity
disorder medications in Castilla y Leon (Spain): Changes in the
consumption pattern following the introduction of extended release
methylphenidate, *Pharmacoepidemiology and Drug Safety*, 21, 435–441.
This paper presents trends and forecasts for or a Spanish region. I will
analyze data for the Netherlands. Forecasts are presented for the users of
ADHD medication for 2012 to 2016. The main conclusion will be that
growth is exponential.

12. Wikipedia (https://en.wikipedia.org/wiki/New_economy) says: "In the
financial markets, the term has been associated with the Dot-com bubble.
This included the emergence of the NASDAQ as a rival to the New York
Stock Exchange, a high rate of IPOs, the rise of Dot-com stocks over
established firms, and the prevalent use of such tools as stock options.
In the wider economy the term has been associated with practices such as
outsourcing, business process outsourcing and business process re-
engineering. At the same time, there was a lot of investment in the
companies of the technology sector. Stock shares rose dramatically. A lot
of start-ups were created and the stock value was very high where floated.
Newspapers and business leaders were starting to talk of new business
models. Some even claimed that the old laws of economics did not apply
anymore and that new laws had taken their place. They also claimed that
the improvements in computer hardware and software would

dramatically change the future, and that information is the most important value in the new economy."

13. I propose this version of the Bass model together with Peter Boswijk in 2005: On the econometrics of the Bass diffusion model, *Journal of Business and Economic Statistics*, 23, 255–268. The motivation for this piece was that the original Bass model is in continuous time, where in practice we only have discretely observed data. We show that going from continuous theory to discrete practice implies that the error terms are autocorrelated.

14. Key references are David A. Dickey and Wayne A. Fuller (1979), Distribution of the estimators for autoregressive time series with a unit root, *Journal of the American Statistical Association*, 74, 427–431; David A. Dickey and Wayne Fuller (1981), Likelihood ratio statistics for autoregressive time series with a unit root, *Econometrica*, 49, 1057–1072; Pierre Perron (1989), The great crash, the oil price shock, and the unit root hypothesis, *Econometrica*, 57, 1361–1401; and Peter C. B. Phillips (1986), Time series regression with a unit root, *Journal of Econometrics*, 33, 311–340.

15. The key reference to the concept of cointegration is the citation classic Robert F. Engle and Clive W. J. Granger (1987), Co-integration and error-correction: Representation, estimation, and testing, *Econometrica* 55, 251–276. The second very important piece is Soren Johansen's (1991) article Estimation and hypothesis testing of cointegration vectors in Gaussian vector autoregressive models, *Econometrica*, 59, 1551–1580.

9 THE TAKEAWAYS

1. The first article on this notion is Robert F. Engle (1982), Autoregressive conditional heteroskedasticity with estimates of the variance of U.K. inflation, *Econometrica*, 50, 987–1008.

2. The Wikipedia lemma https://en.wikipedia.org/wiki/Conjoint_analysis_ (marketing) is very informative and also provides some suggestions for further reading.

Index

Printed in the United States
By Bookmasters